The Citizen Writer

Also by Zachary Michael Jack
and from McFarland

*Rosalie Gardiner Jones and the Long March
for Women's Rights* (2020)

Also Edited by Zachary Michael Jack
and from McFarland

*Participatory Sportswriting:
An Anthology, 1870–1937* (2009)

The Citizen Writer
A Guide to Opinion Writing in a Divided Age

ZACHARY MICHAEL JACK

McFarland & Company, Inc., Publishers
Jefferson, North Carolina

LIBRARY OF CONGRESS CATALOGING-IN-PUBLICATION DATA

Names: Jack, Zachary Michael, 1973– author
Title: The citizen writer : a guide to opinion writing in a divided age / Zachary Michael Jack.
Description: Jefferson, North Carolina : McFarland & Company, Inc., Publishers, 2026. | Includes bibliographical references and index.
Identifiers: LCCN 2025048518 | ISBN 9781476692142 paperback ∞
  ISBN 9781476656410 ebook
Subjects: LCSH: Editorials—Authorship | Essay—Authorship | Op-ed pages |
  BISAC: LANGUAGE ARTS & DISCIPLINES / Writing / General |
  LANGUAGE ARTS & DISCIPLINES / Journalism
Classification: LCC PN4784.E28 J33 2025
LC record available at https://lccn.loc.gov/2025048518

ISBN (print) 978-1-4766-9214-2
ISBN (ebook) 978-1-4766-5641-0

© 2026 Zachary Michael Jack. All rights reserved

No part of this book may be reproduced or transmitted in any form or by any means, electronic or mechanical, including photocopying or recording, or by any information storage and retrieval system, without permission in writing from the publisher.

Front cover image: © Esa fadiat/Shutterstock.

Printed in the United States of America

McFarland & Company, Inc., Publishers
  Box 611, Jefferson, North Carolina 28640
    www.mcfarlandpub.com

To Stu, with long overdue thanks
for a seat at the editor's table

Acknowledgments

Special thanks to North Central College for a research and writing grant—this timely support helped develop this volume. My gratitude also to *The Conversation* for permission to reprint in full "Political cartoonists are out of touch—it's time to make way for memes" by Jennifer Grygiel and "AI 'companions' promise to combat loneliness, but history shows the dangers of one-way relationships" by Anna Mae Duane. Full bibliographic citation and attribution of these and other texts quoted substantively herein can be found in the comprehensive notes at the end of each chapter.

Table of Contents

Acknowledgments vi
Introduction: Your Op-Ed Starts Here 1

Part I—A Piece of Your Mind 5
1. A Citizen Writer's Job Description 6
2. Ready, Set, Op-Ed 16
3. Finding and Framing a Topic 20
4. Ten Steps to Publishing Your Opinions 27

Part II—A Citizen Writer's Toolkit 35
5. Enter the Contrarian 36
6. Ethos and the Art of Sincerity 44
7. Writing the Vox Populi 49
8. Charting a Course of Action 57
9. Finding the "I" in "We" 62
10. The Power of Now 67

Part III—Additional Opinion-Writing Genres 73
11. Advice Columns 74
12. Reviews 85
13. News Analysis 92
14. Arch Cultural Criticism 100
15. Commentaries in Defense 106
16. Commentaries in Praise 112

Table of Contents

17. Humor and Satire	117
18. Writing in Opposition	123
19. Commentaries on Cultural Identity	129
20. First-Person Exposé	137
21. Immersion Commentary	142
22. Polemics and Other Points of Contrast	148
23. Classification Commentaries	153
Part IV—Publishing Citizen Writing	**159**
24. Eight Steps Post-Submission	160
25. A Citizen Writer's Workshop	166
Afterword: And an Exhortation	171
Chapter Notes	173
Selected Bibliography	179
Index	181

Introduction
Your Op-Ed Starts Here

Years ago, a publicist for a Bay Area press asked whether I would consider writing op-eds on topics adjacent to a social justice book I had just published. "Sure," I said, though privately I suspected the publicist's idea amounted to so much pie in the sky.

What chance did I, a mere citizen, have of selling an opinion piece to the *Washington Post*, or publishing an op-ed in *USA Today*, or a commentary in the *Chicago Tribune*—all of which would eventually come to pass. I didn't know any media moguls. The pages of America's newspapers of record were, I suspected, reserved for an elite class of Ivy Leaguers. For me, the mere mention of the term "op-ed" conjured the likes of George Will—PhD from Princeton, personal friend of Ronald Reagan, winner of the Pulitzer Prize for commentary. Even though I'd successfully published hundreds of thousands of words in genres ranging from nonfiction to fiction to personal essay, submitting my citizen opinions for publication felt foreign to me back then, as if it were somehow out of my league.

Many years later, I owe a huge debt of gratitude to the publicist who helped convince me that my opinions merited space on the page. Without her, I would never have had the self-belief to publish my views in North America's best-circulated newspapers and magazines. I wouldn't have had the chutzpah to contract that commentary with the *Washington Post*, or the satisfaction of seeing the op-ed she dragged out of me, kicking and screaming, published in the *San Francisco Chronicle*. Nor would I have had the pleasure of traveling to teach what I've learned, leading citizen writer workshops at community centers, public libraries, and colleges and universities across the country.

In my travels extoling the virtues of citizen writing, I meet countless writers who have been shamed into silence. Most have silenced themselves as a result of a fateful encounter with a gatekeeper that shook their confidence or chilled their free speech.

Introduction

The face of the gatekeeper varies. For some, it's a current spouse or a partner who prefers not to live with the fame or infamy public comment can bring. For others, it's a long-ago teacher who made them self-conscious about their grammar. For still others, it's a disapproving parent or friend whom they worry might abandon them if they make their privately-held beliefs known, or a work supervisor likely to punish them, directly or indirectly, for voicing views that do not conform to the company line. Many more find that the spook that stops them is the specter of their own stifled voice, the one they've neglected for years in favor of propriety, professional politeness, or presumed prudence.

I wrestle with these demons myself. Nearly three decades ago I began working for a local newspaper, first as a cub reporter and later as a section editor. Readers would stop my father at the grocery store to ask if he was related to the journalist who shared his last name, and if he was, to please tell the writer they enjoyed his work. With all due humility, I brushed aside these anecdotes when Dad brought them home. I could tell, though, that while he was proud of me, he also felt a little slighted, and who could blame him? He had worked his whole life in our community and had never been stopped in the produce aisle at Family Foods to be praised for his work. The truth is, Dad deserved ten times as much adulation as I ever earned. To this day, when I write I wonder whether he would agree with me on this or that issue, or if he would instead find me to be a damn fool.

I'm fortunate to have friendly family ghosts inhabiting and inspiring my citizen writing, but my Johnny Appleseed travels across America advocating the genre have shown me others are not so fortunate. Many of the individuals I meet have come to consider citizen writing only later in life. In the intervening years, they've grown mature, deeply-rooted perspectives, resolving to put them down on paper if afforded the opportunity. While they've grown wise, they confess to me that they've also grown rusty, and many, facing the blank page for the first time since they wrote a high school or college essay, confront the phantoms of their youth—those lingering shadows that first chilled their self-expression or undermined their self-belief.

Often, the best way to deal with such apparitions is to call them out in the company of others in an in-person workshop or, asynchronously, in the companionable pages of a book like this one. Dredging up a memory of a spoilsport English teacher who steered us away from a hoped-for writing career is sure to cause others to remember educators, good and bad, who likewise influenced them. Before long, a room full of writers rings with

Introduction

recollections of the sort of specters who, when viewed in the company of others, begin to look more pathetic or comedic than actually intimidating.

In many ways, the practice of citizen writing is about reclaiming our voice and putting that voice to good use while we're still alive and able to use it. Reclaiming it means remembering the people who've supported our writing journey as well as those who've thwarted it. Over time, writing for others, or in the presence of others, usually sends the ghosts fleeing, and the demons that once impeded our growth are soon replaced by a more supportive chorus determined to help us speak our peace.

In this book I hope, first and foremost, to encourage and exhort. In part one, we broach, openly and honestly, the demons of self-doubt and self-censoring that prevent us from taking a public stand on the issues that keep us up at night. In this opening section, the aim is to make opinion writing familiar by comparing it to genres with which we may be better acquainted while simultaneously identifying what makes it truly unique.

Part I covers the steps citizen writers must take to successfully brainstorm, draft, edit, and pitch their work. In Part II, we dig into the specific habits of mind successful citizen writers bring to the opinion page, discussing qualities such as contrariness, charm, sincerity, solidarity, and sympathy for the vox populi—the voice of the people. This part addresses the citizen writer's toolkit—the specific techniques the well-published use to persuade, provoke, invoke, inform, and entertain, while also quoting and analyzing countless works of classic and contemporary opinion. Part III goes beyond the op-ed and commentary to cover the other well-established subgenres freelance citizen writers routinely tackle, such as advice, review, humor, first-person commentary, exposé, immersion, investigation, and so on.

Last but not least, Part IV covers the business of getting our opinions published, from contracts, to copyright, to compensation. It concludes with a writers' workshop on the page, annotating for craft and best practices two contemporary commentaries published in respected outlets ranging from the *Chicago Tribune* to *The Conversation*. Deployed strategically throughout this guidebook readers will find dozens of examples penned by maestro practitioners past and present, such as Charles Dickens, Barbara Ehrenreich, Ernest Hemingway, Langston Hughes, Michael Pollan, Cheryl Strayed, Mark Twain, and many others. Each chapter concludes with two or three opinion-writing exercises designed to thwart writer's block and to kickstart our practice.

PART I

A Piece of Your Mind

1

A Citizen Writer's Job Description

Wanted: Writers willing to speak truth to power. Successful candidates need not be certified, though an experiential credential is strongly recommended. This position celebrates the spirit of the citizen critics who think for themselves yet act on behalf of the public interest, asking difficult questions that challenge the status quo. We seek experienced or aspiring communicators familiar with the value of concision, able to craft opinion pieces totaling less than 1000 words for a variety of popular print and digital media. The successful applicant should be highly motivated, self-aware, and closely observant, with a desire to work remotely on a freelance basis. Diverse voices are strongly encouraged to apply.

If the preceding job description sounds even a little bit like you, you owe it to yourself to give opinion writing a serious try. Few other forms of expression connect the writer so intimately to their readers, and still fewer offer the promise of real-time dialogue on issues of urgent importance to our world. You picked up this book, no doubt, because you've got something to say, something that's better composed as a deeply considered written artifact than hurled as incendiary invective at a public meeting or posted on some random message board in a remote corner of the blogosphere. Whatever it is that gnaws at the edge of your conscience calling to be expressed is bigger than a single tweet or social media post; it's more serious than clickbait, and it requires far more than the three seconds *Wired* magazine claims the average reader spends reading one of the estimated 600 tweets sent every second.[1]

At 500 to 800 words, the conventional opinion piece transcends the fight-or-flight mentality and mind-rot that afflicts so much social media. In opinion, we share, quite literally, something at once sacred and revealing, a "piece of our mind." A well-written citizen commentary offers time to reflect and consider, while utterly refusing to waste the reader's time.

How does citizen writing distinguish itself? In a nutshell, citizen

1. A Citizen Writer's Job Description

writing is *ours*. Rosa Eberly defines the citizen critic as a "person who produces discourses about issues of common concern from the ethos of citizen first and foremost—not as expert or spokesperson for a workplace or a member of a club or organization."[2] Both citizen critics and public intellectuals publish op-eds and commentaries in service to the common good, but public intellectuals do so as acknowledged experts, leaning on their bona fides, their academic degrees, and their professional chops, while the rest of us rely on a passionate heart, a lifetime of practical experience, and an abundance of reciprocal care and common sense.

In sharing our vision for a just and equitable world, we become writers for social change by definition and, in our own way enact the fundamental service a writer performs for society. "Writers get underneath the agreed-upon amenities, the lies a society depends on to maintain the status quo," cultural critic Andrea Dworkin reminds.[3] They do so, she tells us, "by pursuing the truth in the face of intimidation, not by being compliant or solicitous."

The Myth of Glass Houses

"People who live in glass houses shouldn't throw stones," goes the old saying. And while the adage offers the opinion writer a cautionary lesson in humility, its underlying message has stopped many necessary viewpoints from finding their way into print. Far too many citizen critics, worrying what will happen if and when the tables are turned, needlessly pull their punches in public discourse, leaving vital words unsaid for the sake of some imagined decorum.

Surely, then, the first rule of citizen opinion writing is this: be fearless. Having the courage of our convictions means we'll have to stand tall, and bravely bear up, when the people or organizations we call out in print point the finger back at us. Maybe we're complaining about the widespread use of herbicides on corporate campuses, but, truth be told, we used chemicals last spring on a particularly tough weed patch in our lawn. Does such a gap between practice and message expose us as a bit of a hypocrite? Maybe so. Does it disqualify us from speaking or invalidate our opinion? Absolutely not. Suppose you're a cop hoping to share your growing awareness of racial profiling, though thinking back on your early days in law enforcement, you suspect you, too, were guilty of implicit bias. The Glass House crowd would have that otherwise good cop shut their laptop and walk away slowly, choosing a lifetime of silence over sharing.

Part I—A Piece of Your Mind

When the Glass House Gang threatens to dissuade us from sharing hard-won wisdom or well-earned critique for fear of blowback, it's worth asking ourselves how we'll feel if we yield to the myth of Glass Houses and censor ourselves into silence. What will be the cost to our own pride and self-respect if we swallow our tongue just to save face? How might the burden of truth stifled negatively impact our partners, colleagues, and friends who, absent our citizen writing practice, would be the sole audience for our impassioned beliefs and grievances? Won't we, or the causes we advocate, be worse off in the end if we lose faith or turn verklempt on the cusp of important utterance?

In his book *The Soul of a Citizen*, Paul Rogat Loeb reminds how often activists and advocates fall victim to "the perfect standard"—the false notion that the cause must be airtight, the timing must be perfect, and the activist must possess "perfect moral character" in order to speak.[4] Instead, Loeb asserts, the "good-enough activist" must push forward, accepting the possibility that the stones they see fit to throw may indeed be hurled back in their direction. Likewise, the citizen writer succumbs to the perfection standard when they sit on their most time-sensitive views for weeks or months, waiting until every word is right and every argument ironclad and irreproachable, even as the relevance of their topic wanes and the window for timely submission closes. As the saying goes, they're fiddling while Rome burns.

When Glass Houses make us mindful without also making us milquetoast, they serve their purpose, reminding us that words have the power to hurt as well as to heal, and that we should use them wisely. An awareness of Glass Houses means we're not naïve about the consequences our work can have in the real world and that we, as the maker of those words, may be called upon to defend them. Glass Houses are useful to the extent that they remind us that public discourse is a two-way street where turnabout is fair play.

Locating a Language of Praise

As citizen critics we sometimes struggle to express praise on the page. Advised that our work must have conflict to have substance, we're inclined to regard tension, complication, or discord as perquisites for legitimacy. How lifegiving it can be for citizen writers, then, when we are able to find sun where before there was only shade, or to recite a beneficence for readers living lives saturated in sadness or in strife. To write in praise

1. A Citizen Writer's Job Description

of something or someone is to write toward the light, assigning value and meaning.

A closer look at our language suggests the discomfort of the English-speaking world with written public expressions of joy, appreciation, or contentment. Meanwhile, we've coined a plethora of terms for genres whose job it is to criticize, question, or attack. We use formal words like *polemic* to describe a piece of writing that expresses unusually strong criticism or controversial opinion, and *invective* to capture a category of especially provocative, prickly, or willfully insulting work. We still write and publish prose *jeremiads* to recite litanies of woe or complaint—and *philippics* to publicly condemn, in the strongest terms, political actors ranging from presidents to prime ministers to policy wonks. In well-established prose genres like these, we exist primarily to play devil's advocate, while online we generate new buzzwords by the day for the art of taking someone or something down, whether "trash talking," "trolling," or "hate-reading." Where, we may wonder, is the language that describes opinions published to express public praise and extolment?

More to the point, what are we afraid of? That praiseful writing might make us sound weak or effete? If that's true, then benediction, eulogy, and even odes and paeans associated with the poets of old would be classed as second-rate works, rather than the hallmark of literary luminaries from Horace to William Wordsworth to John Keats. Whatever societal forces conspire to keep otherwise concerned citizens quiet and compliant are surely the same that have conflated "expressing an opinion," with spoilsport whining and nattering naysaying. In locating a language of praise in our prose, we remind the powers-that-be that opinion writing is about shining (and sharing) light, not just on inequities and injustices, but on triumphs, successes, and profiles in courage.

Stepping Up, and Hearing Back

On the day when one of my national commentaries is scheduled to run, I'm awfully anxious. I'm hoping people will like it, or, if not like it, at least understand its position. On those days I check the inbox with special trepidation, worried that critics will be waiting with proverbial pitchforks. And yet for all my worrying, I can count on one hand the number of times I've suffered ad hominem attack as a result of publishing my perspectives. Generally speaking, the sort of readers willing to dedicate time to reading thoughtful opinions are respectful of the courage it takes to air one's views

Part I—A Piece of Your Mind

publicly. So, while they may disagree with us vehemently, they seek real dialogue rather than rock fights.

Though I may feel extra anxious on publication day, I feel elated and purposeful, too. I feel strong for having stood up, bucking the societal trend toward compliance if not complacency. In that moment, I'm proud to defy journalist Ray Stannard Baker's contention that, despite our big talk, "most of us are drifters—honest enough, but pulpy; we have no courage to stand up and say what we believe, or to back it up afterwards, if necessary, with hard knocks. We don't like to get our hands soiled, or to have our ease disturbed."[5] Given the alternative—quiet submission to tyranny or chicanery—I'm more than okay entering the fray. At times like these it's natural to steel ourselves, to gird up, and brace for the worse. But we needn't assume a defensive posture. Far better to view the inevitable challenge from others as an opportunity to define what we stand for, and, by extension, the truths we hope the publications that print our work will vigorously defend. Sometimes, when courage fails, it pays to draw on history's intrepid souls for precedents of pluck and inspiration. In this book we'll purposefully resurrect dozens of the brave voices who championed citizen opinion writing in the past, standing for free speech and inclusivity.

Walt Whitman is one such plucky pioneer. In the spring of 1842, corruption rocked New York City, prompting an aspiring young opinion writer who would later become one of America's most celebrated poets to articulate what he believed should be the defining principles of the newspaper he edited, the *New York Aurora*. Contrasting the fighting spirit of his paper with that of the sycophantic yes-men and corruption-kowtowers at the competing *New Era*, Whitman wrote:

> We glory in being true Americans.... We have taken high American ground—not the ground of exclusiveness, of partiality, of bigoted bias against those whose birthplace is three thousand miles from our own—but based upon a desire to possess the republic of a proper respect for itself and its citizens, and of what is due to its own capacities, and its own dignity. There are a thousand dangerous influences operating among us—influences whose tendency is to assimilate this land, in thought, in social customs, and, to a degree, in government, with the moth eaten systems of the old world. [The] *Aurora* is imbued with a deadly hatred to all these influences; she wages open, heavy, and incessant war against them.[6]

Whitman's dauntless mission statement reminds us that citizen writers, then as now, function as a compass aiming to chart a fair and judicious course. Such a job description might seem to lend itself to outsized self-importance, but in truth the citizen commentator and cultural critic

1. A Citizen Writer's Job Description

are opinion leaders by definition. It's incumbent on them to point in a direction, leaving it up to readers to decide whether they will follow. Of course, to be an opinion leader entails some responsibility not just for naming a problem, but for presenting a potential solution, as readers will be inclined to ask, "What would you have us do then?" We as citizen critics should have an answer. The job requires a modicum of ego-strength and a willingness to persuade others of the rightness of the recommended course of action. We might get it wrong, or we might fail to win others to our way of thinking, but we can't simply be another pundit adding fuel to a dumpster fire.

A Time-Honored Path to Publication

Many emerging writers assume literary careers can only be made via the publication of poems or stories in literary journals. And yet, truth be told, even the most established journals have modest readerships when compared to the nation's newspapers and magazines. The numbers tell the story. In the world of contemporary verse, *Poetry* magazine, published by the Poetry Foundation, is arguably the most venerable, and yet, with a circulation of approximately 10,000, the top journal in American verse wouldn't come close to matching the top 100 U.S. newspapers. In fact, poetry's most prestigious publication barely compares to the circulation of newspapers like the *Muscatine Journal* in Muscatine, Iowa, or the *Arizona Daily Sun* in Flagstaff, Arizona. By contrast, America's highest circulating newspapers boast paid subscriptions in the millions.

In her introduction to *The Byline Bible*, writer Susan Shapiro offers corroborating evidence of a tale told often by creative writers who eventually turn to opinion writing. She recalls developing a passionate interest in writing poetry as an undergraduate at the University of Michigan, only to learn that her first published poem would, at best, earn her a free copy of the literary magazine in which it appeared. She felt cheated, and a bit betrayed, and a discussion with her poetry professor only exacerbated her dismay when he informed her that an interest in selling her work to a wider audience only revealed her as an impatient if insufficiently dedicated versifier.

Shapiro recalls of her long-ago student self, "But I *was* serious. And desperate to learn if the obsessions I explored in verse might be expanded to prose I could earn money for. Nobody knew or would tell me. After six years of higher education.... I didn't even know how to craft a cover letter

Part I—A Piece of Your Mind

to submit the pages I'd spent years perfecting."[7] Fortunately, and with the help of a savvier instructor who pointed her in the direction of a paying prose gig at *The New Yorker*, Shapiro found her way into the exciting world of writing opinion on deadline, and a career that would land her work in the pages of *The New York Times*, *Washington Post*, and *The Wall Street Journal*.

In a world where thousands of fly-by-night literary journals and online magazines burst into life one year and die unspectacular deaths the next, it's safe to say that publication of an op-ed, commentary, or column in an established outlet is more likely to earn the citizen writer a slip of immortality than a digital-age poem or short story. *The Wall Street Journal*, for example, has been around since 1889, while *The New York Times* (circulation nearing ten million across its print and digital products) has served as the nation's newspaper of record since 1851.[8] Publishing our freelance opinion in either one of these behemoths practically guarantees that a great-great-grandchild will be able to read our work long after we're gone.

This is not to say that poetry is less important than commentary, but to remind that literary pieces and opinion writing work toward different ends. Poems and short stories may seek to make an aesthetic statement or to push the envelope of language to its natural limits, while op-eds and commentaries attempt to shift public opinion, frame or reframe the headlines, or change an individual or collective course of action. Literary work tackles timeless themes—love, death, beauty, betrayal—and yet all too often the authors who publish such poems and stories in literary journals disappear into obscurity. Conversely, the issues opinion writers address may be topical or time-limited, though the pieces they pen may live on for years or decades in publications that are archived and evergreen. Indeed, many of the most famous quotes in American life began as lines in op-ed pages. "Go West, Young Man," variously attributed to newspapermen Horace Greeley and John Babsone Lane Soule, first appeared in a newspaper opinion section. Meanwhile, the rallying cry of countless Yuletide believers, "Yes, Virginia, there is a Santa Claus," originates with a Francis Pharcellus Church editorial in *The Sun*.

Still more recent examples remind that op-eds and commentaries possess the power to shape public policy and to reshape political fortunes. Witness the bombshell *New York Times* op-ed from 2018 in which an anonymous Trump administration senior official famously sought to reassure worried Americans that there were in fact "adults in the room." Such pieces can and do "change the zeitgeist," social justice author Mary

1. A Citizen Writer's Job Description

Pipher insists, citing the role Bob Woodward and Carl Bernstein played in exposing Watergate.[9] Or consider Roxane Gay's hopeful-yet-critical op-ed written from the heart of the BLM movement in 2020: "How We Save Ourselves." Meanwhile, recent years have commenced a new golden age of cultural criticism, with cultural critics like the late David Foster Wallace and Zadie Smith achieving international acclaim in an opinion-driven genre that, under the label "personal essay," previously languished in its literary silo.

The misconception is in part this: far too many view opinion writing as mere civic duty rather than esteemed literary art, when, in fact, it combines the best of both artforms. It was Whitman the poet-journalist, after all, who famously exhorted America's free-thinking citizenry to sound its "barbaric yawp over the roofs of the world."[10] And no less than the great Irish poet W.B. Yeats opined, "We make out of the quarrel with others, rhetoric, but of the quarrel with ourselves, poetry."[11] The artful commentary—the one that lasts—is two parts rhetoric and one part poetry in prose, as the editorialist queries and challenges their own certainties while simultaneously attempting to win fence-sitting readers to their side of a public debate. It's this distinctive blend that makes the op-ed so winning.

An Op-Ed By Any Other Name

Commentaries, viewpoints, guest essays, first-person pieces, mini-editorials, opinion columns, perspectives—in the brave new world of online and print platforms, we consider each of these terms to be loosely synonymous with the time-honored term "op-ed."

Regardless of nomenclature, the public-facing pieces these terms aim to encapsulate is, generally speaking, a brief guest work submitted freelance—one that advances an individual's take on a timely issue earmarked for the opinion pages. The venerable *Des Moines Register* defines op-ed as "short for 'opposite editorial,'" and, more concretely, as "an opinionated article submitted to a newspaper for publication … written by members of the community, not newspaper employees."[12] The editorial page, by contrast, is reserved for opinion pieces written by editors of a particular publication. And it's important to note that opinion pieces are also a popular fixture in magazines and many other online and for-print outlets. *The New York Times* explains, "At its core, an opinion guest essay provides an argument defined and substantiated with evidence. Rich discussion and debate, combined in a unique way, offer *New York Times* readers a better

Part I—A Piece of Your Mind

understanding of the world."[13] The Merriam-Webster dictionary, meanwhile, echoes the *Des Moines Register*, capturing the essence of an op-ed as "an essay in a newspaper or magazine that gives the opinion of the writer and that is written by someone who is not employed by the newspaper or magazine."

While "op-ed" remains the preferred umbrella term for short pieces of opinion, newspapers and other media increasingly employ a diverse list of synonyms, each inscribing a subtle difference. For example, *The New York Times* prefers the term "guest essay" or "opinion essay," noting: "We believe in the value of creating space for people who aren't journalists and who often have no institutional affiliation with *The New York Times* to speak directly to readers instead of being mediated through a reporter. By design, these arguments and voices often contrast with or challenge those of our newsroom and our own Opinion columnists and editorials."[14]

The *Chicago Tribune* prefers the word "commentary," deeming it more descriptive of the writer's method and content than the somewhat opaque "op-ed." The *Sacramento Bee* and other like-minded publications refer to op-eds as "guest viewpoints" to highlight the powerful personal voices that animate a compelling opinion piece. Meanwhile, the *Sioux City Journal* seeks what it calls "mini-editorials" of 250 words or less written by citizen writers wanting to weigh in on issues of local, regional, or national importance. Closely analogous to a letter to the editor, the mini-editorial frees the writer to set the agenda. *The Boston Globe* prefers the term "perspectives" for its highly regarded *Globe Magazine*, where recent headlines include, for example, "I once nearly died in a pool. Take it from me, kids need swim lessons."

As a descriptor, "perspectives" may indeed feel less exclusively journalistic than "op-ed," and potentially more inclusive of topics mundane and domestic. In fact, some publications prefer "first-person" as the moniker of choice to describe personal experience-driven citizen opinions. For instance, the popular online newsmagazine *Vox* seeks first-person accounts (also sometimes called "first-person narratives") featuring "provocative personal narratives that explain the most important topics in modern life."[15] *Vox* follows a proven formula in generating attention-getting headlines for the first-person opinion pieces it publishes, beginning each with the pronoun "I" followed by what that "I" does that is compelling, controversial, or conversation-begetting. Pieces of this type have run under such first-person-centered headlines as: "I'm Latino. I'm Hispanic. And they're different, so I drew a comic to explain"[16] and "I Own Guns. Here's Why I'm Keeping Them."[17]

1. A Citizen Writer's Job Description

While some individual publications hold tightly to their own in-house nomenclature, the time-honored term "op-ed" remains the umbrella under which most artifacts of citizen opinion writing are submitted, reviewed, and read. In this book, we'll use many of the aforementioned terms, seeking true diversity of practice. To that end, this chapter and many of those that follow conclude with two or three short writing exercises meant to advance our thinking while invigorating our practice.

Voicing Your Opinion

1. As a writer, have you ever pulled punches or softened sentiments for fear of the Glass House Gang discussed in this chapter? What specifically did you fear your critics would say about you if you published the most spirited or strident version of your views? At the time, what made you particularly sensitive to their accusations? Looking back, do you feel your fears were justified?

2. Recollect a time when you published a piece of your writing in a newspaper, magazine, or newsletter associated with your school or organization, with the goal of recapturing some of the joy and self-satisfaction you felt seeing your words on the page. Did that early piece written for publication endure? Did you, your friends, or your family save a copy? Do they still occasionally mention it today? If the piece is accessible, dust it off. Years later, where do you still see yourself—your core personality—alive in its sentiments and subject matter?

2

Ready, Set, Op-Ed

Beyond the personal therapy implicit in reclaiming one's voice, citizen writing helps us enact the familiar social justice mantra, "Be the change you wish to see in this world." If we seek a more inclusive, pluralistic, multi-voiced democracy, we can help make that world a reality by incorporating citizen writing into our practice.

Academic research studies have shown that source-diversity of citizen opinion writing—in other words, diversity among the pool of contributing opinion writers themselves—correlates positively with content diversity.[1] In effect, by contributing our citizen writing to newspaper opinion pages, we increase the percentage of guest content relative to regular columnist content that make up those pages. And the greater the percentage of published material that originates with us—the people—on an op-ed page, the more diverse and inclusive the coverage of issues tends to be. In a nutshell, if we seek more diverse public discourse, one concrete step we can take is to add our voice to the dynamic conversation underway in the nation's opinion sections.

The Long and the Short of It

By now we've identified some self-imposed fears, confronted the ghosts of writing past, and acknowledged, if not embraced, our inner contrarian. We've come to understand, and accept, that while publishing a piece of citizen writing in a widely circulating newspaper or news magazine can help right a wrong or redress a social injustice, it's not for the faint of heart.

As we decide which of the handful of promising ideas are most worth pursuing, we should consider, first and foremost, which of our convictions can best be expressed in a piece of 800 words or fewer. Very likely that modest allotment will mean narrowing our topic—limiting our scope—to something more manageable. We may begin, for instance, with a burning desire to write a viewpoints piece concerning environmental injustice. Then, realizing that's far too broad a topic for such a small canvas, we might home in on the core unfairness of environmental gentrification—the phenomenon by which the underresourced are left to live in the most environmentally vulnerable zip codes. From there, perhaps, we focus further on the gentrification that so often follows catastrophic hurricanes like Helene or Katrina. Perhaps we'll argue that there must be a provision for affordable housing in areas seeking to rebuild with federal funds after a natural disasters.

In citizen writing workshops, I compare this winnowing of topic to opening a series of nested dolls. Inevitably, as each wooden doll is opened, another smaller, more finely detailed representation waits within. One continues opening until they locate the smallest, most precise, most specific iteration—the microcosm. Much like a poem, an op-ed, commentary, or column offers readers a distilled version of a larger issue or question. And, like Matryoshka dolls used in the preceding metaphor, this diminutiveness entails no corollary reduction in meaning or momentousness.

An Art of Proportion

Like a painter who productively fills their canvas without overcrowding it, the well-seasoned citizen writer learns to right-size their topic for maximum effect. A subject that is too large quickly becomes unwieldy, mastering us even as we endeavor to master it. Conversely, a topic that's overly specific, personal, or hermetic (hermit-like) can strike readers as self-indulgent, self-aggrandizing, or simply non-representative. The most impactful artifacts of citizen opinion manage to be both particular and universal—individual and societal—at once. It's a delicate dance, one that depends on tempering self-determination with civic-mindedness.

The key is to locate subject matter we're excited by, and invested in, since our energy, or lack thereof, will be palpable on the page. We'll want to decide in advance what we want our reader to think, know, or believe after reading our opinion, while allowing our piece to surprise even us when, inevitably, it moves in an unexpected direction. We may, for example, begin drafting a commentary with the firm intention of calling for federal guarantees for affordable housing, but decide as we write that any affordable housing mandate must originate at the state or local level.

Part I—A Piece of Your Mind

Arguments Too Complex to Be Won

Once we've tightened our focus, we'll have an easier time rightsizing our thesis. In high school and college English classes, "thesis" was synonymous with persuading others of the rightness of our argument. However, in citizen writing, definitively proving a point is impractical if not impossible, as the arguments we make are too complex to be "won" in 500 or 800 words. No matter how much we might like, most of us won't succeed at changing conservatives into liberals, or vegans into carnivores in the space of a single op-ed or commentary. Rather than vanquish the opposition, a more reasonable, respectful goal is to make the best, most articulate case we can for our position, writing to a reader who's skeptical of those who would attempt to sell them on a new way of thinking. If we can reach the dubious or doubtful sufficient to make them give serious thought to our position, we might consider it an opening victory in the larger battle to change hearts and minds. If the skeptical reader finishes our newspaper column, we can rest assured we've at least been heard. And if they read our last sentence feeling thoughtful rather than accused, scapegoated, or vilified, we should be grateful, since thoughtful consideration is far more likely to produce change in a reader over time than an anger-inducing "hate-read" of words more likely to beget rage than rational reconsideration.

In the final analysis, citizen writing must do more than win or lose. It can sound a warning, flag an injustice, beg us reconsider, call for a subtle or dramatic change in course, prevent or preempt needless conflict, bring to light a little-known fact, or resurrect (or redefine) a forgotten person or cause. It can argue for patience, tolerance, and reason—cooler minds—on one hand, or urgency, action, or immediate intervention on the other. At times, forward-looking opinion writing foreshadows or forecasts while, at others, it reflects, reiterates, and recapitulates. At its heart, the opinion piece is decisive. It understands that readers look to the genre not for a rehashing of the existing questions or a shopworn restatement of persistent quandaries, but for viable answers to pressing problems.

Voicing Your Opinion

1. Make a list of three broad topics about which you feel you could publish a credible citizen's opinion. For example, perhaps heading your list is a topic as big and as broad as fashion or football. Once you have

2. Ready, Set, Op-Ed

your "big three" down on the page, see if you can, following the nested dolls analogy used in this chapter, put a finer and finer point on each until you have the makings of a rightsized 600- to 800-word op-ed, advice column, or commentary. For example, we might unpack fashion into the slightly smaller box "fashion shows." And from fashion shows, we might derive "Paris fashions shows." From Paris fashion shows, we might begin to frame a compellingly concrete opinion. For instance, we might consider pitching a piece to *Teen Vogue* in which we argue that the industry should, on principle, agree to bar children from modeling during Paris Fashion Week.

2. Are you now, or have you ever been, rusty in your writing practice? Have you ever taken a hiatus from the page, or succumbed to a fallow period when you weren't actively writing? How did your self-concept and mental health change when you stepped away? What concrete steps did you take to regain your practice and your motivation?

3. Beyond yourself, for whom do you write at this stage of your life? Who's your most intimate audience—the one behind so many of your words; the one literally or figuratively at your side, or front of mind, as you compose? In what ways does this core audience inspire and motivate you still? Conversely, in what ways, if any, might they limit or inhibit your writing practice.

3

Finding and Framing a Topic

Most writers learned to refine their topic-finding skills in high school or college in service to the writing of formal essays. Fortunately, citizen writers returning to form later in life will be relieved to find those topic-finding chops still evergreen, with one big exception. Back then our adolescent minds were inclined to topics that felt big enough to satisfy the seasoned educators charged with reading our work; hence hot-button subjects like "Euthanasia," or "Performance Enhancing Drugs" or "Body Image."

In one sense, we should be proud of our teenage self; the passionate pieces we penned back then tackled worthy subjects. And yet surely they're an artifact of who we were then more than who we are now. If we're tempted to return to those tired tropes in our current piece of citizen writing, we would do well to consider how much we've grown in the interim. Back then we existed under someone else's roof; now we likely have a "room of our own," to paraphrase Virginia Woolf. When we wrote that cocksure treatise on euthanasia in high school, we were eighteen and perfectly healthy. And yet euthanasia surely looks different to a middle-aged adult caring for a parent with early-onset Alzheimer's or to a 40-something facing a lifetime of chronic disease.

In many ways, reinvigorating our persuasive writing practice is the ultimate act of lifelong learning. Just because we now have a place of our own and a professional calling doesn't mean our hearts beat slowly or that we care less for the world than we used to; in fact, the opposite is often true. As we age, we outgrow our youthful ego, maturing into deep circumspection and a long view. With luck, we're ready to invest in civic arts and public discourse not to please a teacher or impress a would-be lover, but to challenge ourselves to improve our world. We're eager to join the conversation on important topics that feel much more immediate and real to us now than they did back in high school. In the intervening five, ten, or

3. Finding and Framing a Topic

30 years since last we dreamed of a better world in fourth-period English, we've developed a keener sense of self and become a better judge of our own limitations. Better understanding the value of time, perhaps we now write shorter, punchier, stronger. Better acquainted with struggle, we now possess a more finely tuned antennae for systemic injustice. Responsible for rent or mortgage or car payments, we're more adept at cost-benefit analysis.

In short, as mature citizens we're in a better place to tackle persuasive writing on pressing public issues than we might have been as a high school senior or a first-year college student. And yet still, when we sit down to write, we face the same blank page and blinking cursor that so vexed us when we were 16, finding it challenging first to find the right topic, then to successfully wrangle it when we do.

Our Best Topic May Be As Near As a Good Friend

My first teaching job in higher education was as a journalism and English professor at a four-year liberal arts college with a civic arts mission. It was a wonderful crucible for social change writing and service learning, but serving as a faculty advisor to a collegiate newspaper left me little time to pursue my own writing. So when my old friend Mark visited early in my first year teaching at the university, I was ready for a heart-to-heart with a fellow writer whose instincts I'd learned to trust. That day over Cokes and a grilled cheese, Mark mainly listened, and by the end of our old-friends lunch, he had unwittingly helped me find the topic that would become my first book. In patiently listening to me speak my heart and air my grievances, he had, without knowing it, helped me gain a foothold on the steep rock wall I didn't even realize I was climbing: namely, how to balance an impoverished agrarian upbringing with what felt like the uncomfortable privilege of academe.

If we're lucky, most of us have a Mark in our life—someone who knows us well and sympathetically, but not so well as to sacrifice necessary truth-telling. When too many subjects buzz in our heads like rogue electrons—or, worse, when there's no electricity there at all—talking it over with a close pal or trusted colleague can be the best way to achieve clarity. After all, it's the Marks in our world who hear us lament unselfconsciously. They're the sort who truly listen as we decry perceived injustices and the slings and arrows of outrageous fortune. They know exactly what moves us to anger, and what, conversely, tickles our funny bone or

Part I—A Piece of Your Mind

captures our fancy. They know from personal experience what bugaboos and bogeymen keep us up at night and which specific slights get deepest under our skin. It sounds paradoxical, but often the most reliable subjects for our next piece of opinion come from mindful friends reflecting our own minds back at us.

However, there are times in every writer's life when trust in others comes slowly if at all, times when even our most reliable colleagues are busy with projects of their own or otherwise occupied with putting out personal or professional fires. At times like these, we as opinion-makers must learn to query ourselves with the patience and insistence our best friends model for us, refining our own topical compass as we do so. At times like these, when we feel out to sea without a subject, freewriting helps, as does list-making and idea-mapping, but perhaps the most useful technique of all for topic generation is to answer for ourselves a series of open-ended questions, questions like:

1. What's negatively (or positively) impacting our current quality of life or the quality of life of others near or dear to us?

Is it the sixty minutes it takes, roundtrip, to drive to an affordable grocery store? If so, maybe there's an opinion forming concerning the less publicized food deserts in America's small towns and suburbs. Is it the herbicides and insecticides sprayed in the park adjacent to our home that we worry will make our kids sick? Or is it something more systemic, something like the property tax increases that threaten to put homeownership out of reach for the majority of wage-earning men and women? Whatever external forces make our life feel less our own, and, at the same time, less sustainable, pleasurable, or equitable, may be begging for an incisive, razor-sharp act of citizen writing. Conversely, the improvements, inroads, and breakthroughs that make our lives more efficient, joyful, or mindful deserve public praise if we seek to remind the cynical powers-that-be that being a virtuous citizen entails more than just complaining.

2. What person, pop cultural phenom, or popular practice should we reassess or reconsider?

Whom or what are we mindlessly following like lemmings over the cliff? What cultural Kool-Aid do we drink that would be better left on the shelf? Should we, for instance, stop spending precious hours each week mowing our lawn in favor of urban wilding or backyard gardening? Or maybe the argument is that we would all be healthier and better socialized if we scrapped fast-food meals delivered to our door in favor of communal cooking or neighborhood barbequing?

3. Finding and Framing a Topic

3. If history is indeed destined to repeat itself, what present perils does it suggest we're in danger of repeating?

Are we quashing the dream of affordable home ownership with high interest rates reminiscent of the 1970s? Is our current hard line on Russia leading to a second Cold War? Is the spectacle of NFL football simply a thinly veiled simulacrum of Roman gladiatorial contests of two thousand years ago?

4. Whose societal contributions feel unfairly dismissed, devalued, or disparaged?

Are the life-affirming contributions of grandmothers perennially overlooked on Mother's Day? Do teachers deserve more respect at a time when confidence in public schools continues to decline? Can artificial intelligence be reconceived as a savior of humanity rather than as an instrument of its certain doom?

Taking the time to answer such questions—or others we may see fit to pose ourselves—serve to remind, if ever we should doubt, of the depth, value, and diversity of the reasoned opinions we form as citizens moving through the world—viewpoints that, with a little practice, can be shaped into pieces for publication.

Before Hitting "Send"

The moments before hitting "send" on our latest citizen's commentary are always heady. On one hand, they're full of hope and excitement—the odds say our op-ed won't make print; still, we remain sincerely hopeful. To the very last instant we fuss with our syntax and word choice, believing that a small change might make the difference between acceptance and rejection. We read the piece aloud to ourselves, there in our study or home office where we manage to bottle time late at night or early in the morning, or in the window seat of our favorite coffee shop where we do our best thinking, latte in hand, silently mouthing the words as we read them. We listen for lines that are cumbersome or muddled, lingering over sentences that are overlong, overly abstract, or just plain opaque, asking ourselves what we are really and truly trying to say. We edit for clarity, consistency, and concision, for the clean lines that will demonstrate to editors that we've considered shape and structure.

Even as we tinker with the nuts and bolts of our piece, we dream about what it will be like when our citizen's opinion runs in the *Tribune* or the *Times*. Who might contact us out of the blue to communicate their amen?

Part I—A Piece of Your Mind

We allow ourselves to contemplate the myriad small ways the world might change once the public has read our sentiments. More immediately, we wonder what our family, friends, and coworkers may think. Will they like the public version of us they find on the page, or will they find it jarring, at odds with the private person they've come to know and with whom they sit down for lunch? Will they have newfound respect for us—for how deeply we care about the world and its people? Perhaps we take a moment to think back to the friends and family who took the same step before us, mastering their fears to submit an op-ed, commentary, or viewpoints piece to their local newspaper. What personal and professional demons must they have confronted before undertaking that defining act of citizenship?

Many of us falter at the precipice, talking ourselves out of hitting "send," or somehow self-sabotaging our submission. At times like these it's helpful to have a checklist nearby, one that both grounds and guides. Here is the opinion-writing checklist I turn to sometimes when self-doubt threatens to overtake me, or when I've lost the proverbial forest for the trees.

> ✓ Have I generated a short, compelling headline/title, one that captures my subject matter, my perspective, and my takeaway in a dozen words or less? Does the headline include the sort of search-optimized keywords that might help an online reader find my piece?
> ✓ Have I included in my first or second paragraph a rationale for why my opinion is timely or urgent? Likewise, have I expressed my core, animating perspective on my topic by the end of the second paragraph, so readers can anticipate where I'm headed?
> ✓ Have I marshalled some relevant facts, statistics, quotes, or concrete experience to back up claims made in the body of my opinion column—facts that inform my viewpoint without drowning out my voice or slowing my momentum?
> ✓ Have I successfully counteracted, or at least tempered, the holier-than-thou tone that so often makes opinion writing feel preachy or judgmental to those who read it?
> ✓ Have I concluded with a clincher—a resonant line, reverberant question, or definitive statement that puts the finest possible point on it?

What Do Opinion Editors Want?

Now more than ever newspapers are at pains to distinguish between news and opinion, separating the two sections physically within their

3. Finding and Framing a Topic

print editions while also erecting clear boundaries in the minds of readers. *The Wall Street Journal* claims of its newsgathering operation, "We provide facts, data and information—not assertions or opinions—and strive to be a model for ethical, factual and ambitious news reporting," while it describes its opinion section as including "editorials by *The Wall Street Journal's* editorial board, columns from regular contributors, op-eds from outside experts, and letters from readers."[1] *The WSJ's* opinion pages aren't devoid of news and facts; instead, they say, "We cover the major news of the day, often with original reporting, but we also offer a point of view."

Beyond a clear distinction between impartial reporting and perspective-rich opinion, what do the nation's newspapers of record seek in opinion submissions? The *Washington Post* reports, "Among the things we look for are timeliness (is it pegged to something in the news?), resonance (is it something that will interest *Post* readers?) and freshness of perspective (is it an argument we haven't heard many times before?)."[2] They remind would-be submitters, "You don't need to have special expertise in a topic. But explaining how your background or experience informs your point of view can make for a more effective op-ed. You also don't need to have an important [professional] title—and having an important title doesn't mean we'll publish your op-ed."

The New York Times, meanwhile, seeks opinion pieces that "challenge and engage audiences that do not necessarily agree with the writer's point of view," that "give specific and original insight into complicated problems or thorny ideas," and that "anticipate readers' questions and even confusion around news that has an impact on their lives and the world."[3] The nation's newspaper of record wants guest essays that offer abundant context and "clarify and explain the stakes of changes and world events." Commentaries that "start conversations" and "influence policymakers" help *The Times* project its voices into the wider world, while featuring luminous opinions that "open a window to a world they might not otherwise see."

Voicing Your Opinion

1. Locate your best opinion topics by answering each of the four idea-generating questions included in this chapter. After writing a bit on each, which topic do you find most provocative and persuasive? Which of the subjects you've come up with most energizes you, such that you can imagine beginning your piece without delay?

Part I—A Piece of Your Mind

2. Ask a good friend or colleague to write down a list of three headlines for opinion pieces they could easily envision you writing. For example, knowing how strongly you feel about the right to safe drinking water, and how little is being done to ensure it, they might generate, "Finding the Next Flint, Michigan, Before It's Too Late." If your brainstorming session leads you toward levity or laughter, that can be generative, too. For example, conjuring your personal distaste for hot sauce, your opinion writing buddy might suggest: "Not So Hot: Americans Are Infatuated with All Things Spicy." Turnabout is fair play, so if your friend is a writer given to strong opinions, help them generate their own headlines, too.

3. Taking one of the promising topics generated in earlier exercises, find compelling statistics to substantiate your perspective. For example, in the previous exercise, we imagined an op-ed on the drinking water crisis afflicting many of America's cities. As part of our writing process, we might want to research, for instance (a) what percentage of Americans have tap water or well water considered to have unsafe levels of potentially carcinogenic chemicals? Is there any dispute among scientists as to what concentrations of these chemicals are considered suitable for human consumption? As always, seek respected, peer-reviewed, or otherwise fully vetted sources to substantiate your claims. Note that while government publications and .gov websites are generally considered trustworthy, a topic like questionable or controversial government-regulated drinking water standards may require a second opinion from the scientific literature if yours is to be considered a credible and objective piece.

4

Ten Steps to Publishing Your Opinions

As a citizen, getting published in the nation's newspapers of record represents a high bar, with top national outlets accepting less than one percent of the guest pieces sent them. This acceptance rate surprises many writers new to the genre, who assume that because citizen writing often entails volunteer labor, demand would naturally exceed supply. In fact, the opposite is true, with respected newspapers, magazines, and news sites receiving far more opinion than they could ever hope to print.[1]

Citizen critics seeking to get their work into print should take heart, however, as a well-written, well-reasoned, well-researched op-ed will nearly always find a readership if its author proves persistent enough. Here, then, are tens steps that will, if followed, increase the chances one's work will find its way to the page:

1. *Rightsize your piece.* Most opinion pieces published in the popular press fall in the sweet spot between 500 to 800 words, with pieces 400 words or less considered more suitable for a letter to the editor. For example, the *Sioux City Journal* in Sioux City, Iowa, accepts letters-to-the-editor tallying up to 250 words as well as what they call "mini-editorials" of roughly the same length. The takeaway: if our goal is to place a piece of guest opinion in a major newspaper, we will likely want to write our first draft to land in the 600-word range, a just-right number that gives us the ability to edit down to 500 or expand to 800 depending on the specific submission guidelines of our target outlet. However, if after 200 words we feel done—as if we've truly said our piece—we might consider reframing our work as a letter to the editor or the aforementioned mini-editorial. Alternatively, we might search for a daily newspaper, such as the *Des Moines Register,* that prefers op-eds and guest essays of 300 to 500 words.

Conversely, if our piece balloons into the 900- to 1000-word range, we might want to pitch it to a publication's long-form edition. Many daily metro

Part I—A Piece of Your Mind

newspapers run longer editions on Sundays, a day when more pages allow for more in-depth treatments. For example, the *Sunday Register*, published by the *Des Moines Register*, is easily the longest and most eclectic of the newspaper's daily editions, while *The New York Times* publishes a longer-form *New York Times Sunday Magazine*. Opinion pieces of more than 900 words can also be a great match for online news and opinion venues, like *Vox* or *The Conversation*, where attention spans, rather than print costs, are the limiting factor.

2. *Own your subject matter.* Owning your subject matter can sometimes mean having expert knowledge of a subject, but for citizen writers, it more often means making clear what qualifies us to comment, where qualifications can be experiential, circumstantial, or demographical. For example, if we grew up in a city on the banks of the Mississippi or Missouri River, we may have a uniquely informed perspective on topics ranging from catastrophic flooding to river folklore to living with the sometimes dubious choices of the Army Corps of Engineers. Or, if we grew up transgender in an affluent heteronormative suburb, we might have learned something vital about the confluence of sex-based bullying and socioeconomic privilege. In any case, the editors whose job it is to fill opinion pages will be looking for a citizen's sincere connection to their topic. The more lived and seasoned that connection is, the better our publication prospects.

3. *Consider politics.* Though most don't often advertise it, many of the nation's newspapers and news magazines have a pronounced political or ideological lean if not an outright bias. For example, *The New York Times*, the *Washington Post*, and the *Chicago Tribune*, are widely considered to be left-leaning, while the *New York Post* and *Washington Examiner* embrace more conservative views. Trish Hall, former editor of *The Times* op-ed page, argues that would-be opinion writers must first and foremost understand their audience, including "who is most likely to read" the publication to which a piece is pitched as well as what readers' preexisting political or ideological "biases might be."[2] While she agrees with the conventional notion that a liberal opinion writer eager to see their work in print is wise to pitch editors whose views match their own, she insists that exploring the opposite side of the political spectrum is a must. For example, she lists conservative-minded publications such as *The Wall Street Journal*, *The National Review*, *The Federalist*, and *Drudge* as required reading for Progressives seeking a sincere understanding of the right-leaning mind.

Best practices tell us that if our submission is expressly political or ideological, we do well to target likeminded outlets. This isn't to say that, for instance, *The New York Times* wouldn't run an op-ed penned by a fellow of the conservative Hoover Institution on the topic of immigration reform.

4. Ten Steps to Publishing Your Opinions

They can, and they do. But it's understood that conservative input would often be counterpointed by a more liberal piece on the opposite side of the issue and, further, that a highly credentialed, widely known conservative would likely be selected for that right vs. left debate. The takeaway: the citizen opinion writer espousing a conservative view is unlikely to make the pages of *The New York Times* unless they're a recognizable name already associated with the right. On the flip side, if a liberal opinion writer places an op-ed in the pages of a right-leaning newspaper such as the *New York Post*, that writer is likely to be a leading voice, or a lightning rod, on the left.

4. *Leverage geography.* Most news publications remain emphatically place-based, which explains why the host city is often baked into their very title. Overall, that place-centeredness is a boon for citizen writers with deep roots. For example, a resident of Chicagoland is much more likely to place a piece of guest opinion in the *Chicago Tribune* than a commentator currently living in Seattle. This doesn't mean that op-ed pages are reserved for residents of the home city, but that opinion editors put the onus on the submitter to establish meaningful geographic connections.

For example, former NBA star Michael Jordan grew up in North Carolina, but his long association with the Windy City dating back to his days playing for the Bulls would no doubt make his opinion attractive to the *Chicago Tribune* or the *Chicago Sun-Times*. So, while metro newspapers willingly cover national issues, they often do so from a pronounced local or regional perspective. Strong primary ties to a city or metropolitan region include current residence or nativity, while secondary—yet still compelling—connections in the eyes of opinion editors include industry ties (perhaps our work regularly takes us to Chicago), family (maybe our family lived in the city for generations), or geographic adjacency (perhaps we live in neighboring northwest Indiana and want to offer our perspective as a near neighbor).

5. *Plan ahead to ensure timeliness.* Very often we're compelled to craft a piece of citizen writing by something that captures us in the moment. We hear about a controversial school board issue, reflect on the budding controversy during a busy work week, then sit down to scratch out our thoughts on the weekend. We feel as if we've responded quickly to the matter at hand, but opinion editors live at a different pace than the rest of us. For them, six days can feel like an eternity, making an opinion on Monday's news feel stale by the Sunday. Our best chance to place a piece of commentary is to strike while the iron is hot—while the buzz is still buzzing. If circumstances force us to wait or week or two, we may yet find an audience for our work, but we will likely have to reframe it as news analysis or retrospective written with the benefit of hindsight.

Part I—A Piece of Your Mind

Ironically, the times when the busy citizen typically has the most time and mind space to write—weekends and work holidays—are often the times when editors are away from their desks, as they, like us, seek to work well out in front of impending deadlines. For example, maybe we're moved to write a commentary about the importance of honoring the fallen and the dead on the Thursday before the long Memorial Day weekend. We submit the piece on Friday feeling good about the work, and an editor responds that same day to say they would have loved to publish the piece had they received it several days earlier. The editor confesses they had their Sunday opinion page laid out and populated by midweek, hoping to enjoy Memorial Day themselves.

6. *Time the news cycle.* Most industries are in some way seasonal, and journalism is no exception. Late autumn, when inclement weather forces us inside to page- and screen-based pursuits, is an especially busy time in the news cycle in the Northern hemisphere. PR firms have long known the fourth quarter, October through December, to be the busiest season of the year in newsrooms, a time when backlogs are long and editors' attentions spans are short.[3] By October, legislative sessions are in full swing, with election day and its perennial surfeit of public writing in the offing. In the lead-up to election day in November, space in America's newspapers is scarce, with politics vying with sports and entertainment for attention on already crowded screens and pages.

Late October finds a rare confluence of major sports vying for coverage, with football, pre-season basketball, and late-season baseball occurring simultaneously. Publicity demands for a new season of book releases and TV shows exacerbate the autumnal space-crunch. The takeaway: the citizen writer's chances of placing guest opinion in October or November are substantially reduced relative to summer, when the news cycle tends to slow as both readers and editors take hard-won hot-weather sabbaticals.

Summer lulls can be propitious for the freelancer eager to place a piece of opinion. Other auspicious submission windows for citizen writers occur periodically throughout the year. In April, the legislative session is coming to an end, reducing the usual gusher of capitol news to a more manageable trickle. In May, teachers and academicians are focused on tying up loose ends rather than unraveling new threads, meaning the op-ed pages are slightly less crowded with scholars, experts, and pedagogues during that time. Depending on the topic, the period from late December to mid–January can also be a good time for citizen writers to place guest essays, as editors look for personal or anecdotal material that represents a purposeful departure from "if it bleeds it leads" headlines.

7. *Mind your holidays.* Holiday writing is timely by definition, but it

4. Ten Steps to Publishing Your Opinions

comes with an important caveat: many newspapers and new magazines are reluctant to consider commentaries concerning the holidays themselves. Their caution makes sense in a world where an increasing number of readers feel Judeo-Christian values have been promoted by news organizations at the expense of the world's other religions. So, while our holiday commentary on the importance of old-fashioned analog gifts such as board games may be especially relevant to our family and the families in our community, we would do well to consider our piece with religious and spiritual diversity front of mind. For example, we might be wise to prefer the more inclusive "holiday gifts" to "Christmas presents" in our copy.

And if, for example, our piece argues for the old-timey pleasures of a rousing game of Monopoly played at the holiday table with family and friends, we should somehow acknowledge the elephants in the room: that many don't have the luxury of time off on the holidays; that others might have unconventional families or no family at all; still others might object to playing a game centered on corporatist greed in a sacred season. As we parse the fraught syntax of sacred seasons, it's easy to see why opinion editors are reluctant to run holiday-based opinion in the first place. If our holiday perspective is really a keeper, we might instead consider submitting it to a general interest magazine, webzine, or web journal in lieu of a traditional newspaper.

8. *Honor thy editor.* Honoring an editor may sound needlessly deferential, but it's a useful lens through which to view the dynamics involved in freelance submission. How can we respect an editor? We might begin by using their name, if known, when corresponding. Often a cover letter accompanying a guest opinion submission will simply be addressed "Dear Editor." But in instances where the name of the opinion editor is known, or can be found on the masthead, it should be used. The less generic and assembly-line our introductory letter, the more likely it is that our submission will receive the attention it deserves.

We also honor our editor when we follow submission guidelines. Do the guidelines cap our guest viewpoint at 600 words? If so, we'll want to avoid squeaking by with 700. If our target media outlet would like us to use their online form to submit our opinion, we should observe that preference. Editors are gatekeepers, and submission guidelines are put in place to keep the bar equally high for all those who seek entry. As Creatives, we're inclined to plead special consideration, when, in reality, we're likely just one citizen among hundreds submitting a guest commentary to a national opinion editor on any given day of the week.

9. *Prepare to surrender your anonymity.* In summoning the courage to submit opinion for publication, we overcome what is often the engaged

Part I—A Piece of Your Mind

citizen's most difficult hurdle: self-censor and self-doubt. And when—wonder of wonders—a deputy editor replies to express interest in our submission, we face a challenge we perhaps hadn't contemplated previously: the calculus of sharing our personal information.

Most editorial departments refuse to run anonymous opinion, so we'll need to be comfortable providing both our full legal name and street address.[4] Such information is usually submitted for verification purposes only, so that the publishing outlet can confirm that we are who we say we are and not a plagiarist, chatbot, or identity thief. Still, many new to submitting freelance work as citizens are surprised to learn that publications seek still more, potentially privacy-compromising information from guest commentators, including our profession, our employer, and, very often, our headshot.

The reasons for these requests are common-sensical rather than conspiratorial. We're asked to provide our profession because knowing it can help establish (a) our expertise and (b) any perceived biases or conflicts of interest, especially if we're employed by a company with a financial interest in, or connection to, the publication to whom we've pitched our work. We may also be asked to email our headshot both to confirm our identity and, in many cases, to run alongside our commentary, as author pictures help readers feel connected to a contributor with whom they are unfamiliar.

10. *Craft a concise cover letter.* Begin with a no-nonsense salutation such as "Dear Editor" or "To the Editors." Insert the name of the opinion or public engagement editor, if known, or if ascertainable via online research. The opinion editor's name may be found in the masthead of the target outlet—either in the print or online edition—or may be listed under the "Newsroom" or "Contact Us" link on the publication's website. If the name of the specific editor can't be located in a cursory search, it's okay to proceed with one of the more generic alternatives. Some publications do not have a dedicated opinion editor, meaning the review of our citizen's submission could fall to the managing or chief editor, to another section editor doing double duty, or to a multi-person editorial board.

Include a title and word count somewhere in the first paragraph of your query, as word counts function as an industry-standard measuring stick. In the body of your letter, briefly summarize any specific credential—whether experiential, professional, or circumstantial—that qualifies you to write your piece. Be sure to identify any conflicts of interest that might need to be disclosed. Finally, take care to close your letter in a way that doesn't imply expectations of follow-up. Since the vast majority of opinion submissions never receive a personal reply, there's no need to insert the formulaic "I look forward to hearing from you" or "Please let me know if you are interested."

4. Ten Steps to Publishing Your Opinions

Instead, thanking an editor for their time and consideration is a good thing to do, since most op-ed page editors audition guest opinions on top of their everyday duties. As a term, "cover letter" may in fact be a bit of a misnomer in the digital age, since the short introductory missives we write to accompany freelance submissions are now mostly sent via email or, increasingly, submitted via an online submission portal.

For reference, here is a sample of the cover letter I emailed to the *Chicago Tribune* to pitch the op-ed printed in full later in this volume:

> As a writer for young adults and a former children's librarian, I've marveled at the success of *Oh, the Places You'll Go!* by Dr. Seuss as graduation gift juggernaut, and yet its phenomenal success has crowded out many other worthy contenders written for adults. Included below for your consideration is an approximately 700-word op-ed in which I tackle what has become a graduation gift-giving cliche. With the commencement season in full swing in Chicagoland area schools these next few weeks, I feel the piece is an especially timely one, both for graduates and those who support them. Additionally, the op-ed could represent an occasion for interactivity, with *Trib* readers weighing in on their favorite graduation reads. As the headquarters for the American Library Association, Chicago is a national center for good advice for readers.
>
> Thanks so much for your time and consideration.

As this sample suggests, a cover letter functions as a personal and professional introduction, so it's okay to curate the information you find most relevant. Just as you might when chatting with a newfound seatmate on an airplane, you should feel free to filter personal information for relevance to audience and occasion. For example, in the preceding cover letter, I emphasize my experience as a former youth librarian and writer for young adults, as those aspects of my life speak most directly to an informed perspective on Seuss. In a different submission to a different venue, I might instead choose to feature my scholarly research or teaching.

For instance, you may have spent the first 20 years of your career teaching industrial education to high school students, and the last ten in semi-retirement as a home inspector. If the citizen writing you're submitting concerns allegedly hasty building inspections of the sort that made national news in the Florida condominium collapses of the early 2020s, your experience as a building inspector trumps your time as a teacher. In workshops, college students often ask if they should feel obliged to include their student status in the cover letter accompanying their commentary. They worry that the mere mention of "college student" makes them sound like novices or neophytes. My advice is to note their student status only if it's relevant to their topic—for instance, in the case of an op-ed on campus protests. If not, I recommend using the introductory letter to relay an alternate, more germane experiential credential. For instance, if a student writer waits tables on weekends and pens a perspectives piece on the boorishness of today's in-restaurant diners, their weekend gig is likely more relevant than their full-time student status.

Note that cover letters themselves are typically considered optional. So while a well-written one can help our case and solidify our credentials, in effect, greasing the wheels of our submission, a poorly written one that rambles or overshares might wreck otherwise promising prospects.

Voicing Your Opinion

1. Following the advice in the preceding chapter, leverage a meaningful geographical connection into an original piece of citizen opinion writing. Consider how the reputation of the neighborhood, city, county, or state, in which you grew up might amplify or augment your take in the eyes of opinion editors and the general reading public. For example, if you grew up along the Rio Grande in Texas, or live there now, your experience may lend itself to an on-the-ground perspective on immigration.

2. Flip your calendar forward six to eight weeks to a prominent event or perennial cultural fixture about which you could advance-pitch a piece of timely citizen writing. For example, looking ahead to the Fourth of July, perhaps you decide to write an op-ed in support of the full legalization of consumer fireworks in your state. Or, if the summer reading season is in the offing, maybe you elect to pen a guest essay on while you'll be listening to your books this summer rather than reading them. In keeping with the counsel given elsewhere in this chapter, it might be wise to avoid centering your commentary on a sacred holiday or religious observance.

3. Draft a cover letter for an opinion piece you have firmly in mind but have not yet written. For the purposes of the exercise, it's okay to generate a speculative yet attention-getting title for the piece you pitch. Following the advice given in this chapter, take care to emphasize those aspects of your personal or professional biography that most credential you to comment on the topic at hand, while also making mention of previous pieces, if any, you may have published. Make the case that your take is timely and relevant, in particular, to the target publication's readership. The shorter and more informative your cover letter, the better.

Part II

A Citizen Writer's Toolkit

5

Enter the Contrarian

Above all, the citizen writer must be an independent thinker, querying our conscience before counting our chickens. The commentaries we pen are often corrective. Like steering a plane that has gone badly off course, the citizen writer steps in when responsible parties fail to solve urgent problems.

Opinion writers function as counterweights. Imagine a Boeing 737 in which 80 or 90 percent of the passengers are seated on the same side, seeking the scenic view; by analogy, the opinion writer would be the first to point out that the aircraft is imbalanced and unsafe, and the first to move to the less populated side for the good of all. In theory, we lead by example, even when the course we recommend may be misunderstood, inconvenient, or unpopular.

Ideally, the author of the most trenchant opinion is independent in thought, action, and deed. While the editorialist is often on the masthead of the publication in which their work routinely appears, the citizen writer of the op-ed or commentary is a freelancer in deed if not in name, an independent contractor free to follow their conscience. At the same time, our hard-won freedom of action and thought can make us suspect. We're sometimes presumed to be hell-raisers, troublemakers, contrarians, or worse merely for our penchant for speaking truth to power.

In the hands of a skilled writer, however, contrarianism is a tool more than an all-consuming character trait. Citizen writers of provocative guest essays, op-eds, and commentaries opt to go against the grain, in part, because, as writer Phillip Lopate explains, they want to make it "more difficult for the reader to identify frictionlessly with the writer." In so doing, they often cultivate the curmudgeonly, since "there is no quicker way to demonstrate idiosyncrasy and independence than to stand a platitude on its head."[1]

5. Enter the Contrarian

The Nail Sticking Up

In their best-selling work *The Big Sort*, coauthors Bill Bishop and Robert Cushman relay a sobering social psychology experiment from the 1950s that speaks to the steep price paid by nonconformists who resist entrenched orthodoxies. Bishop and Cushman describe how the study's chief author, Stanley Schacter, divided student participants into clubs at the University of Michigan—for example, a radio club, a theatre club, and a movie club.[2] He then embedded two key undercover participants in each group. The first was a "slider" who began discussion on a controversial news item before gradually staking out a middle ground. The other secretly played the role of the "deviant" charged with maintaining the opposite view throughout the discussion—in effect, playing the vital role of contrarian. Later Schacter asked the group to nominate members for (a) an honorific executive committee and (b) members who could be downsized with little or no negative effect on the club. Unsurprisingly, the contrarian was never nominated for a place on the executive committee and was frequently mentioned by others as the member the group could most afford to lose. Bishop and Cushman report that the contrarian character was gradually excluded from the conversation entirely, "effectively turning him into a nonperson."[3]

The University of Michigan experiment offers a cautionary tale for independent thinkers who refuse on principle the go-along-to-get-along mantra, or who reject a commonly held belief or majority position: we're not likely to win any popularity contests or to earn promotions reserved for those who walk the company line. The need to foster opposing views is precisely the reason why defenders of free speech and spirited public debate argue that space must be reserved in op-ed pages for public dissent. In fact, some of the most acclaimed newspapers and news magazines employ a kind of objectivity ombudsman to ensure that there is an approximate parity of conservative and liberal (read: Red and Blue) commentaries published each year.

While North America's publications of record are at great pains to convince readers that their opinion pages are the last bastions of free speech and uncensored opinion, the reality for true renegades and radical thinkers may be somewhat less rosy in practice. In the 1990s and early 2000s, cultural critic Andrea Dworkin claimed that newspaper and magazines systematically suppressed or ignored the work of true radicals, opining, "We think that contemporary Western democracies are different but we are wrong. The society will mobilize to destroy the writer who opposes

Part II—A Citizen Writer's Toolkit

or threatens its favorite cruelties."[4] Dworkin complained bitterly that the progressive publications that should have been most open to publishing the views of a radical feminist on topics as diverse as pornography and patriarchy instead systematically ignored her work; she called out publications like *The Atlantic* and *Harper's*, in particular, that only "presume to intellectual independence."[5]

Difficult as it is to be the proverbial nail sticking up, the satisfactions for contrarian citizen writers are many, chief among them self-respect and the satisfaction that we did not stay quiet in the face of inequity or injustice. Instead, we ask others to pay heed, to pay attention, and to act where action may be required. The writer of the op-ed or commentary stands watch, their sensitive antennae sensing what the general public sometimes cannot.

Op-Eds in Defense of the Public Interest

Regardless, the writer of opinion must have a thick skin, one capable of taking arrows. Mark Twain, a.k.a. Samuel Clemens, serves as a guiding example. On his way to becoming the iconic author of *The Adventures of Huckleberry Finn* and *The Adventures of Tom Sawyer*, Twain cut his teeth scratching out opinions in California boomtowns such as San Francisco and Sacramento, where he began cultivating the incisive voice of the satirist and consummate puncturer of pretense and presumption. The young Twain refused to let anything stop his dogged pursuit of transparency, speaking truth to power at every opportunity at a time when his age and status as recent émigré to the Golden State might have silenced a less audacious scribbler.

Had young Samuel Clemens been involved in Schacter's experiments at the University of Michigan, he surely would have played the role of deviant. The piece that follows offers an excellent example of the way the opinion writer, then as now, serves as watchdog in the public interest, rising to indignation without losing reason. In "A Small Piece of Spite," a young Twain takes on the coroner's office in his adopted hometown of San Francisco, calling out public officials for what is now sometimes called "Fake News."

> Some witless practical joker made a false entry, a few days ago, on a slate kept at the dead-house for the information of the public, concerning dead bodies found, deaths by accident, etc. The *Alta*, *Bulletin*, and *Flag*, administered a deserved rebuke to the Coroner's understrappers, for permitting the entry

5. Enter the Contrarian

to remain there, and pass into the newspapers and mislead the public, and for this reason the slate has been removed from the office.

Now it is too late in the day for such men as these to presume to deny to the public, information which belongs to them, and which they have a right to demand, merely to gratify a ridiculous spite against two or three reporters. It is a matter of no consequence to reporters whether the slate is kept there or not; but it is a matter of consequence to the public at large, who are the real injured parties when the newspapers are denied the opportunity of conveying it to them.

If the Coroner permits his servants to close the door against reporters, many a man may lose a friend in the Bay, or by assassination, or suicide, and never hear of it, or know anything about it; in that case, the public and their servant, the Coroner, are the victims, not the reporter. Coroner Sheldon needs not to be told that he is a public officer; that his doings, and those of his underlings at the coffin-shop, belong to the people; that the public do not recognize his right or theirs to suppress the transactions of his department of the public service; and, finally, that the people will not see the propriety of the affairs of his office being hidden from them, in order that the small-potato malice of his employees against two or three newspaper reporters may be gratified.

Those employees have always shown a strong disinclination to tell a reporter anything about their ghastly share in the Coroner's business, and it was easy to see that they longed for some excuse to abolish that slate. Their motive for such conduct did not concern reporters, but it might interest the public and the Coroner if they would explain it. Those official corpse-planters always put on as many airs as if the public and their master, the Coroner, belonged to them, and they had a right to do as they pleased with both.

They told us yesterday that their Coronial affairs should henceforth be a sealed book, and they would give us no information. As if they—a lot of 40-dollar understrappers—had authority to proclaim that the affairs of a public office like the Coroner's should be kept secret from the people, whose minions they are! If the credit of that office suffers from their impertinence, who is the victim, Mr. Sheldon or the reporters? We cannot suffer greatly, for we never succeeded in getting any information out of one of those fellows yet. You see the dead-cart leaving the place, and ask one of them where it is bound, and without looking up from his newspaper, he grunts, lazily, and says, "Stiff," meaning that it is going to an inquest of the corpse of some poor creature whose earthly troubles are over. You ask one of them a dozen questions calculated to throw more light upon a meagre entry in the slate, and he invariably answers, "Don't know"—as if the grand end and aim of his poor existence was not to know anything, and to come as near accomplishing his mission as his opportunities would permit. They would vote for General Jackson at the "Bodysnatchers' Retreat," but for the misfortune that they "don't know" such a person ever existed.

What do you suppose the people would ever know about how their interests were being attended to if the employees in all public offices were such unmitigated ignoramuses as these? One of these fellows said to us yesterday, "We have

Part II—A Citizen Writer's Toolkit

taken away the slate; we are not going to give you any more information; the reporters have got too sharp—by George, they know more 'n we do!" God help the reporters that don't! It is as fervent a prayer as ever welled up from the bottom of our heart.

Now, a reporter can start any day, and travel through the whole of the long list of employees in the public offices in this city, and in not a solitary instance will he find any difficulty in getting any information which the public have a right to know, until he arrives at the inquest office of the Coroner. There all knowledge concerning the dead who die in mysterious ways and mysterious places, and who may have friends and relatives near at hand who would give the world and all its wealth for even the poor consolation of knowing their fate, is denied us. Who are the sufferers by this contemptible contumacy—we or the hundred thousand citizens of San Francisco? The responsibility of this state of things rests with the Coroner, and it is only right and just that he should amend it.[6]

When he penned his public-interest piece, Twain had lived in the Bay Area less than six months and had not yet reached the age of 30. On an occasion when most cub reporters would retreat to the sidelines to let more seasoned scribes take the bullets, he willingly enters the fight, not so much on behalf of his brethren newspapermen and women, but on behalf of the commonweal. His tone reveals itself in his unsparing word choice—*ignoramus, underlings, understrappers*—the latter a term for a junior official or assistant. His point: the coroner's office ought to serve the people, not the other way around. Moving seamlessly between colloquialism ("understrapper," "stiff," "dead-house,") and high diction such as "contemptible contumacy" (the later defined as refusal to comply with authority), Twain is at his iconoclastic best when he deploys both high and low diction, as when he describes the "small-potato malice" of the coroner's office, the colloquial "small potato" pairing beautifully with the high falutin' Latinate noun "malice." It's worth noting that many of the terms Twain uses in his shot across the bow were old or archaic even when he fired them at his target, including "understrappers" and "contumacy," while the popular American idiom "small potatoes" had been coined as recently as the eighteenth century. To properly expose the suppression of information at city hall, he needed both old and new arrows in his inimitable quiver.

Today's style-forward commentators and cultural critics draw liberally from Twain's playbook, mixing new words with ancient ones as circumstances dictate. The dramatic resurgence in the use of the word "bloviate" by twenty-first century commentators offers a case in point. Coined in the mid–1800s to mean "to talk at length, especially in an

5. Enter the Contrarian

inflated or empty way," the term remained relatively rare in print until the late 1990s when its use in print soared, no doubt to roast the culture of long-winded politicians and pundits who had come to dominate public discourse. After yet another mass shooting event in 2023, commentator James C. Nelson offered readers of *Counterpunch* a Twain-worthy litany of condemnations of a gun-centric culture consisting of "press conferences; school classes cancelled; politicians falling all over each other with their thoughts and prayers—and, choreographed for the evening news, bloviating frustration and rage."[7]

Notes From the Underground

Contemporary style-forward commentators and cultural critics continue to draw liberally from Twain's playbook, mixing new words (known as "neologisms") with ancient ones, slang with streetwise soliloquy. The underground press of the late 1960s signified their parting of ways with the mainstream not just via the publication of alternative views but by pushing the boundaries of free expression itself, aiming to write with absolute fidelity to self while exposing falsity and flim-flam in failed institutions. Jeff Shero, editor of the New York-based alternative *The Rat*, conjures the best of the Beat style in a 1968 opinion piece distributed across the country via the Liberation News Service. Walking through Manhattan on his way to participate in a WNDT-TV 13 panel about underground media, Shero can't help himself from puncturing the pretense of the Lower East Side in highly opinionated prose that borders on the poetic: "The aloof pressed white shirt and tie men, eminently respectable, seem all the more like sanitized robot creatures who uncomprehendingly misperform the function of maintaining the machinery of the city."[8]

In this first-person opinion, the remarkable editor of *The Rat* recounts with colorful language what ensues when Steve Roberts of *The New York Times* asks him what's different about the underground press, and, at that very instant the WNDT studio is stormed by a group of free press advocates in a moment immortalized in the headline "Storm Channel 13: Hippies Turn TV Tubes Blue." Shero records the moment as: "Bedlam. The show is no longer a show, real human tensions flash across the screen. Real anger. Real sweat from the moderator. Incoherence. The chaos of the virile ghetto crashed into the programmed calmly classified discussion.... The first underground assault on the airwaves.... Packaged issues give way to the real confrontation of life sensibilities. That's it. Liberal educational

Part II—A Citizen Writer's Toolkit

TV meets the mob. The scalpel pairs away the façade and bares the man beneath."

Whether Twain in the nineteenth century or Shero in the late twentieth, the writer's scalpel aims to scrape away the last vestiges of pretense, politeness, and perfunctory politeness or sham professionalism in service to truth, for, as Shero argues, the "chaotic spontaneous" is infinitely preferable and "more simulating than the well prepared canned variety" of opinion that aims only to amplify an official message or mouthpiece.

Shero's commentary, so reminiscent of charismatic gonzo journalists and cultural critics such as Hunter S. Thompson, reminds us to loosen and enliven our language when called upon to document the roiling or topsy turvy—to travel through the looking glass, as writer Lewis Carroll put it. When viewed through a contrarian lens, the world we know often begins to feel upside down or backwards, shot through with the most meaningful kind of irony, inanity, or imbecility. It's easy to see why opinion writing and expressive writing meld so readily, as both invite the writer to summon their bravery while bucking journalistic conventions. Both make allowances for close observation and keen perception, on one hand, and extreme, sometimes ecstatic subjectivity on the other. When we unshackle our syntax on the page, we simultaneously liberate our minds.

Voicing Your Opinion

1. Generate a list of the attitudes, people, or forces that you feel prevent you from sending that simmering citizen op-ed or guest opinion piece to your local newspaper or news outlet of choice. Make your initial list freely and without censor, jotting down whatever or whomever comes to mind as a real or imagined impediment. Once you've generated your list, review it in its entirety. Which of the inhibiting forces or attitudes most surprise? Which would you highlight as the most significant factors in your self-censorship? What action might you take to reduce, dimmish, or work around the most daunting of these barriers?

2. Recall a time when you positively and productively refused to bow to public opinion or peer pressure. What price did you pay for your conscientious objection or contrarian behavior? What pleasure or praise did you earn in return for pushing past your fear and trepidation?

3. After the fashion of Mark Twain, consider an agency or office that deserves to be exposed in a prescient piece of citizen writing. Do

5. *Enter the Contrarian*

you, like Twain, have firsthand or secondhand experience with this failed institution that you would consider sharing with fellow citizens in an unflinching op-ed? While Twain directs his ire at the county coroner, it's possible to apply similar techniques to an office less official but no less relevant to your life and the lives of others—for example, a private homeowners' association, a rental agency, a school or college, an airline, or any other entity that claims to advocate for the public good while too often falling short.

6

Ethos and the Art of Sincerity

Though opinion writers earn their keep by pointing out difficult or inconvenient truths, we can be likeable, too, manifesting the all-important appeal ancient rhetoricians called "ethos." Of course, ethos is about more than just being likeable; it's about being credible on our topic and good in our craft, where "good" can be taken to mean both virtuous and skilled. Indeed, one of my favorite professors once distilled the fraught concept of ethos to "a good man or woman writing well." Put another way, ethos involves not just the writer's book-learning or long-time experience with their subject but also their winning word choice, tone, and audience awareness.

Occasionally, citizen writers record the virtue, beauty, and goodness they feel others take for granted. They might distill the defining spirit of a season or a decade or shed light on the most overlooked yet important events of a week or a year. In such instances, their goal is to exhort readers to appreciate more fully, or to defend that which deserves defending. The writer of the op-ed or commentary stands watch, their sensitive antennae sensing and feeling what the general population, the "gen pop," may be too preoccupied or numb to notice.

An Art of Sincerity

Every persuasive writer is part performer at heart, perhaps explaining why pundits, public speakers, and politicians are so often accused of playing to the crowd. Still, for all the stereotypes about communicators who change their stripes, chameleon-like, to please, propitiate, or placate their audience, the most natural stance for most scribes is sincerity. Our fundamental inclination to earnestness is efficient if nothing else, since sustaining the illusion that we are someone other than ourselves would consume

6. Ethos and the Art of Sincerity

the energy we need to make our work right and true. "Socially conscious writers want authenticity and transparency to saturate every page of their work," social change Mary Pipher reminds us, clarifying that we aim to teach readers "how to think, not what to think."[1]

As we've seen, pure logic and prodigious intellect can be winning, but they can also be cold, cruel, and cutting. In his columns and commentaries, Pete Davis urges his fellow writers toward an earnest view of the world, their craft, and their civic responsibility. While Davis would go on to publish the best-selling book *Dedicated: The Case for Commitment in an Age of Infinite Browsing*, in the late 2010s he was a student at Harvard Law who found himself sincerely troubled by the uber-competitive, cutthroat ways of his classmates. Rather than turn snarky or cynical, Davis remained earnest in his convictions, writing soul-searching perspectives for *The Harvard Law Record*.

In one especially memorable column, he urges his fellow students to eschew participation in higher education's "cult of smart": "See, from the very beginning of your time here, there will be a push to hold those with the sharpest and narrowest analytical skills in acclaim, regardless of their moral or civic orientation."[2] Davis takes his readers inside the hallowed halls of Harvard Law, where he tells us: "It is not uncommon to hear classroom comments like 'I might disagree, but this argument is so clever and well-written,' or 'Say what you want about what he advocated for, he was a genius.'" The author's sincere opinion is that the dangerous separation of intellect from civic virtue even extends to the physical environment of Ivy League classrooms as well, wherein paintings of legal scholars and acclaimed jurists, "as opposed to clinicians and courageous reformers" adorn the walls.

Standard dictionaries define *sincerity* as honesty of mind, but in opinion writing the elusive quality is probably best captured by its close synonym: *earnestness*, a word which connotes a kind of intense and often unmitigated conviction. Unsurprisingly, usage of both *sincerity* and *earnestness* in print have declined dramatically in the past 150 years; presumably because as the world grows more complicated, ulterior motives and biases are presumed in nearly every act of communication. Sincerity thereby becomes something of a shibboleth. And in a digital age the bar for sincerity seems higher than ever. At the same time, however, the value of this heirloom quality grows greater as it grows rarer in public discourse.

For many contemporary commentators, cultivating sincerity amounts to an act of recovery, taking us back to roots and origins. Who were we before we became the many things we must be now: worker,

Part II—A Citizen Writer's Toolkit

partner, citizen, colleague? Who are we beneath the many masks we're compelled to wear in our various spheres and silos? I don't mean to imply any New Ageisms—that somehow our childlike self is purer and more virtuous—but that achieving absolute authenticity and earnestness on the page is, even on the best days, an effort requiring a kind of conjuration—a movement away from complex and conflicted freneticism to core convictions. At times, sincerity can feel so deeply buried that we can only properly illuminate it by pairing it with its antithesis:

> Belief versus cynicism
> Quiet conviction versus bombasticism or bloviation
> Faith versus cynicism or nihilism

No twenty-first-century opinion writer or critic can articulate such sentiments without feeling a twinge of self-consciousness. In the presence of sincerity, the voice of the cynics, those "Muppets in the balcony," grows increasingly loud, and we can only imagine the vitriol our earnestness might meet in a post-postmodern world. What is belief, sincerity's critics say, other than personal bias or bullying dogma? To lionize quiet confidence over too-loud bombasticism, they insist, is old-fashioned and ethnocentric. And as for *faith*, well, that's a word so loaded with baggage that merely seeing it in print produces in some a series of triggering associations. However, if effective opinion writing is in large part a societal corrective or counterweight, and if the general public does indeed conflate opinion with complaint, we can surely do with more earnestness in public discourse to balance the surfeit of desultory philippics and lamentations crowding today's editorial pages.

Opinion writing's most powerfully earnest piece may well be the 1897 editorial written by newspaperman Francis Pharcellus Church in response to Virginia O'Hanlon, who writes in her famous "Dear Editor" letter: "I am 8 years old. Some of my little friends say there is no Santa Claus. Papa says, 'If you see it in *The Sun*, it's so.' Please tell me the truth, is there a Santa Claus?" Church jumps at the chance to address his dubious young reader, walking the fine line between truth and "white lies" in his famous opinion-cum-reply:

> Virginia, your little friends are wrong. They have been affected by the skepticism of a skeptical age. They do not believe except they see. They think that nothing can be which is not comprehensible by their little minds. All minds, Virginia, whether they be men's or children's, are little. In this great universe of ours, man is a mere insect, an ant, in his intellect as compared with the boundless world about him, as measured by the intelligence capable of grasping the whole of truth and knowledge.

6. Ethos and the Art of Sincerity

Yes, Virginia, there is a Santa Claus. He exists as certainly as love and generosity and devotion exist, and you know that they abound and give to your life its highest beauty and joy. Alas! How dreary would be the world if there were no Santa Claus! It would be as dreary as if there were no Virginias. There would be no childlike faith then, no poetry, no romance to make tolerable this existence. We should have no enjoyment, except in sense and sight. The eternal light with which childhood fills the world would be extinguished.[3]

Keeping It (Charmingly) Real

How can one be both charming—a word which implies enchantment and even beguilement—and sincere at the same time? Humor is one method, as it uniquely mingles charm and virtue, explaining why a good sense of humor is routinely listed as one of the qualities we most seek in a mate. Viewed in this light, the value of humor to a citizen writer makes an intuitive kind of sense. To be witty or funny is to be alert, engaged, astute, and alive to nuance just as it is to be observant, salient, salty, and sensitive to incongruity or anomaly. It's to not miss a beat. Like a news commentator, a humorist must be "on" all the time, lest the punchline or present moment pass them by. Commentary and kind-hearted humor are kindred arts requiring proportion, speed, and timing.

In his commentary "Going Out for a Walk," English social critic Max Beerbohm endears himself by puncturing the smug superiority of exercisers, thereby aligning himself with his less physically ambitious everyman or everywoman reader. By tackling the pomposity and presumption of exercise-shamers who think less of a person that refuses physical activity, Beerbohm picks a well-intentioned bone with his brethren Englishmen, specifically those who zealously insist on an evening stroll or a morning constitutional. While an inveterate walker declares that their daily stroll clears the mind and renews the vigor, charming Beerbohm sincerely claims the opposite, arguing that he is seldom more of a mindless idiot than he is during the glorified act of walking.

Beerbohm opines: "Even if you go to some definite place, for some definite purpose, the brain would rather you took a vehicle; but it does not make a point of this; it will serve you well enough unless you are going for a walk. It won't, while your legs are vying with each other, do any deep thinking for you, nor even any close thinking."[4] In Beerbohm's humble opinion, the compulsory fitness "powerwalk" stands to lower I.Q., not raise it.

In commentaries like "Going Out for a Walk," the writer turns on the charm to underscore their ethos. In this case, Beerbohm convinces

Part II—A Citizen Writer's Toolkit

his reader that a man who could be so sincere in his distaste for an English institution must be honest-to-a-fault and therefore authentically himself. And the reader surely grants Beerbohm bonus points for his use of bathos—the classical move by which the writer punctures pretense and pomp with their gift for leveling humor.

Voicing Your Opinion

1. After the fashion of Francis Pharcellus Church's famous editorial "Yes, Virginia, there is a Santa Claus," pen an opinion in which you lead with sincerity, perhaps defending that which you consider wholesome, pure, or sacred. As you write, keep your eyes on the sharpshooters—those so-called Muppets in the balcony that would accuse you of being juvenile or jejune.

2. Inspired by the example of Pete Davis, write an earnest op-ed or commentary in which you caution colleagues, coworkers, or fellow citizens against a trap you have good reason to believe they have fallen victim to, or might soon. Maybe you agree with Davis that your age cohort is overly enamored with "keeping their options open," and "infinite browsing." Or maybe you feel young workers have fallen into what he calls in a separate commentary written for *Fast Company* "the Cult of Busy." Your goal is to reach others with an earnest plea that comes straight from the heart.

3. Led by the example of Max Beerbohm, be charmingly real regarding your opinion about something you concede may be good for you or for society, but which has, in your sincere estimation, been taken too far. Perhaps you feel the move away from meat to plant-based proteins is a bridge too far. Or maybe you, an avowed dog-lover, offer your readers an earnest confession that the cult of dog worship threatens to overrun common-sense prohibitions against animals in restaurants and grocery stores. Whatever you choose, avoid simple snark in favor of an astringent approach that maintains its good humor.

7

Writing the Vox Populi

Vox populi, or voice of the people, is bedrock for the citizen writer seeking to discern the voice of the everyman and everywoman amid a cacophony of special interests, sanctimonious sentiment, and sanitized messaging. It's the vox populi, the theory goes, to whom the truly civic-minded editorialist owes their most profound allegiance. Granted, the opinion writer must first serve, and answer to, their individual conscience. But it's also true that the commentator or columnist who isolates themselves from public sentiment in favor of their own idiosyncratic view is no more in touch than the intellectual in the ivory tower or the artist in the garret. It makes sense, then, that a majority of opinion writers have populist leanings, having seen over a lifetime that the will of the people is too often subverted by those that only claim to champion the common man or woman. In such a climate, the independent, unaffiliated writer of op-eds is the closest thing to an impartial citizen-advocate We the People could ever hope to find.

What does it mean, in practice, to be a vehicle for the vox populi? First and foremost, the public-serving writer must respect the collective wisdom of the people while at the same time seeking solutions that transcend simple common sense. It entails an understanding that the will of the *demos* in democracy is a difficult thing to discern in op-ed pages populated by the kind of self-centered authors who only pose as representatives of the masses. This doesn't mean, however, that citizen writers must yield to the tyranny of the majority or bow to the will of the collective. In some instances, the job entails serving as a counterweight to conventional wisdom, or calling out the implicit biases and blind spots of otherwise loyal readers and subscribers.

Author-journalist Ambrose Bierce frequently calls the vox populi into question. Such is the case in his aptly titled commentary "Public Opinion Is Responsible for Many Fallacies." Bierce's piece, penned for the *San Francisco Examiner*, begins:

Part II—A Citizen Writer's Toolkit

> Surely the "average man," as everyone knows him, is not very wise, not very learned, not very good.... It seems to me that the average man, as I know him, is very much a fool, and something of a rogue as well. He has only a smattering of education, knows virtually nothing of political history, or history of any kind, is incapable of logical, that is to say, clear thinking, is subject to the suasion of base and silly prejudices, and selfish beyond expression. That such a person's opinions should be so obviously better than my own that I should accept them instead, and assist in enacting them into laws, appears to me most improbable. I may "bow to the will of the people" as gracefully as a defeated candidate, and for the same reason, namely, that I cannot help myself; but to admit that I was wrong in my belief and flatter the power that subdues me—no, that I will not do. And if nobody would do so, the average man would not be so very cocksure of his infallibility and might sometimes consent to be counselled by his betters. In any matter of which the public has imperfect knowledge, public opinion is as likely to be erroneous as is the opinion of an individual equally uninformed. To hold otherwise is to hold that wisdom can be got by combining many ignorances.[1]

Bierce offers some tough medicine in this acerbic passage, as the picture it presents of the average Joe or Jane is far from flattering. From it, one can clearly see how the opinion writer's fundamental view of We the People colors and shapes their prose style. A writer sympatico with Bierce's worldview prepares themselves to confront the "many ignorances" masquerading as popular sentiment. Conversely, the writer with a predisposition to find people essentially good and virtuous finds themselves inclined to defend the vox populi when it is dismissed or disparaged. Writers of both types can succeed as citizen critics, though their success taps into very different wellsprings.

Sympathy For the Common Man

Part of a belief in the vox populi is the understanding that much of a nation's essential work is done by a working class owed greater appreciation. Highlighting unsung heroes is, therefore, very much in the job description of the equity-minded citizen writer.

A prime example is a commentary written by journalist Stephen Crane, celebrated author of *The Red Badge of Courage*. As a war correspondent stationed in Cuba during the Spanish-American War, Crane saw countless common soldiers give their lives with little fanfare. Indeed, the lack of regard for their sacrifice led him to write one of the most memorable opinions of his time. In columns written for the *New York World*, Crane took great pride in honoring the prototypical nameless infantryman,

7. Writing the Vox Populi

calling him the "best man standing on two feet on God's green earth." At the same time, he understood that the exploits of the ordinary Army grunt in Cuba held little fascination for the American public. This disconnect, in fact, lends impetus to the commentary excerpted below, "Regulars Get No Glory," a piece with both feet planted firmly in the camp of the common man. Crane insists:

> The public wants to learn of the gallantry of Reginald Marmaduke Maurice Montmorenci Sturtevant.... Whereas, the name of the regular soldier is probably Michael Nolan and his life-sized portrait was not in the papers in celebration of his enlistment. Just plain Private Nolan, blast him—he is of no consequence. He will get his name in the paper—oh, yes, when he is "killed." Or when he is "wounded." Or when he is "missing." If some good Spaniard shoots him through he will achieve a temporary notoriety, figuring in the lists for one brief moment in which he will appear to the casual reader mainly as part of a total, a unit in the interesting sum of men slain. In fact, the disposition to leave out entirely all lists of killed and wounded regulars is quite a rational one since nobody cares to read them, anyhow, and their omission would allow room for oil paintings of various really important persons, limned as they were in the very act of being at the front, proud young men riding upon horses, the horses being still in Tampa and the proud young men being at Santiago, but still proud young men riding upon horses. The ungodly Nolan, the sweating, swearing, overloaded, hungry, thirsty, sleepless Nolan, tearing his breeches on the barbed wire entanglements, wallowing through the muddy fords, pursuing his way through the stiletto-pointed thickets, climbing the fire-crowned hill—Nolan gets shot.[2]

In fiery passages like this one, it's easy to see with whom the author's sympathies lie, and why. The gentrified officer class, Crane implies, already have legions of supporters and sycophants ready to sing their praises and to make certain their heroic deeds are duly noted for posterity. By contrast, the Michael Nolans of the world have only frontline war correspondents like Crane to ensure their fleeting lives are recorded. Crane obviously takes great pride in this role. Even as he celebrates Nolan's fighting spirit, he chastises a public that prefers propagandistic accounts of gallant young men of wealth and class.

Crane's work of opinion succeeds in large part due to its ability to draw a sharp contrast between two characters—the fictional Michael Nolan, on the one hand, and the hyperbolic Reginald Marmaduke Maurice Montmorenci Sturtevant on the other. Without these sobriquets, it's possible his commentary would fizzle for want of concretion or exemplification. The difference between these two soldiers is evident in their names—one being plainly American, the other sounding aristocratically European. The commentator clearly sides with Nolan, as does the reader.

Crane concludes his column by confronting Jane and John Doe even as he praises the unsung American dying in the fields of Cuba, scolding: "And shame, deep shame, on those who, because somebody once led a cotillon, can seem to forget Nolan—Private Nolan of the regulars—shot through, his half-bred terrier being masterless at Reno...; Nolan, no longer sweating, swearing, overloaded, hungry, thirsty, sleepless, but merely a corpse, attired in about forty cents' worth of clothes. Here's three volleys and taps to one Nolan, of this regiment or that regiment, and maybe some day, in a fairer, squarer land, he'll get his picture in the paper, too."

Making the Invisible Visible

Like Stephen Crane, commentator Dorothy Thompson held a healthy respect for the average man and woman on the streets whose plight she examined in countless newspaper and magazine columns. Thompson had a special gift for making the invisible visible while seeing to it that those less fortunate were seen and heard. In her work one senses genuine fondness for the vox populi, and a concomitant dedication to the idea of America as a worthy home for the needy as well as the free and the brave.

An example of Thompson at her egalitarian best is "Our Ghostly Commonwealth," a commentary first published in the *Saturday Evening Post*. Thompson begins her piece with this compelling assertion: "There exists in the United States, alongside our so-called normal social and economic life, another commonwealth, a ghostly one—ghostly because it is largely invisible to those who are not its members, and ghostly in the vague uneasiness which its haunting presence provokes." Prefiguring the "Two Americas" trope later made famous by President Barack Obama, Thompson goes on to describe the invisible citizens—men, women and children—languishing in poverty and stigmatized by need.

"Our Ghostly Commonwealth" demonstrates the many ways in which language is used to categorize, shame, and silo working-class Americans who depend on government relief. In Thompson's view, words are just one of several instruments used to systematically disenfranchise a group euphemistically called "The People." She writes, "The people on relief are not usually referred to as 'people.' The society in which they live has a nomenclature of its own, as well as a social and economic organization of its own. They are usually referred to as 'clients' or as 'cases,' and, in

7. Writing the Vox Populi

groups, as a 'case load.'"[3] Thompson points out that despite their sociological depersonalization, these "clients" and "case loads" do the work of the nation, from construction to manufacture to transportation.

Ironically, these denizens of the ghostly republic are not endowed with privacy in return for their anonymity. Instead, the opinion writer claims, their lives are relentlessly documented and cataloged, to the point that "more is known about them than about any other part of the population—about their race, and skills, work histories, diseases, even about their personalities—but the knowledge is in the files of state and federal government agencies.... In so far as the rest of our society is conscious of them, the attitude is a combination of bad conscience and hostility, and of this attitude they are also aware—and repay it, on their part, with a feeling of frustration and hostility."

As much as she empathizes with the working poor, Thompson's advocacy is not blind or uncomplicated. Using words like "frustration" and "hostility," she makes it clear that the people on relief are not always charitable or kind in return. She allows for the possibility that a small minority of welfare recipients may file fraudulent claims. Such occasional transgressions do not reduce Thompson's sympathy, though they do inform her empathy. The writer's goal is not to further mythologize those on the welfare rolls, but to humanize them, which necessarily means making mention of failures and even frauds. In sum, "Our Ghostly Commonwealth" succeeds in making the invisible visible, pointing out that the language used to name a societal injustice can prove critical in finding a solution. Thompson's piece is an argument both for the generosity of language and a call for its intentional, precise use. If indeed our republic is populated by human ghosts denied recognition as individuals, then the answer must partly lie in revising an injudicious or unjust nomenclature.

Applying a similar logic, contemporary commentators have sought to raise awareness of homelessness by redirecting the language used to describe it, preferring, for instance, "unhoused person" to the more conventional "homeless." Detractors decry such changes as political correctness, but to many who experiencing the condition, "unhoused" feels more precise, since it's possible to feel "at home" or "homed" without actually having a roof over one's head.

A Case Study in Courage

In his long career, Pulitzer Prize–winning commentator Ray Stannard Baker exemplified not only a belief in the newspaper and magazine

Part II—A Citizen Writer's Toolkit

as instruments of civic life but also in the courage requisite to challenge a complacent or compromised vox populi. Combining the unflinching truth-telling of Ambrose Bierce with the patriotic sympathies of Dorothy Thompson, Baker treats the public with a mixture of praise and punitive comment. Is it possible to critique the very person or institution one is sworn to uphold? Baker's work suggests it's not only possible but necessary, with the understanding that true love and loyalty require absolute honesty.

In his famous piece "The Lone Fighter," Baker tackles the ascendant power of "Bosses"—the class of monopolists and middle managers that exploit a sometimes gullible workforce. Refusing to mince words, he begins with what might be called fightin' words, asserting, "We Americans are not a free people, and this is not a free country."[4] The founding myth inscribed in America's so-called War for Independence is just that, he insists, adding, "Whatever may have been the dream of 1776, no thoughtful American will venture to assert that we have, today, a government by the people." Instead, he declares, the audacious sentiments expressed in the Declaration of Independence have devolved into "a government of the Bosses, by the Bosses, and distinctly for the Bosses ... not only in politics—our gall sores there have even begun to callous—but in other departments of our life."

Bosses, Baker argues, are "the very disease of democracy," multiplying like virulent strains of an insidious virus. Even the leaders of trade unions, when they became all-powerful, behave like monopolists and machine politicians. Meanwhile, financial bosses like steel magnate John D. Rockefeller began to direct the business of government, serving as a kind of "extra-constitutional cabinet." In essence, Baker declares, We the People are ruled by what he calls "usurping middlemen; the Boss is a middleman, a sort of broker in government to whom we assign our obvious and personal rights and duties (allowing him to take his own percentages) because we are too busy making money or spending it, to care whether we are free or not." Later in his muckraking commentary he doubles down on his thesis, opining:

> No, this is not a free country, because we, the people, are not intelligent and honest and brave enough to use freedom. What we do have in this country to a degree unequaled elsewhere in the world is the opportunity of freedom. That is the triumph of the American democracy; it insures the people freedom if they wish to take it; but it cannot force freedom upon any man who does not want it, or who is too lazy or too selfish or too ignorant to take it. Half of our reformers are today engaged in the utterly stupid task of trying to make people free by new laws. It is like trying to legislate a man happy.

7. Writing the Vox Populi

It is safe to say that a majority of the people in this country would prefer an honest free government to boss-rule, but most of us are drifters—honest enough, but pulpy; we have no courage to stand up and say what we believe, or to back it up afterwards, if necessary, with hard knocks. We don't like to get our hands soiled, or to have our ease disturbed.[5]

Later in this remarkable piece of opinion, the truth-telling commentator blunts his critique, pointing to the "lone fighter" as America's most potent weapon against monopolies and plutocrats. No doubt wanting to leave his readers with a potential solution to the problems named, he reminds us of a central American tenet that "everything worth doing in this world has been done by the man who believed something strongly enough to fight for it alone."

As a commentary, "The Lone Fighter" plays for keeps, rejecting polite euphemism. The opinion writer concludes that if the vox populi cannot call out the despotism of monopolists and bosses, then American workers might as well surrender their country along with their freedom: "It is a dead man who does not thrill when he reads of the citizens of Chicago and New York and other cities who, setting aside their business interests, having no hope of reward, subject to misunderstanding and abuse and foul questioning of their motives, have yet gone on doggedly fighting political corruption, because something inside of them was honest and angry."

Together, Baker, Bierce, Crane, and Thompson write with a healthy respect for the voice of the people and an attendant willingness to confront citizens who have lost sight of the core creed of their nation.

Voicing Your Opinion

1. Following Stephen Crane, generate your own "Michael Nolan," a composite character embroiled in a struggle much larger than themselves. For example, suppose you want to write a guest opinion piece about immigration-resistant ranchers living on the Southwest border. What representative character name might you generate to stand in for the whole, and to serve as the face of the problem or its solution? As you write, be aware that names can serve as vehicles for harmful stereotypes, especially where race and ethnicity are concerned.

2. Using Dorothy Thompson's "Our Ghostly Commonwealth" as scaffolding, produce a citizen's viewpoint piece on a population you feel has been "ghosted"—forgotten, maligned, or neglected. In your

Part II—A Citizen Writer's Toolkit

opinion, why are they so often forgotten and who is most complicit in their forgetting? Take care to avoid excessive pity or pathos as you draw attention to a neglected demographic.

3. Is America truly a free country? Does the vox populi really rule? Following the brave example of Ray Stannard Baker, dissect the myth of American exceptionalism in an original opinion. In what ways has twenty-first-century American democracy remained true to its founding ideals? In what ways has it forgotten its sacred promise to its people? As you draft and re-draft, make a point of weaving compelling facts with provocative opinions.

8

Charting a Course of Action

At one time or another, nearly every opinion writer gets labeled a windbag, wonk, or worse. "Easy for you to say," a reader might say (or think) in response to a commentator's bold assertion. "Why don't you come down from your high horse and fix it then, know-it-all."

In many ways, the exasperated reader is entitled to their cynicism, journalists being better known for high-minded decrees than for life-changing deeds. Fortunately, writers of opinion have long been held to an accountability standard: if we name a problem in the course of our column, we're expected to conclude with a potential solution, or, at the very least, a plausible path forward. It's by this means that the critic on their high horse is brought back down to earth, where decisions must be made and action must be taken.

Sometimes the burden of saying nothing, of turning the other cheek on a known injustice, is one the conscientious citizen writer simply cannot bear. Such is the case with Richard Harding Davis, the intrepid war correspondent who reported from the frontlines in Cuba and in Germany, where he was held captive. Davis begins his op-ed in the *New York Tribune* with an unabashed statement of intention, writing: "I feel very deeply, therefore, that if I did not earnestly try to convince Americans that they should not be neutrals I would be shirking a responsibility."[1]

Neutrality was the official American stance in 1914, yet Davis hopes to make the case to an isolationist nation that it should confront German aggression before it is too late. Germany, he maintains, is fighting dirty, ignoring international conventions of war and committing crimes against humanity. "If we are convinced that one opponent is fighting honestly and that his adversary is striking below the belt, or gouging and biting," he declares, "then for us to maintain a neutral attitude of mind is unworthy and the attitude of a coward." Resorting to metaphor, the writer compares Germany to a mad dog run amok in a peaceful village, insisting, "It is the duty of every farmer to get his gun and destroy it, not to lock himself indoors."

Perhaps sensing that his argument relies too heavily on outmoded codes of honor, Davis quickly moves to clarify. America should not make an enemy of the German people, but instead train its weapons on the military-industrial complex ruled by men badly out of touch with their people. He continues:

> This is not a war against Germans, as we know Germans in America, who are among our sanest and most industrious and most responsible fellow countrymen. It is a war, as Winston Churchill in his interview last Sunday explained, against the military aristocracy of Germany, men who are six hundred years behind the times; who, to preserve their class against democracy, have perverted every great invention of modern times to the uses of warfare, to the destruction of life.
>
> These men are military mad. Their idea of government is as far opposed to our own as is martial law and the free speech of our town meetings. Every belief of these high-born butchers is opposed to every principle that is to us most dear.

Less than 500 words into his opinion, Davis deftly changes his tack such that the man or woman unwilling to fight Germany is cast as a de facto underminer of American democracy.

Choosing a More Equitable Path

In 1919 American soldiers of many colors and creeds were returning from fighting the very enemy Davis calls to account. America and its allies had secured an armistice, and yet thousands of Black soldiers who had fought the Germans in the trenches felt defeated on returning to their home country. Enter activist-author W.E.B. Du Bois, whose column "Returning Soldiers" aims to raise awareness among White Americans. The writing of Du Bois, who is more exuberant in his prose than Richard Harding Davis, reads like a series of impassioned pleas. His objective is to help the nation see the hypocrisy of urging its African American citizens to war against a racist regime overseas while overlooking the way citizens of color are lynched and brutalized at home.

What could the United States do to remedy the injustice? It could appreciate the sacrifice of its returning soldiers of color. It could take urgent action against fascism and racism on its own soil, showing itself strong enough to confront domestic peril and prejudice. Du Bois's powerful

8. Charting a Course of Action

commentary must be read in full to appreciate the force and skill of its appeal:

> We are returning from war! THE CRISIS and tens of thousands of black men were drafted into a great struggle. For bleeding France and what she means and has meant and will mean to us and humanity and against the threat of German race arrogance, we fought gladly and to the last drop of blood; for America and her highest ideals, we fought in far-off hope; for the dominant southern oligarchy entrenched in Washington, we fought in bitter resignation. For the America that represents and gloats in lynching, disfranchisement, caste, brutality and devilish insult—for this, in the hateful upturning and mixing of things, we were forced by vindictive fate to fight.
>
> But today we return! We return from the slavery of uniform which the world's madness demanded us to don to the freedom of civil garb. We stand again to look America squarely in the face and call a spade a spade. We sing: This country of ours, despite all its better souls have done and dreamed, is yet a shameful land.
>
> It *lynches*.
>
> And lynching is barbarism of a degree of contemptible nastiness unparalleled in human history. Yet for fifty years we have lynched two Negroes a week, and we have kept this up right through the war.
>
> It *disfranchises* its own citizens.
>
> Disfranchisement is the deliberate theft and robbery of the only protection of poor against rich and black against white. The land that disfranchises its citizens and calls itself a democracy lies and knows it lies.
>
> It encourages *ignorance*.
>
> It has never really tried to educate the Negro. A dominant minority does not want Negroes educated. It wants servants, dogs, whores and monkeys. And when this land allows a reactionary group by its stolen political power to force as many black folk into these categories as it possibly can, it cries in contemptible hypocrisy: "They threaten us with degeneracy; they cannot be educated."
>
> It *steals* from us.
>
> It organizes industry to cheat us. It cheats us out of our land; it cheats us out of our labor. It confiscates our savings. It reduces our wages. It raises our rent. It steals our profit. It taxes us without representation. It keeps us consistently and universally poor, and then feeds us on charity and derides our poverty.
>
> It *insults* us.
>
> It has organized a nationwide and latterly a worldwide propaganda of deliberate and continuous insult and defamation of black blood wherever found. It decrees that it shall not be possible in travel nor residence, work nor play, education nor instruction for a black man to exist without tacit or open acknowledgment of his inferiority to the dirtiest white dog. And it looks upon any attempt to question or even discuss this dogma as arrogance, unwarranted assumption and treason. This is the country to which we Soldiers of Democracy return. This is the fatherland for which we fought! But it is *our* fatherland.

Part II—A Citizen Writer's Toolkit

It was right for us to fight. The faults of *our* country are *our* faults. Under similar circumstances, we would fight again. But by the God of Heaven, we are cowards and jackasses if now that that war is over, we do not marshal every ounce of our brain and brawn to fight a sterner, longer, more unbending battle against the forces of hell in our own land.

We *return*.
We *return from fighting*.
We *return fighting*.

Make way for Democracy! We saved it in France, and by the Great Jehovah, we will save it in the United States of America, or know the reason why.[2]

Du Bois's rhetorical toolkit includes the use of anaphora (repeated words used at the beginning of successive clauses) to detail a litany of racial transgressions. He uses exclamation points to lend immediacy and urgency to his argument while leveraging parallel structure to bring order to a commentary that might otherwise feel overwrought. The use of dynamic verbs used in parallel such as "lynches," "disenfranchises," and "steals" puts the focus on the negative actions the nation takes toward its Black citizens rather than making more abstract claims about what America is or isn't. For example, to label the United States a racist country would have been to alienate many readers in 1919, but to state plainly that many of its most vulnerable citizens were lynched within its borders was simply to state a matter of public record.

In fewer than 600 words, Du Bois manages to summon his patriotism, his fighting spirit, and his sense of indignation. "Returning Soldiers" is a brave commentary, in that it was written at a time when Americans were feeling especially patriotic and proud. To confront them with a litany of the nation's transgressions against its own people was to risk alienating citizens committed to a return to normalcy. Still, its conspicuous timing is exactly what makes the piece so courageous; the writer honors the courage of returning veterans with a courage all his own. In that way and in others, his ringing piece of opinion meets the moment.

Voicing Your Opinion

1. Generate an opinion piece lauding a group, subculture, or demographic that deserves more. For example, do you, like W.E.B. Du Bois, believe that your country owes its veterans more wholehearted support? For the sake of diversity, consider for your op-ed or commentary the service of other groups the country fails to support in reciprocal fashion.

8. Charting a Course of Action

2. Invoke the citizen writer's compass by suggesting a course of action that your organization, community, state, or nation would be wise to follow. In so doing, you could argue for a complete 180 degree turn in direction, or a more modest redirection of time, energy, or resources. Or, following the example of Richard Harding Davis, you might make your argument by detailing the dramatic consequences of collective inaction.

9

Finding the "I" in "We"

For well over a century, journalists have been trained to avoid the first-person "I." The prohibition against the "I" was so strong in the nineteenth century, in fact, that commentators wanting or needing to reference their own experience would often resort to awkward constructions like "the author," "the reporter" or "this journalist."

Fortunately, twenty-first-century opinion writers have a longer leash when it comes to using "I" and the first-person plural "we," and the most well-versed practitioners distinguish themselves by knowing exactly when to use each. After all, the line between the two pronoun cases is often a fine one; "I" is a powerful pronoun when used as an emblem of self-knowledge and self-assurance, while "We" is powerfully inclusive and communal. At the same time, a strongly self-possessed "I" who presumes rather than earns the use of the collective "We," risks misappropriation certain to alienates readers.

Community journalists know better than most just how fraught is the "I"/"We" tango. I learned this lesson firsthand many years ago while working at a family-owned weekly in the heart of the agrarian Midwest. As a section editor, I penned regular opinion columns on local and regional events ranging from sports to politics. On occasion, I availed myself of the first-person plural "We" when expressing a widely held view in the half dozen towns I regularly covered. When using the first-person plural, I felt buoyed and empowered; I wrote with a sense of solidarity, of togetherness, of all-for-one and one-for-all that, while fleeting, felt real. At other times, I grew trepidatious before the fraught pronoun, worrying that I had presumed a mandate rather than fairly earned one. At such times, I found the knowable "I" less presumptuous and more honest than "We." I found the personal pronoun especially useful on those occasions when I wanted or needed to separate my views from the views of the community, or to challenge them.

Citizen writers seeking to master the delicate dance of "I" and "We" do well to take their cues from the community journalists charged

9. Finding the "I" in "We"

with fairly representing the views of their neighbors even as they articulate their own. In the heart of the Civil Rights movement, the push-pull between "I" and "We" voices was felt acutely by the columnists writing for America's African American–owned newspapers. In St. Petersburg, Florida, for example, the Black community turned to *The Weekly Challenger* during a time of tumultuous social upheaval. Founded by businessman Cleveland Johnson, Jr., in 1967, the paper vowed to be a positive voice in a sea of otherwise discriminatory news coverage in the Deep South. By the early 1970s, however, its small stable of regular opinion writers felt pressured by those in the community who wanted *The Weekly Challenger* to fight for civil rights and racial equity with greater ferocity.

In her popular eponymous column "Mabel Writes of This 'n' That," Mabel Cooper decided to take the bull by the horns in the October 6, 1973, edition, addressing those readers who had long wanted her to be more critical of the White establishment. Cooper's response expertly blends the first-person singular and first-person plural in a column that simultaneously manages to reinforce community at the same time that it defends the writer's personal views. She writes: "You see, I am not a preacher. Nor a teacher. I am simply Mabel Cooper, citizen. A black woman fortunate enough to speak up and speak out and reach hundreds of people through *The Weekly Challenger*. Still, I am only a single voice, trying to remain. You and me and all of us, know how important it is to constantly re-examine our attitudes and solutions to black problems."[1]

Cooper confesses that she has been labeled a "Tom"—short for "Uncle Tom"—by some, and because her personal phone number is printed alongside her column's headshot, she's heard from plenty of detractors. She doesn't believe in using her commentaries to stoke the fires of racial enmity, she tells us. Instead, she aims to cultivate "sensitivity" and "sensibility." She closes her column with a renewed resolve to speak her mind while at the same time being mindful of reader reactions, opining, "I do hope, though, that when I communicate my way, more and more of us will give just a little honest thought to what we are all doing—what we can do—to more realistically solve more of the problems facing the black community. If I get congrats and comments because of it…. I must be doing something right. At least, someone out there is reading and thinking." The sheer diversity of the pronoun cases used in Cooper's short piece—*me, you, we, our, us,* and *I*, with the latter used well over a dozen times—show that she practices exactly what she preaches, as her citizen writing walks the fine line between self and society.

Part II—A Citizen Writer's Toolkit

"We" Shall Overcome

As a pronoun, "we" came to epitomize the collective action and advocacy of the American Civil Rights movement. Historically, "we" serves for solidarity, especially when wielded by a writer with the confidence to presume a mouthpiece and a mandate. However, there's also power in "we" when it articulates a difficult truth or unpopular view back to the close-knit constituency that engenders its use in the first place.

A case in point is the opinion "Shooting of Mr. Wallace Deplorable" written by C. Blythe Andrews, editor and publisher of the African American semi-weekly the *Florida Sentinel Bulletin*. An ardent segregationist and candidate for the Democratic presidential nomination in 1972, George Wallace was viewed as public enemy number one by many in the Black press. And yet when a gunman attempted to assassinate the former Alabama governor that spring at a Maryland shopping mall, Andrews unequivocally condemned it, articulating a difficult truth under the bold headline "Shooting of Mr. Wallace Deplorable." Andrews turns to "we" and the first-person plural possessive "ours" to walk the fine line between decrying the candidate's racist views to his predominately Black readers while also condemning in no uncertain terms acts of retaliatory political violence.

In just his second paragraph, the courageous editor of *Sentinel Bulletin* lays it on the line, writing: "We fought and will continue to fight everything Mr. Wallace stood for, but certainly respect him as a politician and his individual right to have opinions different from ours."[2] Indeed, Wallace opposed just about every single thing Andrews's newspaper stood for, from school integration to affirmative action. Still, Andrews boldly labels the attempt on Wallace's life "wanton and unwarranted," while also returning to the shelter and safe haven offered by the umbrella use of "we" as an emblem of collective action, observing: "We all must work together for a strict gun control law and tell the masses the truth about where the country is headed if we continue to polarize along racial lines, war lines, and segregated lines."

Where did the editor find the humanity to speak up for the sanctity of the life of a politician who served as the antithesis of all Andrews held dear? Empathy must surely have played a role, as Andrews knew what it meant to be targeted for the beliefs he dared express. Six months earlier his office at the *Sentinel Bulletin* had been burglarized and looted, the thieves stealing the very symbol of an editor's persuasive power: his typewriter.

9. Finding the "I" in "We"

A Case for Pronoun Cases

Another journalist who consistently puts his pronouns to productive use is the great Ray Stannard Baker. Writing for *McClure's* circa the early twentieth century, Baker uses his national platform to expose the ongoing problem of lynching in America to his primarily White readership. Taking a first-person approach that uses both the familiar "I" pronoun and the first-person plural "We" in addition to the second-person "You," he writes with a sense of restrained indignation, sharing his experience traveling to "lynching towns" that only seem distant to readers ensconced in a protective bubble:

> You and I imagine that a lynching somehow could not possibly take place in our town; our people are orderly and law-abiding; our officials, whatever may be said of their politics, may be depended upon to do their duty; you and I are truly civilized. And conversely, we imagine that the people in towns where lynchings occur must be somehow peculiarly barbarous, illiterate, lawless. A lynching, like death, is a great way off until it strikes us.
>
> I have just been visiting a number of "lynching towns" in this country, both in the South and in the North. I went primarily to formulate, if I could, a clear idea of what one hundred and fifty lynchings a year—the average in the United States for the last twenty-two years—might really signify, to discover in what way a lynching town is different from my town or your town, what classes of citizens constitute the mobs, and what is the underlying cause of such murderous outbreaks.
>
> And as I visited the various towns I was more and more impressed with a sense of their homely familiarity; they were all American towns, just like yours and mine. I saw no barbarians. On Sunday morning I heard the church bells ringing, on weekdays there was the same earnest political buncombe; I found the same sort of newspapers and fraternal societies and woman's clubs, the same talk—and nothing but talk—of "political graft" in this gas deal or that water company, the same soaring local pride over the tallest stand-pipe, or the most wonderful spring, or the greatest factory.
>
> In each successive place they pointed out the ... pole or tree from which the mob's victim had dangled, or the stake at which he was burned to death; they showed me the jails which had been broken open; they told me the awful and gruesome details of the crimes committed. And I heard and saw these things with a strong sense of the unreality of it all; one cannot easily believe that such upheavals could really happen in these orderly, busy, familiar American towns. Yet they have happened, both in the North and in the South, with incidents of unimaginable horror and brutality; and they will happen again—next time, perhaps, in your town or mine. No, lynching is not a crime of barbarians; it is not a Southern crime, nor a Western crime, nor a Northern crime; it is an American crime.[3]

Baker's status as a White commentator writing for an established magazine affords him a collegial "You and I" tone largely unavailable to

Part II—A Citizen Writer's Toolkit

Black journalists writing to White readerships. Still, the commentator puts his privilege to good use in "What Is a Lynching?" by enacting a sort of solidarity that helps make his point: lynching is an American humiliation. His opinion piece is further empowered by his willingness to travel to the scene of the crime, and to point out the beguiling normalcy of American places with blood on their hands.

In a world marked by corruption, opportunities to expose injustice are endless. The thoughtful citizen critic chooses their battles carefully by homing in on a manageable aspect of a larger problem viewed in microcosm. Baker might instead have commented on a topic as broad as racial injustice. Solid journalistic instincts, however, guide him to a more specific focus on racial violence committed against African Americans, and, in particular, to the horrific crime of lynching. Far from being a hedge or a sell-out, shorter commentaries all but require a tighter focus, one that takes a larger problem and breaks it down into component issues whose resolution feels sure to move the needle in the right direction.

Voicing Your Opinion

1. Inspired by the courage of Civil Rights–era columnist Mabel Cooper of *The Weekly Challenger*, write an opinion piece in which you speak directly to members of your individual community, both as a community spokesperson of sorts and as an individual with a strong sense of self and conscience. What do members of your community criticize you for? How do your expressed opinions sometimes disappoint or irk them? Conversely, what do they feel you consistently get right, despite their criticism? Like Cooper, consider ending your short column with a statement of your goals for yourself and for the community to whom you write and speak.

2. After the fashion of Ray Stannard Baker, consider writing a social justice-vested piece on a problem you're willing to experience personally. If you're writing on a tight budget, it's likely impractical to travel, for example, to the U.S.-Mexico border to ascertain conditions there. However, chances are good that an equally urgent injustice is occurring across the river, the railroad tracks, or county from where you are now. If at all possible, go there to live the problem and its solution, at least for a short time, while writing an opinion that reports to your readership what you found there and why it should matter.

10

The Power of Now

To earn the widest possible readership, successful opinion pieces appeal to what the ancient Greeks called *kairos*, a term that loosely translates as the right or critical moment or an auspicious or propitious moment for decision, discussion, or action. In an age of social media and round-the-clock news and status updates, citizen scribes working in a digital age must become orchestrators of time—coincidence, coalescence, concomitance, conjunction. And yet, if we wait for the proverbial planets to align, we may find the moment for comment has passed. The timely citizen critic must entertain past, present, and future all at once, managing time by thoughtfully moving through it.

Following is the text of the commentary I referred to in the introduction of this volume—the one whose existence I owe to the book publicist who first urged me to write for a national audience. The particular challenge I faced in drafting my breakthrough op-ed was to take a historical interest—in this case the pioneering voting rights marches of the early twentieth century that served as the subject of my book—and make it relevant to contemporary readers determined to redress present-day inequities. To succeed I would need to devise a hook provocative enough to capture the attention of a newspaper readership primarily focused on current events, one capable of helping them see that past and present are inextricably bound. The women's protest marches planned for the inauguration of then president-elect Donald Trump served to bridge then and now, offering what journalists call a "news peg" whose job it is to pin the topic of a piece to current events. Here's the original commentary in its entirety:

> On January 21st, the day after Donald Trump's planned inauguration, two hundred thousand women plan to march on Washington in support of the women's rights agenda threatened by the incoming administration.
>
> It wasn't until I published a book on the last such large-scale women's marches on inauguration week in Washington—those led by the inimitable "General" Rosalie Gardiner Jones and Inez Milholland in the winter of

Part II—A Citizen Writer's Toolkit

1913—that I understood how rare such gatherings of American women have been in history.

As a historian of the votes-for-women movement what interests me most about the coming March on Trump is not necessarily the way history rhymes, as Mark Twain put it, but how little seems to have changed in the palpable fear many men still feel when women don their marching boots. It's an abiding cultural if not biological anxiety that seems to emerge every time the issue of women in combat (read: militant women) bubbles up in public discourse, as it did this past year with the Obama administration's support of women registering for selective service.

Why is it that when women put boots on the ground and march, military-style and en masse, that they tend to meet with ideological if not physical violence, as they did in 1913, when the inauguration march turned out to be as much about men's fears as about women's rights. Is it women's displays of physical and intellectual strength that men historically fear, or widespread women's community, solidarity, and mobilization?

In 1913 votes-for-women activists stormed Pennsylvania Avenue on the occasion of Woodrow Wilson's inauguration, hoping to serve notice to the president-elect. Then as now marchers came from across the country for a grand parade led by Milholland wearing a white cape and riding a white horse at the front of a woman's army. Milholland's forces included five mounted brigades, twenty-six floats, and between 8,000 and 10,000 marchers.

Back then what most unsettled American men was the militant metaphor of Jones's and Milholland's march. Jones dubbed herself a "general" while her right-hand woman, Ida Craft, described herself as a "colonel." The reporters following the march of "Rosalie's army" were widely known as "war correspondents." Though the votes-for-women processions were peaceful (Jones actually carried doves), so-called "militant" suffragists such as Alice Paul understood that great gains in civil rights seldom arrived without first confronting the powers-that-be with their deepest (and often darkest) fears.

Brigades of "troops" advancing up Pennsylvania Avenue by the tens of thousands will always get the attention of institutionalized power-holders. And if president-elect Donald Trump's past disparagement of women is at root an expression of some deep-seated fear of them, this latest march will surely succeed, as it did in 1913, in drawing out and identifying the latent sexism and bigotry in Washington, D.C.

The boots-on-the ground marchers of 2017 do not expect to be greeted with violence on the National Mall come Saturday. Still, history reminds us that the activists of 1913 did not anticipate mob violence either. Saturday's marchers have the right to protection by law enforcement and to a peaceful and productive protest. They have the right to expect that the wrongs of the past will be righted.[1]

While my kairos-minded opinion piece wasn't perfect—no commentary ever is—it cleared its most formidable hurdle: demonstrating, in just over 500 words, how women's rights marches past and present form an

10. The Power of Now

important historical rhyme. The final version published by the *San Francisco Chronicle* was very close to the draft I originally submitted with one key difference: the final paragraph, which originally read:

> In 1913 mostly male fear of a mobilized and marching women's army resulted in mob violence in Washington, and a public outcry that ended in an eleven-day Congressional inquiry whose results, in part, helped secure Congressional passage of the 19th Amendment six years later in 1919. And while the boots-on-the ground marchers of 2017 do not expect to be greeted with violence on the National Mall come January 21st, history tells us their exceptional solidarity should leave the Trump administration sobered if not shaken.

After reading the original conclusion, the opinion editor wrote, "As far as I can tell, there is fear the 2017 marchers will encounter violence. Can [you] rework the last paragraph? I don't want to sow fear but I don't want to say there isn't fear when there is concern. Can you get this back to me tomorrow morning ... reworked?"

Initially, I balked at the revision the editor proposed, not to mention the twelve-hour timeframe I was given to revise and resubmit. I felt the requested edits risked turning already dramatic events into melodrama. By the next morning, however, I could better see the editor's point. My original conclusion perhaps put a bit too much faith in government restraint. It ended in a relatively risk-averse statement of fact (that the Trump administration would be "sobered if not shaken") while my rewrite issued a time-sensitive call-to-action—namely, the need for advance assurances of law-enforcement protection for marchers.

A Thing Worth Saving

At root, an op-ed assigns value, and very often that assignation applies to something that is undervalued, underestimated, and urgent. While commentaries that focus on earthshaking issues such as politics, war, and global economies tend to dominate op-ed pages, treatments of less publicized struggles sometimes achieve greater traction.

Just as commentators and columnists tackle issues of social and economic justice, so too must they address environmental justice. A case in point is naturalist John Muir, who realized that the preservation of nature could only be achieved if words on the page joined boots on the ground. Those who would disrespect Mother Nature would have to be reached rationally as well as emotionally. While Muir strongly preferred tramping through the high Sierras to the studied domesticity of his writer's desk,

Part II—A Citizen Writer's Toolkit

he understood that both the pen and the rucksack were needed to turn the tide in favor of Mother Nature in an otherwise rapacious age.

In his opinion "Save the Redwoods," Muir lodges his appeal through ethos, pathos, logos, and, most importantly, kairos, as he begins with a timely assessment of the growth of the environmental movement. "We are often told that the world is going from bad to worse, sacrificing everything to mammon," he commences, adding, "But this righteous uprising in defense of God's trees in the midst of exciting politics and wars is telling a different story, and every Sequoia, I fancy, has heard the good news and is waving its branches for joy."[2]

Muir's opening move toward optimism is a judicious one, as his readers—primarily fellow environmentalists—are surely weary of the never-ending battle to save the nation's most endangered plants and animals. He begins with a badly needed burst of optimism determined to see the good in people. "The wrongs done to trees, wrongs of every sort, are done in the darkness of ignorance and unbelief, for when light comes the heart of the people is always right," he writes, refusing to cast blame. Muir succeeds in this viewpoints piece in part because he makes the bold decision to personify the trees, comparing them to humans at every opportunity. When he describes a giant sequoia whose bark was stripped and shipped overseas for sale, he claims the tree is "skinned alive."

When he responds to those who justify the slaughter by claiming the giant sequoias offer the very best wood for building and industry, he offers a poignant analogy by way of rebuttal, opining, "No doubt these trees would make good lumber after passing through a sawmill, as George Washington after passing through the hands of a French cook would have made good food." Though the giant sequoia are mighty and noble, Muir wisely emphasizes their vulnerability before exploitative humans. They have survived for Millenia, and yet they are helpless before lustful lumbermen hell-bent on profit. On this subject, America's great preservationist proves particularly prescient:

> Any fool can destroy trees. They cannot defend themselves or run away. And few destroyers of trees ever plant any; nor can planting avail much toward restoring our grand aboriginal giants. It took more than three thousand years to make some of the oldest of the Sequoias, trees that are still standing in perfect strength and beauty, waving and singing in the mighty forests of the Sierra. Through all the eventful centuries since Christ's time, and long before that, God has cared for these trees, saved them from drought, disease, avalanches, and a thousand storms; but he cannot save them from sawmills and fools; this is left to the American people.

10. The Power of Now

What course of action would Muir have Americans take on behalf of these aboriginal giants? First, he argues, protectors must stay vigilant against an insatiable and insouciant industry. Second, Californians, sole American host to this remarkable species, must lead the fight in their defense:

> This righteous and lively indignation on the part of Californians after the long period of deathlike apathy, in which they have witnessed the destruction of other groves unmoved, seems strange until the rapid growth that right public opinion has made during the last few years is considered and the peculiar interest that attaches to the Calaveras giants. They were the first discovered and are best known. Thousands of travelers from every country have come to pay them tribute of admiration and praise, their reputation is world-wide, and the names of great men have long been associated with them—Washington, Humboldt, Torrey and Gray, Sir Joseph Hooker, and others. These kings of the forest, the noblest of a noble race, rightly belong to the world, but as they are in California we cannot escape responsibility as their guardians. Fortunately the American people are equal to this trust, or any other that may arise, as soon as they see it and understand it.

In the final analysis, the environmental writer's appeal to save the redwoods is both logical and passionate, pessimistic and optimistic. Californians have been awakened to the need for preservation, but their success has been limited to small conservation set-asides and areas, like Calaveras, where the trees are officially protected. Outside those borders, however, their wanton slaughter continues. Muir's urgent call to action is to defend the noble tree wherever it sinks its root. On a deeper level, his is a demand for government intervention in the fate of the species, the lumber industry having demonstrably failed to protect it. The time to act—the kairos of the issue—is now, since, as the citizen writer points out, their destruction is ongoing. "While the iron of public sentiment is hot," he exhorts, "let us strike hard. In particular, a reservation or national park of the only other species of Sequoia, the sempervirens, or redwood, hardly less wonderful than the gigantea, should be quickly secured."

Voicing Your Opinion

1. Like John Muir, use the power of the press to make an impassioned plea for the health and well-being of a nonhuman entity that, in your opinion, needs the public's help now before it's degraded or decimated beyond restoration. For example, suppose you want to write an op-ed defending the richly forested peaks of the Appalachian

Part II—A Citizen Writer's Toolkit

Mountains against mountaintop coalmining, or make an appeal for continued support of gray wolf reintroduction efforts in the West. Consider choosing a topic with which you have firsthand experience or long-standing research interest.

2. Locate a chapter in history that fascinates you—like the pioneering women's rights marches captivate me—and generate an opinion piece that hears a historical rhyme in a present-day analogous event. For example, suppose, in your mind, the current quest for transgender rights rhymes with the Civil Rights protests of the 1960s. Craft a succinct piece of opinion that, in fewer than 750 words, educates us on an overlooked history even as it alerts us to a contemporary congruence or resurgence of that prior ordeal or ideal.

Part III

Additional Opinion-Writing Genres

11

Advice Columns

Since the days of pioneers Emily Post and Beatrice Fairfax, advice columns have grown more diverse and inclusive. In their earliest incarnation, advice columnists tended to follow what we might call the Dear Abby template, one in which a distressed, directionless, or lovelorn letter-writer reaches out to the all-knowing columnist for much needed advice. Very often the writers of such letters express frustration at the powerlessness they feel, stuck in an exploitative relationship, a loveless marriage, or a dead-end job. More recently, however, a new generation of advice columnists has pivoted from offering shopworn advice on relationships to dispensing career and professional advice as well as counsel on ethical and philosophical dilemmas.

In a post-postmodern age suspicious of authority, readers are inclined to ask *who are you to give me advice?* of traditional counsel-givers. The very fact that any Joe or Jane could, in theory, oversee an online or print advice column partly explains why publications like *The New York Times Magazine* have raised the bar on contributor credentials.

Philosophical Opinions

Consider the case of Kwame Anthony Appiah, author of the popular *Times* feature "The Ethicist." Offering "advice on life's trickiest situations and moral dilemmas," Appiah, a trained philosopher with a PhD from Cambridge, brings a lifetime of academic experience in his field to bear on life's most persistent questions. In recent columns written for "The Ethicist," Appiah has tackled readers' real-life philosophical dilemmas in pieces titled "Should My Wife and I Tell Our 8-year-old How Much Money We Make?" and "Is It Okay to Get Food Stamps When You're Just Pursuing Your Passion?" In the latter, *The Times* ethicist responds to a concern shared by "Name Withheld" about a young artist friend's willingness to pay for her food with food stamps despite

11. Advice Columns

financial support from parents, an upper-middle class upbringing, and a part-time teaching job. Name Withheld feels that her young friend, who is able-bodied and possessed of a degree in her field from an elite university, should not avail herself of government benefits just to subsidize her passion for painting.

Appiah sees both sides, but ultimately advises Name Withheld, "If those activities aren't earning her enough money to feed herself adequately, I don't see why she shouldn't take the help our society has decided to offer."[1] In another piece, Appiah addresses the quandary of a reader, Mary Anne, who wonders if a local clothing boutique that quietly employs slimming mirrors is behaving ethically in the eyes of its customers. These examples demonstrate both the diversity of twenty-first-century philosophical debates and the utility of the advice-giver having a modicum of academic training to put such questions in proper context.

Career and Professional Advice

Many newspapers and trade magazines now provide thought-provoking opinion pieces on best practices, and very often these commentaries are first-person takes directly from the trenches of a profession, pieces in which the workplace citizen shares hard-won experience with newer hires. For example, several publications covering education regularly print career advice pieces in which seasoned practitioners share opinions on what to do, and what not to do, within the world of academe. Topics run the gamut from practicing self-care to advice on how to write performance reviews, and everything in between.

In a recent piece entitled "I no longer grade my students' work—and I wish I had stopped sooner," long-time professor Elisabeth Gruner shares her recommendation of a practice known as "ungrading."[2] Gruner's goal in this Creative Commons advice piece is to share current research on grading and at the same time, to recommend what she considers to be a more mindful evaluative practice. She articulates her reasoning in three parts: First, she wants students to focus on the feedback offered rather than simply tuning out once they receive their grade. Second, she aims for a more inclusive brand of teaching that refuses to assess achievement without first considering prior educational privilege. Third, she's delighted to substitute meaningful dialogue with her pupils in place of what she calls "the tyranny of determining a grade." Bruner's is a classic career advice piece in that it (a) articulates a problem with the current status quo and

Part III—Additional Opinion-Writing Genres

(b) identifies to readers what the writer sincerely feels to be a more enlightened option—in this case, "ungrading" student work.

On the surface, career advice would seem to be the easiest of opinion writing subgenres to tackle. Most writers work a day job, and most of us, by virtue of our discerning eye, develop strong opinions on what works, and what doesn't. However, an advice column that's actually heeded by working professionals—that gets real traction—is a much more difficult proposition. And while there's no hard-and-fast recipe for success, there are a handful of best practices, including:

✓ Choose a topic about which there is meaningful or energetic disagreement. For example, educators often have very strong opinions about grading. Many resent the workload; others lament the inevitable inequity of the evaluation, while still others find value and satisfaction in benchmarking students and their work.
✓ Demonstrate to readers what's wrong, unjust, or unfair about the current system, standard practice, or modus operandi.
✓ Present a reasonable, implementable alternative that could be liberating for open-minded reader-practitioners open to new ways of thinking.
✓ Close the loop by sharing results achieved.

Gruner's advice piece closes the loop beautifully, as she shares the results achieved in her implementation of the ungrading policy in her own classroom. She reflects, "Now, I see students from all backgrounds recognizing their own growth, whatever their starting point. They benefit from my coaching, but perhaps even more from the freedom to decide for themselves what really matters in their reading and writing. And I benefit too, from the opportunity to help them learn and grow without the tyranny of the grade." As career advice columnist, Gruner demonstrates sound craft. She expertly pairs antithetical words with strong connotations such as "freedom/tyranny." She wisely avoids attacking educators who continue to use the letter-grading system, since they remain the overwhelming majority, even as the connotation of her word choice strongly links conventional grading with tyranny.

Unconventional Advice

Author-journalist Cheryl Strayed would go onto to publish the best-selling memoir *Wild*, but circa the early 2010s she was busy penning a

11. Advice Columns

popular weekly advice column on the website *The Rumpus*. Writing under the nom de plume "Sugar," Strayed answered hundreds of soul-seeking letters in her time at the helm of "Dear Sugar," transforming the advice column forever. While countless columnists had used sobriquets before, including Dear Abby and Beatrice Fairfax, Sugar broke new ground with her liberal use of both profanity and profundity in lengthy, sometimes philosophical rejoinders. *The New Yorker* critic Sasha Frere-Jones summarizes her appeal thusly: "Sugar doesn't coddle her readers—she believes them, and hears the stories inside the story they think they want to tell. She manages astonishing levels of empathy without dissolving into sentiment, and sees problems before the reader can. Sugar doesn't promise to make anyone feel good, only that she understands a question well enough to answer it."[3]

While many of Strayed's letters of advice cover conventional relationship topics, others address more idiosyncratic or individualistic life challenges. "Ashamed and Afraid" writes Sugar to describe how his lifelong bout with stuttering has caused him to move from San Francisco to New York in an attempt to start anew, only to find that the shame of stuttering traveled with him. Sugar's reply demonstrates both her desire to be of service and her characteristic empathy, telling him that it's "heart-squinchingly terrible" that he's been alone for 28 years with such a deep-seated and sometimes desperate personal dilemma.[4] Still, she reminds him, "You have the power to end your isolation in ten seconds if you choose to. Just click on over to the National Stuttering Association, where you will find oodles of information that will help you connect with others who stutter ... and access other resources that will very likely play an important role in your ability to overcome the shame and fear you've gathered around you like a tomb constructed of the shame that has buried you alive."

The small sample of a much longer body of work demonstrates what makes Sugar so appealing. It's expressive ("heart-squinchingly"), instructive, informal ("oodles of information") and at times beautiful (the richly metaphoric "tomb constructed of the shame that has buried you alive.") In her candid response to "Ashamed and Afraid," Strayed does more than just rehash or restate the problem identified by the letter-writer, she reframes it, using new language and fresh expression to help clear the logjam inside the letter-writer's head. Sugar doesn't refer exclusively to the advice-seeker by their chosen moniker either, instead turning to words like "dear one," and "darling," to personalize her reply while at the same time infusing it with affirmation and affection.

Part III—Additional Opinion-Writing Genres

Life Lessons on the Opinion Page

Generally speaking, the tone and subject matter of advice columns reflect the unique demographics of the host publication. *The Rumpus* skews young, with a preponderance of readers in their 20s, 30s, and early 40s. Little surprise, then, that "Dear Sugar" is hip, highly literate, and occasionally profane. Many of the life dilemmas readers bring to Sugar reflect the problems and preoccupations of 20- and 30-somethings coming to terms with cultural and sexual identities.

Conversely, advice columnist Carolyn Hax writes for the *Washington Post*, a publication whose largest concentration of readers falls in the 55- to 64-year-old range.[5] As a consequence, Hax fields far more letters dealing with the questions and conundrums of middle age as experienced by empty-nesters. In one recent column, for instance, she fields a query from "Baited and Switched," who has booked an expensive adults-only vacation with several friends and their significant others only to learn that at least two of her friends have reneged on their pledge not to bring their children along. "Baited and Switched" loves the kids but resents the change in plans, so much so that she no longer wants to go on the trip. Hax is honest—and honesty is an absolute prerequisite for advice columnists—in reply, writing: "Baited and Switched: I am so angry on your behalf that I can't think of an answer right away. You lost something significant, but if you speak up, you're an ogre."[6] She goes on to inventory the "bad options" as she sees them. As an additional step, Hax crowdsources the question, inviting reader input to, as she puts it, "make up for my blind spots." The crowdsourcing move is generous, transparent, and a surefire method by which the digital age columnist can check individual instincts against collective wisdom. It's also a great way to boost reader engagement, as impassioned readers adding their two cents add layers of context, content, and opinion at no additional expense to the *Washington Post*.

Relationships and Romance

Relationships remain the advice columnist's bread and butter. In their inherent uncertainties and insecurities, relationships generate an endless supply of just the sort of queries and questions that keep the advice-dispenser in business.

Amy Dickinson makes an excellent case study of today's Dear Abby–styled columnist, welcoming letters on all manner of relationship

11. Advice Columns

quandaries. In one recent column, "Alarmed Wife" asks whether she should be concerned about her husband's new social media correspondence with a woman half his age. Alarmed Wife becomes worried when the younger woman begins sending her husband virtual hugs and kisses. "Husband has a close Facebook relationship with younger woman" demonstrates the timeless role the advice column plays in the lives of readers who submit their dilemmas for public adjudication. While jealousy and infidelity within relationships are age-old bugaboos, the prospect of a virtual infidelity is very much of the now. And while "free" counsel can now be found across the Internet in online forums and relationship-specific sites, the societal role filled by the advice columnist is in some ways more precious than ever, precisely because advice columnists become known and trusted quantities in ways fly-by-night Internet sources can never be.

Dickinson points out to Alarmed Wife that while the virtual relationship may seem innocent enough it is nevertheless already impacting the wife's psyche. She opines, "I'm suggesting that the relationship is already happening, that it is already interfering in your marriage, that you don't trust your husband and that you are surveilling him in secret." Dickinson also feels obliged to mention to the letter-writer that her husband could be getting "catfished" by someone with a fake identity.[7]

Like Cheryl Strayed and Carolyn Hax, Amy Dickinson follows a model playbook in her popular column, a playbook we might distill to a checklist of best practices:

- ✓ *Read between the lines.* An advice columnist must go beyond restating the letter-writer's predicament to actually perceiving it, while locating appropriate language to cast the core problem in a new light.
- ✓ *Cut to the chase.* Columnists can't afford to hedge their advice or pull their punches, as their replies need to be succinct and to the point. While it's fine for the columnist to admit uncertainty, or to crowdsource a potential solution, waffling, wavering, or wish-washy counseling only risks confusing the issue.
- ✓ *Affirm but don't excuse.* While some columnists find satisfaction in confronting their interlocuter, or breaking down their defenses, advice-givers who alienate their readers aren't likely to last long. Though most advice-seekers are anonymous, they do make themselves vulnerable; thus the effective advice-giver must acknowledge and affirm the courage it takes to seek help in such a public venue.

Part III—Additional Opinion-Writing Genres

✓ *Make a referral.* There's no degree, certification, or credential required to dispense advice in newspapers, websites, and magazines, and most columnists aren't trained therapists. Instead, digital age advice columnists can serve as resource gatherers on behalf of concerned readers.

✓ *Answer the question.* Like a judge, columnists are expected to render a verdict, and failing to do so is likely to disappoint. For example, in her letter to "Ask Amy," Alarmed Wife is essentially asking whether she should be worried about her husband's Facebook relationship. The answer is an unequivocal yes.

Pioneering Women: Marie Manning and Elizabeth Meriwether Gilmer

Marie Manning, writing under the pen name Beatrice Fairfax, is widely considered the pioneer of the quintessential advice-to-the-lovelorn column. Manning broke plenty of glass ceilings en route to the top, not only at the *New York Evening World*, where she was one of a very few female writers when her "Dear Beatrice Fairfax" column began in 1898, but also in Hollywood, where her weekly self-titled film series appeared in theaters.

Even a cursory read of Fairfax's timeless advice demonstrates the deep roots of the most enduring tropes of the genre. Her takes are decided yet fair-minded, while still leaving room for some diagnostic uncertainty. For example, when a young man, engaged seven years to the same young woman, writes to ask Fairfax whether he should dutifully follow through on the engagement, or break it off to pursue a new love, she refuses to mince words, beginning with the gentle chastisement: "Seven years of courtship is surely long enough time for even the most undecided young man to make up his mind quite decidedly."[8] While Fairfax focuses her energies, as any good romance columnist must, on the plight and predicament of the young man whose fiancée has twice previously broken off the engagement, she responds objectively, refusing to take sides. She reminds the love-riven young man that he owes "a great deal to a girl who has given you her time for seven years," while remaining appropriately circumspect about the young woman in question—"Any girl is foolish who lets a courtship and engagement drag on for seven years without taking some sort of definite stand." In the end, Fairfax waxes poetic as she reminds the letter-writer, "To marry one woman while your heart belongs to another

11. Advice Columns

is to hopelessly entangle three lives." Refusing to judge harshly, or without all the evidence, she wishes the young man well in seeking new love, though with the caveat that he should absolutely avoid another seven-year engagement.

Even as "Dear Beatrice Fairfax" whet reader appetites for profound personal advice publicly dispensed, Fairfax contemporary Elizabeth Meriwether Gilmer penned a rival advice column that would eventually make the long-lived scribe, writing under the pseudonym "Dorothy Dix," the world's highest paid woman writer.[9] Dix earned fame and fortune not just for the "Dorothy Dix Talks" column, which was syndicated in hundreds of newspapers by 1940, but also via her time as crime reporter for William Randolph Hearst's *New York Evening Journal*.

Like Fairfax, Dix dishes unapologetically, serving up unconventional advice to those that seek her counsel. In one memorable column, she is queried by a young businesswoman who is still living at home, quite unhappily, with her mother and sister. While the customs of the time might dictate that the well-seasoned columnist criticize the young woman for disrespecting her elders, Dix defies expectation by instead encouraging the young professional to stop living under her mother's roof. Her sage advice is delivered firmly yet kindly: "No fiction dies harder than the theory that family ties are silken ones.... They are just as often iron fetters that cut into our flesh, and make life a curse and torment for us. Nor is there any truth in the supposition that because people are of the same blood, and have been reared in the same environment, that they are necessarily congenial to one another."[10]

Dix waxes philosophic at times, too, quoting Oliver Wendell Holmes on the enmity that can exist within families, and, in so doing, beats back the pernicious stereotype that romance columns are little more than pulp or pablum for the masses. In the end, she refuses to point the finger at the letter-writer's mother or sister, but instead speaks to the larger principle animating the domestic conflict: "Because mother and daughter or two sisters do not get along together is no reflection on either, but it is a reflection upon their intelligence for them to persist in making each other miserable by dwelling under the same roof when they could both achieve happiness by the simple expedience of parting." The idea that a dutiful family must live under the same roof even when they are at one another's throats is one of several "false and idiotic domestic fetishes" that should be undone, Dix argues, for the sake of personal happiness. "Family life is only beautiful when it is harmonious," she writes, adding, "but it is the most hideous thing on earth when it is filled with bickering and bitterness."

Part III—Additional Opinion-Writing Genres

At its best, the advice column tackles timeless dilemmas using current language and a contemporary cultural lens. For example, in a 2024 *Chicago Sun-Times* column entitled "I wish my mom spoke to me like a parent instead of a friend," Dear Abby (Jeanne Phillips) offers twenty-first-century wisdom on precisely the topic Dix counseled advice-seekers on nearly a century earlier: erecting healthy boundaries between adult parent and child. In the piece, "Son, Not Friend, in Washington" asks Abby what he should do to discourage his middle-aged mother from oversharing her personal life via texts messages received while he is at work. Addressing her reply, "Dear Son," Abby indulges in some necessary truth-telling, calling the mom in question "needy" and "emotionally immature," and suggesting that her son restrict the times his mother can text him during work hours.[11]

As a genre, the advice column lends credence to the old adage "the more things change the more they stay the same." While text messages may have replaced telegrams and personal letters as the vehicles of choice for meddling parents, the issue of where the parent begins and where the child stops remains current, like so many advice column topics, as relevant now as it was in the days of Beatrice Fairfax and Dorothy Dix.

Celebrating the Good Things

Not all advice columns are filled with heartache and strife; some celebrate a personal breakthrough or shine a light on an exemplar. In his classic column "Rich Dads and Poor Dads," columnist Damon Runyon does just that when a 41-year-old father writes that he and his two living teen-aged sons (the third has died tragically in a car accident) still play baseball together in the backyard. The letter-writer is proud to say he is best friends with his teenagers in addition to serving as their father.

In his timeless response, Runyon springboards from the father's letter to a larger meditation entitled "Rich Dads and Poor Dads." The letter-writer is the titular "poor dad"—a manual laborer—who expresses his determination to bring up his boys to be strong, principled men. Runyon seizes on the opportunity to celebrate and redeem lower- and middle-class dads who, while they cannot always fulfill their sons' every material need, are nevertheless willing to engage with them in ways a rich, absent father cannot. Runyon writes of the poor man's sons:

> They will have a finer rearing, a better training, than the sons of millionaires, because millionaires can't afford the time from their millions these days to play with their sons.

11. Advice Columns

> That's one of the sad features of a great deal of money.
> The average rich man is so busy with his affairs he loses intimate touch with his family, especially with his children.
> Only too many of the boys of the rich nowadays spend their young years away from home at fashionable prep schools, or under the guidance of private tutors.
> Their fathers rarely know what they are doing, how they are doing. Their playmates also are the sons of rich men. They are brought up in a soft, easy atmosphere.
> Their fathers are greatly astonished, greatly mortified, when they suddenly turn to the son for assistance in carrying on the business that made the millions, to find they have on their hands, not the useful citizen, the manly man they expected, after a prodigious expenditure of money in education, travel—but a total loss.
> This isn't a lecture, it's a statement of fact.[12]

The columnist goes on to characterize the archetypal wealthy father, whose family is often scattered to the four winds, with children away at boarding schools or on vacation to warmer climes with their mother. The rich man's house may be larger and more impressive, the columnist claims, but it's devoid of edifying intimacy and interrelationship by comparison. Runyon concludes his column with an unabashed question: "How well do you know your son, Mr. Father, who reads this?" In the end, the writer makes his feelings clear: that the 41-year-old father who works with his hands and loves his boys enough to interact with them daily is the father more worthy of esteem, in his eyes, than the dad who buys his children's affection with trinkets and toys.

Voicing Your Opinion

1. Guided by the advice columns discussed in this chapter, put your columnist skills to work by writing a piece of counsel in reply to a question or quandary you've heard good friends express. While you will write with the real-life addressee firmly in mind, assign them an identity-protecting sobriquet of the sort that might appear in the pages of a newspaper or website advice column, i.e., "Dear Confused College Student," or "Dear Insomniac Gamer." To rid yourself of the inhibiting effects of ego, generate an advice-giving nom de plume, just as Chery Strayed does with her alter-ego "Sugar."

2. Pen a piece of advice from you to you. Begin by making a list of life questions that have preoccupied you recently, and add them to a collection from which you pick at random. Once you have your

Part III—Additional Opinion-Writing Genres

question in hand, respond to it as if you were writing to a sincerely curious stranger similar to yourself. The goal is to underscore the difference between ourselves as fundamentally flawed humans unable to see our own predicaments clearly, and the surprisingly wise voice that often emerges in response to others' earnest and open-minded questions.

12

Reviews

As consumers we swim in a sea of unsolicited evaluation. Thankfully, the well-practiced citizen critic offers a different kind of assessment, though—one that is hopefully more purpose-based, informed, and nuanced. The goal is advisory—to let reader-viewers know whether the product is worth their hard-won money, time, and trust. In this way and in others, thoughtful reviews exemplify the opinion writer's art.

Too often, whether a reader considers a review useful or worthless boils down to whether they agree with its judgment of the product on offer. Fortunately, consensus distinctions in quality are available on aggregate sites, where established reviewers writing for publications of record bump up against the unvarnished assessments of passionate citizen critics. Consider as a case study reviews of the blockbuster film *Barbie* collected on the popular film and TV website Rotten Tomatoes. On his website entitled Smart New Media (tagline: "Groupthink doesn't live here, critical thought does") reviewer Cole Smithey bills himself as the "smartest film critic in the world." Smithey writes that he hates *Barbie*, calling it the worst movie he has ever seen while assigning it "less than zero stars."[1] He finds the film overly derivative of the franchise, and calls director Greta Gerwig a "hack screenwriter and a remedial filmmaker at best." He adds: "'Barbie' is nothing more than a (nearly) two-hour commercial, designed to send hordes of potential customers to Amazon to purchase an endless array of plastic toys. And you thought only Marvel could play in that crap-infested sandbox." Elsewhere he decries *Barbie* as a "diarrhea stain on humanity."

Is Smithey fulfilling the essential function of the citizen critic? Yes, in the sense that he's acting in an advisory capacity, protecting the public from frauds and other flimsily made products. In his obvious determination not to mince words, he also shows he's not likely to have his opinion swayed by studio propaganda or paid sponsors. His assessment bristles with verbal energy and moves easily between tonal registers—from the colloquial, to the critical, to the quasi academic. Smithey proves himself

Part III—Additional Opinion-Writing Genres

unafraid to lodge a negative review of a film that earned widespread critical acclaim.

But these short excerpts also demonstrate some less-than-textbook review-writing techniques. First, it's surely inaccurate to call an Academy Award-nominated director of many films "remedial" in any sense of the word. Second, the notion that *Barbie* is a two-hour long commercial for its maker, Mattel, defies logic, as *Barbie's* PG-13 rating suggests that the audience for the film and the doll are demographically distinct. Finally, lines like "crap-infested sandbox" and "diarrhea stain on humanity" may be fun to write, but as metaphors they have little to do with the world of *Barbie*, and have the unintended effect of making the reviewer, rather than the film, feel juvenile.

Contrast Smithey's review with this lead sentence from Christy Lemire's take on Roger Ebert's website: "'Barbie,' director and co-writer Greta Gerwig's summer splash, is a dazzling achievement, both technically and in tone. It's a visual feast that succeeds as both a gleeful escape and a battle cry. So crammed with impeccable attention to detail is 'Barbie' that you couldn't possibly catch it all in a single sitting; you'd have to devote an entire viewing just to the accessories...."[2] What's good here? First, the prose is chockful of sonic devices ranging from sibilant "s" sound in "summer splash" to the alliterative pairing of "technically" and "tone." The long "e" sounds in "feast" and "gleeful" evoke a pleasing assonance. The overriding metaphor Lemire employs is more subject-appropriate than Smithey's sometimes vulgar analogies, as words like "summer" "splash" and "accessories" invoke the trademark Barbie vibe. Lemire concludes her opening paragraph with a full flowering of the metaphoric conceit: "It's not just that Gerwig & Co. have recreated a bunch of Barbies from throughout her decades-long history, outfitted them with a variety of clothing and hairstyles, and placed them in pristine dream houses. It's that they've brought these figures to life with infectious energy and a knowing wink."

Reviewing Performances

At root, the reviewer's task is to manage expectations, detailing for consumers exactly how and why a product, or a pitchman, succeeds or fails. Mark Twain offers us a classic example of exactly this kind of performance review in his evaluation of superstar novelist Charles Dickens. Pulling no punches, an underwhelmed yet undaunted Samuel Clemens assesses both the person (the flesh-and-blood writer himself) and the

12. Reviews

product (Dickens's public reading from *David Copperfield*). Does Dickens disappoint or exceed expectations? Twain leans toward disappointment, as he finds the Great Man all too human in his stage presence:

> Promptly at 8 P.M., unannounced, and without waiting for any stamping or clapping of hands to call him out, a tall, "spry" (if I may say it), thin-legged old gentleman, gotten up regardless of expense, especially as to shirt-front and diamonds, with a bright red flower in his button-hole, gray beard and moustache, bald head, and with side hair brushed fiercely and tempestuously forward, as if its owner were sweeping down before a gale of wind, the very Dickens came! He did not emerge upon the stage—that is rather too deliberate a word—he strode. He strode—in the most English way and exhibiting the most English general style and appearance—straight across the broad stage, heedless of everything, unconscious of everybody, turning neither to the right nor the left—but striding eagerly straight ahead, as if he had seen a girl he knew turn the next corner. He brought up handsomely in the centre and faced the opera glasses. His pictures are hardly handsome, and he, like everybody else, is less handsome than his pictures. That fashion he has of brushing his hair and goatee so resolutely forward gives him a comical Scotch-terrier look about the face, which is rather heightened than otherwise by his portentous dignity and gravity. But that queer old head took on a sort of beauty, bye and bye, and a fascinating interest, as I thought of the wonderful mechanism within it, the complex but exquisitely adjusted machinery that could create men and women, and put the breath of life into them and alter all their ways and actions, elevate them, degrade them, murder them, marry them, conduct them through good and evil, through joy and sorrow, on their long march from the cradle to the grave, and never lose its godship over them, never make a mistake! I almost imagined I could see the wheels and pulleys work. This was Dickens—Dickens. There was no question about that, and yet it was not right easy to realize it. Somehow this puissant god seemed to be only a man, after all. How the great do tumble from their high pedestals when we see them in common human flesh.[3]

Twain offers a masterfully ambivalent review of England's great man of letters. Reading between the lines, it's clear that he admires Dickens's work, so much so that he might consider him a literary genius. There's a hint of professional envy here, too, especially in the passage where the writer reflects on the godlike powers of the consummate novelist. Finally, there's a palpable sense of disappointment, articulated in the line "How the great do tumble from their high pedestals when we see them in the common human flesh." And beneath all this runs Twain's profound subtextual commentary on human nature, one that suggests that putting literary figures on so high a pedestal inevitably leads to their disparagement, degradation, or downfall.

Part III—Additional Opinion-Writing Genres

After an opening paragraph in which he offers readers a kind of broad-brush assessment, Twain unspools a loosely chronological account of the evening in which the English author reads from *David Copperfield*. He says of Dickens: "He is a bad reader, in one sense—because he does not enunciate his words sharply and distinctly—he does not cut the syllables cleanly, and therefore many of them fell dead before they reached our part of the house." He continues:

> I was a good deal disappointed in Mr. Dickens' reading—I will go further and say, a great deal disappointed. The *Herald* and *Tribune* critics must have been carried away by their imaginations when they wrote their extravagant praises of it. Mr. Dickens' reading is rather monotonous, as a general thing; his voice is husky; his pathos is only the beautiful pathos of his language—there is no heart, no feeling in it—it is glittering frostwork; his rich humor cannot fail to tickle an audience into ecstasies save when he reads to himself. And what a bright, intelligent audience he had! He ought to have made them laugh, or cry, or shout, at his own good will or pleasure—but he did not. They were very much tamer than they should have been.

It's worth noting that Twain, well-known as a spellbinding raconteur, is in many ways evaluating Dickens by his own measuring stick, almost ensuring that Dickens will be judged to have come up short. If Twain is an American folk hero in the making, Dickens, by contrast, comes off as a stuffy Englishman out of touch with the reading public. Is Twain biased as a reviewer? No doubt he is. But to the degree that he positions himself as an average American with strong likes and dislikes—a citizen critic—and without much tolerance for pomp and circumstance, his biases match those of his audience. He's also clearly conjuring his inner contrarian. If America's newspapers of record were enthralled by the great man, and said so, there's little use in Twain constructing an equally fawning review.

Twain is careful to conclude his review with a modicum of humility, addressing the limitations of his assessment. While he adheres to his thesis in saying "every passage Mr. D. read, with the exception of those I have noted, was rendered with a degree of ability far below what his reading reputation led us to expect," he also admits that he has only given "first impressions" that might change if he had the opportunity to hear the great novelist read on multiple occasions.

Reviewing En Masse

At times it's more efficient for the citizen writer to review an entire class or category of product—the best of this year's new cars, say, or the

12. Reviews

must-see touring acts or Broadway shows of a given season. This subgenre of review writing tends to be longer and more comparative, as the opinion-maker evaluates a handful of products or texts simultaneously. Patterns of similarities and dissimilarities inevitably occur in a multi-product review, as do patterns of judgment. For example, while there may be bright spots, perhaps five of the top six *New York Times* bestsellers fail to meet the reviewer's expectations. Or maybe the year's summer blockbusters disappoint across the board. In his aptly titled review "Various Bad Novels," critic H.L. Mencken tackles multiple reviews in one, returning an unflattering view en masse:

> In order to save your arm, a humane surgeon saws off your little finger, or even your thumb; in order to buttress you against smallpox, a wise physician gives you cowpox. The reviewer of books, if he would serve his customers well, must sometimes serve them as ruthlessly. In the present case, I bore you with 5,735 words of review, at a cost to you of less than two cents, in order to warn you away from some 1,200,000 words of cheerless, uninspired, machine-made fiction, which would cost you about $23.50 in the department stores. The 1,200,000 words of fiction I have swallowed myself, deadhead and willingly—a nobler act than the vaccinator's, for he flees from the smallpox as precipitately as his patient.[4]

The opening of "Various Bad Novels" is vintage Mencken—eloquently unfettered, self-important, darkly humored. The takeaway is clear—the novels under review are long without earning their length, and they're costly without meriting their price. In so judging, Mencken fulfills his advisory role with gusto, and with the reader front of mind. "Is it possible to imagine any more witless, preposterous bosh—any more puerile, overladen nastiness?" the exasperated reviewer asks, adding, "And yet such garbage is pouring from the presses day in and day out, and multitudes of the feeble-minded seem to read it and enjoy it."[5]

In passages like this one, it's easy to see how adroitly Mencken lambasts not just subpar novels but also the unfortunate simpletons who mistake them for worthy literature. He offers what amounts to a double-edged sword, one that cuts both ways. His project in this review essay is not to balance the ledger by finding, say, four new novels out of eight that are worth readers' time, but to point out that there's something wrong, wholesale, with the kind of dross being written, and also with consumers' willingness to swallow it whole hog. Thus does he become a wider cultural critic as well as an evaluator of particular texts. He concludes with a sweeping condemnation: "So much for the novels that have come to me this month—five mildly good ones and sixteen bad ones, not to mention

Part III—Additional Opinion-Writing Genres

the half-dozen so wholly bad that I haven't even mentioned them. My advice to you, if you yearn for fiction on these lazy afternoons, is that you pass over all of them, and go to the better things of yesteryear."6

In this statement and in others, Mencken reveals an essential conservatism, which might be distilled to "just because something is new, doesn't mean it is better." In such a worldview, progress is often delusional, since the best-made, most sturdy and functional things may have been built a lifetime ago. It's worth noting that even though Mencken is on his high horse he is not without humility, as he opens the piece by expressing the notion that he fears his review will be rather dull, though not as dull, he's quite certain, as the works that prompted it. As we've seen, even resident curmudgeons benefit from a moment or two of self-deprecation, if for no other reason than to remind readers that the reviewer is also an imperfect machine.

As Mencken and Twain suggest, memorable reviews are themselves an artifact of style. Most reviewers, at least those who seek to be read, err on the side of dramatic takes because they know that writing a bland review is a bit like serving up tasteless food. Far better to offer big, bold flavors even if a reader finds them difficult stomach. In an era when thousands of citizen reviews are posted each day for products ranging from the latest dipping sauces to the newest running shoes, establishing a strong, distinctive voice is more important than ever.

Voicing Your Opinion

    1. Try your hand at writing an art or performance review of the kind offered by Mark Twain and H.L. Mencken in this chapter. Choose an artistic product—book, film, dramatic performance, sporting event, video game, public speech—about which you hold strong opinions. Before beginning, consider whether or not you feel your reader will agree with your assessment. If you will likely be preaching to the choir, the language you use in your review will need to be just as charismatic and memorable, but you will be able to presume your reader's shared knowledge of, and esteem for, the product or subject you feature, while still taking care to mention one or two of its deficiencies. If, on the other hand, you draft a dissenting opinion of a popular, critically acclaimed product, be prepared to work extra hard, writing with precise, connotatively rich language and abundant examples to prove your point.

12. Reviews

2. Identify a product or service you feel sure is poorly made or underperforming, and write a review that holds it to account for its flaws. Here's the twist: your goal is to roundly condemn the product without resorting to the standard evaluative adjectives such as "bad, awful, flawed, faulty, inept, erroneous, inaccurate, unreliable" etc. Instead, trying infusing your verbs with negative connotations to cast all due shade on your subject. For example, if in reviewing the latest gee-whiz vacuum, you deem the suction "inadequate" or "anemic" (both adjectives), you might instead draft a sentence like "TurboX's suction underwhelms," wherein the verb carries the tone of your assessment.

13

News Analysis

News analysis has long vexed lay readers, scholars, and critics. The question such a hybrid genre begs borders on self-evident: is it news or is it analysis? Can it be a bit of both? More to the point, is news analysis better suited to news pages or is it more at home in the opinion section?

To sort out the question it's helpful to begin with the views of editors working in the trenches. *The Wall Street Journal* editorial page editor Paul Gigot notes, "*Wall Street Journal* readers want information, but they also want to make their own judgments about what they are learning. Our commentary is intended to inform on the issues of the day, with the added purpose of stirring debate and helping readers decide for themselves what they think."[1] Captured under the heading "News vs. Opinion," Gigot's comments suggest news analysis falls under the umbrella of opinion.

Meanwhile, writing for "The Journalism Blog," Spencer Izen defines news analysis as an "in-depth interpretation or explanation of a news story through a close examination of the facts and their contextual significance or meaning."[2] News analyses, he adds, are written by those with "experience or knowledge in a specific subject, qualifying them to make observations based on the facts of a story"—a description that sounds closely akin to the experiential credentials of the expert opinion writer. "For years," Izen confesses, "journalism scholars and public editors have cautioned that while increased contextualized coverage has its benefits, the differences between analysis and opinion can and have at times blurred to obstruct the lines distinguishing them."

Concurrently, he notes that while the rise of explanatory and analytical journalism has muddied the once well-established lines between news and opinion, a better informed reading public has benefited from increased interplay between the two. For the purposes of this chapter, we'll emphasize the brand of news analysis that draws heavily on the opinion writing skillset detailed in this book—offering the kind of personal take or perspective that only a skilled writer with a compelling experiential credential can bring to the table.

13. News Analysis

A prime example is the Daniela J. Lamas piece from *The New York Times* entitled "I'm a Doctor and a Voter. Here's How I'm Thinking About the Health of Trump and Biden." *The Times* originally ran the explanatory piece as a guest essay, locating it firmly in the opinion camp. And yet, as its title clearly shows, Dr. Lamas, a contributing opinion writer and a pulmonary and critical-care physician, is at the same time analyzing headlines exploring the age and mental acuity of aging presidential candidates. Her piece challenges and contextualizes the news concerning the candidates' fitness for office, while also availing itself liberally of first-person pronouns—both the singular "I" and the plural "we." In claiming that the public should have as much knowledge of their president's health as a physician would of a patient entering intensive care—at the very least age and comorbidities—Lamas frames her opinion, namely that voters should have access to the basic health information of candidates not to be used as "a political weapon, but one more factor alongside political views and experience that we need to weigh."[3] She reminds us that "illness and aging do not need to be synonymous with weakness or hidden from public view."

Evidence-Based Analysis: A Personal Case Study

Years ago, I developed a relationship with a section editor of an influential news and opinion site, despite having my first submission there rejected. In the wake of the Uvalde, Texas, school shooting in which two teachers were killed, I felt a powerful need to write in solidarity with the growing threat dedicated educators faced in the classroom. In the weeks that followed the mass shooting, the media focused on the presumed failures of the teachers and administrators to stop the gunman, while glossing over the heroic actions taken by Irma Garcia and Eva Mireles, both of whom lost their lives attempting to safeguard the well-being of their students. In a year during which school shootings reached record highs, I wanted to draft an opinion informed by news analysis in which I argued for the need to name the particular form of violence faced by educators around the country.

As I began to formulate the analysis, I struggled to properly frame the indignation and heartbreak I felt. As a teacher myself, I knew I wanted to advocate for the bravery exhibited by my fellow educators. I knew I wanted to offer a solution, however imperfect, to the problem of public indifference to the risk teachers increasingly take when they walk into the classroom. While it's sometimes recommended to write a pitch for an opinion

Part III—Additional Opinion-Writing Genres

piece before writing the commentary itself, in this case I felt the need to get my ideas on paper first, so that my hybrid opinion-analysis piece could, in effect, educate me about the complicated, even conflicted feelings with which I proposed to grapple on the page. After I had a first draft of the piece in front of me, I reasoned I would be in a better position to distill its central themes and arguments.

My next step was to choose an outlet to which I would pitch my evidence-based piece, and here I reached a crossroads. If, as originally intended, I submitted the piece to the usual suspects, *The New York Times*, the *Washington Post*—I worried that the commentary I'd drafted would be viewed as too teacher-centric. If instead I decided to propose the piece to a trade publication—for example, one of a handful of national outlets specializing in education—I entertained the opposite concern: that the piece would be perceived as too focused on current events and not enough on pedagogical practice and the scholarship of teaching. Then, too, if I submitted my opinion to an education-specific publisher, would I pitch it to the part of the industry I know best—higher education—or would I dig deeper, and look harder, for the relatively rare trade publications open to submission from professors about middle school and high school public education?

In the end, I decided on one of a very few widely visited websites featuring news analysis written by folks working in higher education. Per the outlet's stated submission guidelines, I broke my proposal into four requisite sections: Section, Story, Significance, Timeliness (selected from options provided in a drop-down menu) and Key Points. The pitch I made follows below:

> Section: Education
> Story: As a society we've begun the difficult work of discussing the special brand of violence committed by, and against, law enforcement officials—cop-killers and cops-who-kill. And yet teachers, who increasingly die in the line of duty, have largely been left out of such discussions, the particular threat they face going unnamed.
> Significance: The self-sacrificial nature of educators only partly explains the tragic lack of attention given their professional vulnerability. Like police persons, many teachers would willingly give their lives to shield those they are charged with protecting. And yet this same tendency toward self-sacrifice may explain why the deaths and injuries they increasingly suffer as a result of their professional calling continue to lack society's most specific acknowledgment.
> Timeliness: Now
> Key points: Much has been written on the tragedy in Uvalde, but I approach the question from a new angle, using disciplinary expertise to focus on how, and to what extent, we as a society name the particular violence educators face.

13. News Analysis

My pitch, coupled with my credentials, must have worked, because I heard back from the editor overseeing the education section that very same day. He was sufficiently interested to request that I send the full piece. I ended the day—a Friday as I recall—full of the hopefulness the editor's note had stoked while also hoping an acceptance would arrive in my inbox on Monday.

Unfortunately, the hoped-for acceptance never arrived, and a week later, after exchanging several emails and undertaking significant additional research, I opened my email to read the "thank you for thinking of us" consolation note that all writers dread. Where had my piece failed exactly? Editors are characteristically tight-lipped about the precise reasons for rejection, and I didn't want to be that particular pest who presses the issue. I inferred from his comments that the piece, written only a week after the Uvalde shooting, might have been a bit "too soon." Maybe we as a nation were still too deep in our grief to achieve critical distance. Or perhaps, per my point, readers were still more interested in the stories of the student victims and responding police offers to have the mind space necessary to contemplate the vulnerability of educators.

Looking back, I see validity in each of the proposed rationales for rejection; my commentary may well have been too soon, and it might have been a smidgen too spirited in its solidarity with the teachers who gave their lives on that tragic day in Texas. I see, too, that my op-ed might have been too abstract for the moment, asking readers to entertain the subtle connotations of language at a time when many of us were still viscerally angry at what we had witnessed. It's also possible that my piece, prepared at just under 600 words, was too brief to give voice to the nuanced argument I hoped to make and might have been better suited to a longer-form publication with more room for reflection.

Still, I take heart in knowing that I didn't write the piece in vain. Conceptualizing it helped me better reconcile my own strong feelings on a complex issue; by all accounts my piece had made an impression on the dozen or so individuals who read it—not just the education editor at the outlet I'd pitched, but also the colleagues with whom he had he had eagerly shared my work. Having engaged in a true back-and-forth dialogue via email, we had established a rapport that would surely not have been achieved had he simply said "yes" and run my piece, pro forma, a week or two later. And I had come away with a much more concrete sense of what the publication I'd pitched seeks in freelance work, meaning that my next submission could be better tailored to its needs.

Part III—Additional Opinion-Writing Genres

News Analysis as Opinion

As we've seen, it's not uncommon for experts to weigh in with opinions and observations on a news topic adjacent to their area of academic or professional expertise. While many opinion pieces relay solely on anecdotal or circumstantial evidence to make their point, evidence-based analysis, in its purest form, brings real, firsthand research to the table—research the writer has sometimes conducted themselves. Of the major online news outlets, *The Conversation* is perhaps the best example of evidence-based opinion penned by leading scholars. *The Conversation* captures the flavor of the pieces it publishes in its tagline: "academic rigor, journalistic flair." Imagine, for example, that you are a professor of social media in a communications department at a major university. After yet another controversy over the alleged bias of a prominent political cartoon or cartoonist, you feel compelled to share your research with the public and at the same time express your reasoned opinion: that traditional political cartoons themselves are part of the problem. That's exactly what communications professor Jennifer Grygiel sets out to do in the evidentiary piece that follows.

> "Political cartoonists are out of touch—it's time to make way for memes"
> by Jennifer Grygiel, Assistant Professor of Communications (Social Media) & Magazine, News and Digital Journalism, Syracuse University
>
> Originally published May 17, 2019, in *The Conversation*

The New York Times came under fire after a political cartoon appeared in print on April 25, 2019. In it, a blind President Donald Trump, wearing sunglasses and a yarmulke, is being led by Israeli Prime Minister Benjamin Netanyahu, who's depicted as a guide dog with a Star of David around his neck.

The Times later issued an apology, called the cartoon "anti–Semitic," and announced that it would discipline the editor and enhance its bias training. The newspaper also indicated that it will no longer use the syndication service that supplied the cartoon.

To some, this might appear to be a significant move. But it fails to address larger problems with editorial cartooning—namely, the ranks of cartoonists are too White, too old and too male.

As a scholar who studies social media and memetics, I wonder if political cartoons are the best way to connect with today's diverse readership. Many crave searing, cutting political commentary—and they're finding it in internet memes.

What if internet memes were elevated—not only as a serious art form but also as an important form of editorializing that's worthy of appearing alongside the traditional cartoon?

Behind the times

Newspapers and magazine editors still rely on political cartoons to capture readers' attention and to deliver some lighter material alongside heavier news

13. News Analysis

stories. The need for this content isn't going away, nor is the need for forms of communication that challenge governments and open up important public discussions—a role the political cartoonist has long held.

But in many ways, political cartooning can seem like a relic of a bygone era.

A 2015 Washington Post report also underscored the lack of diversity among political cartoonists in newsrooms, noting how not a single black individual was employed as one.

Then there's journalism's top prize, the Pulitzer.

An extensive 2016 study by the Columbia Journalism Review unveiled how the ranks of editorial cartoon Pulitzer winners have been largely dominated by White men. Since 1922, only two women have received a Pulitzer in this category, and it wasn't awarded to an African American until this year, when syndicated cartoonist Darrin Bell became the first to receive the award.

One roadblock to diversifying the ranks of political cartoonists is that the potential pool of candidates is limited. Few have the technical skill to draw pen-and-ink drollery, the common style for political cartooning.

Another has to do with industry trends. A 2017 study found that many newspapers don't even employ an editorial cartoonist anymore. Instead, they've come to rely on less expensive syndication services.

A more democratic form

Given the important function of the political cartoon, simply discontinuing their use serves no one, including publishers.

But the field's high barrier to entry—not to mention the time it takes to actually produce a cartoon—clearly poses a problem. A new, quicker and more inclusive solution to political commentary is needed.

The political cartoon is technically a meme, which is simply any piece of culture that can be copied or replicated.

A different sort of political cartoon, the internet meme, dominates on social media. Often crudely constructed, they're far easier to create than, say, your typical New Yorker political cartoon. Many simply appear as a photo with text overlay, something that can be made within a few minutes via an online meme generator or mobile app. But the lack of technical skill needed means that they're democratic in nature—and those that resonate the best will get shared the most and rise to the top.

Memers of the world, unite!

Cartooning is undoubtedly a skilled art form. But in 2019, an ugly internet meme that uses a screen grab from "The Office" and quippy text overlay can have just as much clout—if not more—than a sophisticated political cartoon.

Internet memes increasingly play a role in politics and even have the power to influence elections. Facebook groups with hundreds of thousands of followers are dedicated entirely to propagating and spreading political internet memes, such as the Bernie Sanders Dank Meme Stash and God Emperor Trump.

Politics has become, in many ways—as campaign strategist Doyle Canning put it—"a battle of the memes."

Part III—Additional Opinion-Writing Genres

Some publishers and media outlets understand the value of user-generated content in political discourse and news gathering. For example, BuzzFeed occasionally posts lighthearted political internet memes on its social media platforms that speak to a younger audience. The Associated Press employs user-generated content editors who comb social media platforms for important images associated with news events.

Memers, meanwhile, are beginning to see their role in driving internet traffic—and ad revenue—and are beginning to formalize their work and employment as content creators. They're even beginning to organize, with some groups seeking union status. It's possible that new syndication services may develop for political memes out of these efforts.

But there have been few signs of anyone printing a meme in a physical newspaper or magazine unless it's controversial enough to become the topic of a news story. To serve print needs, what if publishers hired staff memers or freelance memers—individuals with a pulse for viral content and an understanding of what resonates with younger readers, who could construct stylized, more professional-looking memes that could appear in print and on the web?

Again, this isn't to say that traditional political cartoons no longer have a role. But it's time for publishers to anoint the internet meme as worthy of publication.

After all, the best political commentary is just as likely to be found on Tumblr as the pages of the Times.[4]

What distinguishes this provocative piece of evidence-based analysis from traditional op-ed or commentary? First, the commentator is an expert in their field, a publisher of original research, and well-credentialed to render an informed opinion. Second, the piece's length—nearly 1000 words—exceeds the 500 to 800 words customarily afforded an op-ed, commentary, or column. Third and finally, the piece is significantly more inclined to cite published studies and scholars to frame the debate than is a traditional op-ed, which seeks greater accessibility.

And yet for all its scholarly traits, Grygiel's opinion is a far cry from the sort of work she might publish in an academic journal in her field, indicating that she has modulated her tone and adjusted her approach to reach a broader audience. For instance, "Political cartoonists are out of touch" utilizes extremely short paragraphs—some totaling as few as seven words—to enhance readability while ramping up reader-engaging rhetoric. The writer makes modest use of the first-person, too, to personalize the cartoon controversy, in ways that would typically be verboten in an academic journal. True to the hybrid genre it exemplifies, "Political cartoonists are out of touch" exists as something of a centaur.

While it's true that evidence-based analysis published by scholars and academicians stretches the definition of citizen writing, it's important to note that pieces like this one are circulated widely in popular platforms like

13. News Analysis

Facebook/Meta, where they reach a wide audience of general readers. Thanks in part to *The Conversation's* generous republishing agreement, which allows the work featured on its site to be republished online or in print for free subject to its guidelines, Grygiel's article has been shared on Facebook well over a thousand times since its original publication, "Political cartoonists are out of touch" clearly speaks for the many who embrace memes as a preferred form of communication. Its author offers her readers a closely argued evidence-based analysis that never loses sight of its topic. The piece is sufficiently compelling to convince even conservatives and traditionalists of the limitations of the old-fashioned political cartoon and the cartoonists who make them. Moreover, the commentator's plea that the work of meme writers be recognized and even renumerated for their digital artistry strikes us as reasonable.

Importantly, Grygiel's analysis makes no claims of neutrality, as the writer freely mixes a modicum of academic research with a generous dose of opinion. In places the piece does feel more than a bit biased in favor of the mostly younger population of meme artists, and carries with it a strong, almost ageist critique of conventional cartoonists. The piece might pull back a bit on the implication that the political cartoonist should simply be put out to pasture to instead consider what common ground exists between memes and cartoons, and how memers might productively share the op-ed pages with more traditional, hand-drawn illustrations. However, a less provocative view would surely have reduced the number of documented "shares" the work received.

Voicing Your Opinion

1. Consider writing a news analysis piece in an area you follow closely from within an established discourse community. Suppose, for example, that you follow politics closely enough that you dedicate a personal or professional blog or social media account to expressing your takes on the subject. With a news analysis piece in mind, revisit the day's headlines in your subject area to see what current events may benefit from the kind of analysis and context you, uniquely, can offer.

2. Inspired by the Jennifer Grygiel piece featured in this chapter, consider a subject area or scholarly discipline in which you can fairly say you've conducted some original research or are otherwise well-versed in the academic literature. Next, connect that demonstrated expertise to a news controversy currently making headlines, rendering an opinion informed by your prior study or reading.

14

Arch Cultural Criticism

The dictionary defines "arch," from the English root meaning "rogue," as "deliberately or affectedly playful and teasing." As the definition suggests, the arch cultural critic is an opinion writer unafraid of playing cat-and-mouse with their reader, of "getting their goat," as the old saying goes.

The master of arch commentary is surely H.L. Mencken, the twentieth-century cultural critic who served as the founding editor of the *American Mercury*. At its helm Mencken routinely poked the strange bird that is the average American, dubbing them "boobus Americanus" for their relentless gullibility and defining optimism. Mencken writes boobus Americanus with intimate familiarity, and more than a bit of playful fondness, as a creature of lovable predation.[1] Indeed, a hasty reader of America's archest arch critic might easily mistake Mencken's tone for jolliness, so willfully provocative is his treatment of our national frailties. Initially, he masks his fear at our profound innocence—or is it ignorance?—in language so dopamine-drenched that it feels almost intoxicated:

> It is my contention that, if this definition be accepted, there is no country on the face of the earth wherein a man roughly constituted as I am—a man of my general weaknesses, vanities, appetites, prejudices, and aversions—can be so happy, or even one-half so happy, as he can be in these free and independent states. Going further, I lay down the proposition that it is a sheer physical impossibility for such a man to live in These States and not be happy—that it is as impossible to him as it would be to a schoolboy to weep over the burning down of his schoolhouse. If he says that he isn't happy here, then he either lies or is insane.[2]

As the lengthy commentary gathers momentum, it becomes clear that Mencken is in large part facetious, treating serious issues with a kind of trademark flippancy soaked in irony. In his own arch way, Baltimore's most iconic critic makes clear that we, as citizens, ought to question our idiotic glee and glib self-satisfaction, for, as we laugh at circus-level amusements, we are, he implies, fiddling while Rome burns. He continues:

14. Arch Cultural Criticism

Here, more than anywhere else that I know of or have heard of, the daily panorama of human existence, of private and communal folly—the unending procession of governmental extortions and chicaneries, of commercial brigandages and throat-slittings, of theological buffooneries, of aesthetic ribaldries, of legal swindles and harlotries, of miscellaneous rogueries, villainies, imbecilities, grotesqueries, and extravagances—is so inordinately gross and preposterous, so perfectly brought up to the highest conceivable amperage, so steadily enriched with an almost fabulous daring and originality, that only the man who was born with a petrified diaphragm can fail to laugh himself to sleep every night, and to awake every morning with all the eager, unflagging expectation of a Sunday-school superintendent touring the Paris peep-shows.[3]

Achieving Necessary Distance

Often citizen writers morph into arch critics when the foolishness of the thing they hope to broach is so genuinely alien to them that they feel compelled to insert an ironic distance between themselves and their subject. The resulting commentaries can feel darkly comedic or even bathetic, the latter from the Greek root *bathos* meaning to move from the sublime to the ridiculous. The hyperaware citizen critic understands that life can easily oscillate from luminous to lunatic in a single day's news cycle. However, those of us given to ironic commentary should be advised that adopting a satiric tone is considered risky business in newspapers and news magazines associated with serious comment. While staff commentators and regular contributors might be afforded the luxury of black humor strategically deployed within otherwise serious columns, guest contributors, freelancers, "stringers," and citizen critics may be unknown quantities by comparison, making it more difficult for readers to detect and decode ironic intent.

The arch commentator is nothing if not a genuine risktaker. And while a well-developed sense of irony may be an allowance made to seasoned commentators who've paid their dues and earned their chops, recent history offers several compelling examples of arch critics who've made their reputations in their thirties and forties, chief among them the late David Foster Wallace. In his quasi-journalistic piece penned for *Harper's* magazine, "Shipping Out," Wallace comments on the inanity of luxury cruises while undertaking one himself. The result is an ecstatically arch opinion essay that manages to be highly exuberant and critical all at once, a tonal pas de deux captured in his subtitle: "On the (nearly lethal) comforts of a luxury cruise." Consider the shot across the bow inscribed

Part III—Additional Opinion-Writing Genres

in commentator's lead paragraph: "I have now seen sucrose beaches and water a very bright blue. I have seen an all-red leisure suit with flared lapels. I have smelled suntan lotion spread over 2,100 pounds of hot flesh. I have been addressed as 'Mon' in three different nations. I have seen five hundred upscale Americans dance the Electric Slide. I have seen sunsets that looked computer-enhanced. I have (very briefly) joined a conga line."[4] Wallace's introduction bristles with the paradoxical animus of the arch critic, as he seems to say, simultaneously (1) that luxury cruises do indeed offer travelers an unprecedented series of experiential firsts and (2) that such experiences can also be cringeworthy or painfully self-conscious.

In an ironic age, "arch" would seem to come naturally to most critics. And yet getting its tonal nuances right proves exceedingly difficult for those who reduce archness to simple sarcasm, unsubtle irony, or cheeky wit that does little to complicate a writer's ambivalent take. The productively ambivalent critic often finds themselves of two minds about their subject, as Mencken is about America optimism and as Wallace is about the sublime and sometimes sadistic pleasures of pleasure boating.

The commentator sufficiently daring as to query their mixed mind is likely to find a trove of tonally rich material. The opinion writer works hard not necessarily to be likable—an instinct that can quickly degenerate into virtue signaling or sycophantry—but to be down to earth, embodying an appeal to bathos. The bathetic writer, in turn, delights in puncturing pretense, cutting the pompous or presumptuous down to proper size. The most artful arch critics remind us, for instance, that even presidents and prime ministers can be as fallible and as foolish as the rest of us.

Rhetorical Matters

In modulating tone, the well-versed commentator makes use of a toolkit as venerable as classical Greek oratory. Overstatement, understatement, enumeration, antithesis, rhetorical questions—all are classical moves seasoned citizen critics make to spar with skeptical readers as they seek to win the battle for hearts and minds. Since the citizen writer hopes to persuade, their entreaties and appeals amount to a kind of courtship dance with a disinterested or distracted audience, like a bird that pirouettes in order to convince others that it is worthy of their attention. To extend the analogy, individual figures of speech amount to the stylish moves in the dance, and to be effective they must be a finely calibrated combination of the familiar with the unfamiliar, the expected with the

14. Arch Cultural Criticism

unexpected. Stylish syntax consists, after all, of both the pattern and the artful breaking of that pattern, hence figures of speech.

Consider author-critic Ambrose Bierce, who made a living pointing out the inanities of American culture, a culture he once proudly served as a soldier in the Union army. An unconventional thinker possessed of a trenchant wit, Bierce relishes pointing out hypocrisies big and small, whether his own or someone else's. In his *The Cynic's Word Book* (later aptly retitled *The Devil's Dictionary*), he compiles a series of arch commentaries, quips, and snippets from early in his career, organized after the fashion of a dictionary positively dripping with ironic intent. In Bierce's bathetic book, *absurdity* is defined as noun meaning "A statement or belief manifestly inconsistent with one's own opinion"; *accuse* as a verb signifying "to affirm another's guilt or unworth; most commonly as a justification of ourselves for having wronged him"; and an *abstainer* amounts to: "A weak person who yields to the temptation of denying himself a pleasure.[5] A total abstainer, meanwhile, is one who abstains from everything but abstention, and especially from inactivity in the affairs of others."

Bierce's ironic view of human nature may be unusually dark, but it is realistic. By pointing out inconsistencies and absurdities, he holds up a mirror in which we as readers can readily see our own foolishness and, hopefully, a path to its eventual remediation or revision. Far from being idlers or nihilists, arch commentators enact their reform agenda on the page.

In the piece that follows, Bierce tackles an American trait he loves to loathe: the impromptu introduction of one person to another. As the piece makes clear, the commentator considers such social happenstance to be anything but a happy accident: "The devil is a citizen of every country, but only in our own are we in constant peril of an introduction to him. That is democracy. All men are equal; the devil is a man; therefore, the devil is equal."[6] Bierce describes the offending scenario at length:

> You incautiously meet your friend Smith in the street; if you had been prudent you would have remained indoors. Your helplessness makes you desperate and you plunge into conversation with him, knowing entirely well the disaster that is in cold storage for you.
>
> The expected occurs; another man comes along and is promptly halted by Smith and you are introduced! Now, you have not given to Smith the right to enlarge your circle of acquaintance and select the addition himself; why did he do this thing? The person whom he has condemned you to shake hands with may be an admirable person, though there is a strong numerical presumption against it; but for all Smith knows he may be your bitterest enemy. Smith has never thought of that. Or you may have evidence (independent of the fact of the introduction) that he is some kind of a thief—there are one thousand

Part III—Additional Opinion-Writing Genres

and fifty kinds of thieves. But Smith has never thought of that. In short, Smith has never thought. In a Smithocracy all men, as aforesaid, being equal, all are equally agreeable to one another.

That is a logical extension of the Declaration of American Independence. If it is erroneous the assumption that a man will be pleasing to me because he is pleasing to another is erroneous too, and to introduce me to one that I have not asked, nor consented, to know, is an impudent evasion of my rights—a hideous denial and limitation of my liberty to a voice in my own affairs. It is like determining what kind of clothing I shall wear, what books I shall read, or what my dinner shall be.[7]

Do Bierce's sentiments make him an antisocial lone wolf or an incorrigible curmudgeon? Surely not, though in a commentary this dark he surely risks such accusations. There's no disputing, however, that this former soldier is a writer of great rhetorical aplomb. In fewer than 750 words, he uses a variety of figures of speech, including ironic wordplay in his call for "a system of disintroductions"; neologism in his coinage of the term "Smithocracy"; syllogism in his claim that "all men are equal; the devil is a man; therefore, the devil is equal"; and logical fallacy when he asserts: "If it is erroneous the assumption that a man will be pleasing to me because he is pleasing to another is erroneous too." These moves and many others help the cultural critic argue his point that forced socialization is no socialization at all. Notice how timely Bierce's critique remains. His lambasting of false or forced friendships cannot help but remind contemporary readers of the false promise of virtual buddies.

Voicing Your Opinion

1. Summon your most colorful language to describe the average citizen of your nation, state, or neighborhood with insight and empathy. Your take could be laudatory, critical, or, like H.L. Mencken's or David Foster Wallace's, an entertaining mix of both. Don't shy away from ironic characterizations, as true familiarity often produces a knowing kind of ambivalence.

2. Inspired by Ambrose Bierce, tackle an annoying or irksome custom or habit that springs from regional or national identity. For example, maybe you want to challenge enduring regional stereotypes like "Midwestern nice" or "Southern hospitality."

3. Generate your own ideas for arch pieces like Mencken's and Wallace's by posing yourself a series of paradoxical questions to be answered in an archly critical commentary or column, for example:

14. Arch Cultural Criticism

What's so bad it's almost good? (B-movies? Black Friday doorbuster deals? Fast-casual food?) What's a guilty pleasure (Video games at work? Ice cream in bed? Sweaters for pets?) What's a group or demographic we're loath to confess we enjoy belonging to (Audio book listeners? Frequent flyers? Grammar police?)

15

Commentaries in Defense

Citizen writers habitually rise in defense of something or someone badly overlooked, underestimated, or dismissed. Perhaps it's the sentimentalist in us that makes it so, or the nostalgic, or the indefatigable advocate for the oppressed. Whatever the case, defense is an important weapon in the commentator's equity-minded arsenal.

Fortunately, one need only fill in the blank after "In Defense of…" to be off and running with a plum idea: "In Defense of the Little Black Cocktail Dress," "In Defense of Military Intelligence," "In Defense of Babysitters." A botanist might draft a piece in defense of plant-based psychedelics while an astronaut might pen an impassioned defense of government-funded space exploration. In an era of viral trends and cancel culture, in-defense commentaries serve a vital societal role, reminding us that some things are worth preserving even if they seem outmoded or old-fashioned. The citizen writer need only look around them for erstwhile fixtures rapidly or silently disappearing to locate poignant subject matter. Perhaps we notice the crossing guards that once ushered schoolchildren across busy streets have gone missing; or that the outdoor clothesline that was once a fixture in suburban lawns has gone AWOL. In every conspicuous absence, the perceptive opinion writer sees a chance to redeem the unfairly condemned.

Sometimes the object needing defending is as common as dirt. Consider the web copy for journalist Michael Pollan's book *In Defense of Food: An Eater's Manifesto*. The blurb begins with the elephant in the room: "Food. There's plenty of it around, and we all love to eat it. So why should anyone need to defend it?"[1] Reading further, we find that the answer depends on how one defines food. Pollan's blurb offers this rationale: "Because most of what we're consuming today is not food, and how we're consuming it—in the car, in front of the TV, and increasingly alone—is not really eating. Instead of food, we're consuming 'edible foodlike substances'—no longer the products of nature but of food science."

Pollan succeeds in naming the tragic irony of our diets—abundant food but less abundant health—while advancing his argument a step

15. Commentaries in Defense

further. From whom does food need defending? The answer: "From the food industry on one side and nutritional science on the other. Both stand to gain much from widespread confusion about what to eat, a question that for most of human history people have been able to answer without expert help." Decades of sometimes dubious nutritional advice, the book argues, has only made Americans "sicker and fatter," while simultaneously making the act of eating less pleasurable.

In theory, any phenomenon locked in a pitched battle for legitimacy or survival could be apropos for an in-defense piece. If landfills and charity shops overflow with discarded microwaves, perhaps a savvy citizen critic cooks up an "In Defense of Microwaves" piece arguing that microwaves should be saved rather than tossed. If school bus routes are declining as urbanization increases, the school bus may need defending. Of course, defense isn't just relevant to the material objects—the iconic yellow school bus—but also to that object's historical, psychological, physiological, and social legacies. It might seem difficult to defend a microwave, for example, until one considers the profound way it has liberated millions of moms and dad from the sweaty chore of oven-cooked meals.

Standing Up for the Overlooked

E.B. White's debut piece for *The New Yorker*, "In Defense of the Bronx River," announced his keen eye for the natural wonders that New Yorkers tended to pass over in their relentless pursuit of industry and profit. The premise for White's commentary is discernible at a glance: In a city famous for waterways ranging from the East River to the Hudson, the lowly Bronx River is easily overlooked.

The writer opens his piece with a bracing statement of the problem: "The Bronx River rises in Valhalla and flows south to Hell Gate. The people I have mentioned this to, from time to time, have always said 'What of it?' This cynical indifference is something I resent in New Yorkers, for if this town is ever going to get anywhere, it must study its heritage of natural beauty."[2] The thesis is clear from the outset: here is a literary river, full of symbolic import and folklore, that is characteristically passed over by unsentimental New Yorkers too busy to notice the nature right under their nose. In the final paragraph, White's tone resolves to elegy and earnest defense of a waterway mostly known to the old-guard train commuters who travel into the city. The train commuter, he says, "know it of old by reputation and of late by name." He continues:

Part III—Additional Opinion-Writing Genres

And they stand up for it. In Spring the willows on the shore turn a pleasant shade of yellow, and the stream takes their color, and the little tributaries of the Bronx come rushing down from the hills in pipes and empty into the main stream, augmenting it and causing white rapids at Bedford Park. I have seen commuters forsake their newspaper and flatten their nose on the window as the train glided along the Bronx River. And I have seen a strange light come into their eyes, especially if there was a duck or something like that floating on the water. And here is one commuter who wouldn't trade this elegant little river, with its ducks and rapids and pipes and … willows for the Amazon or the Snohomish or La Platte or the Danube, or the Mississippi, even though the latter does rise in Lake Itaska and flow south to the Gulf of Mexico, and is wider.

New Yorkers may have found White's piece poetically overwrought or patently overzealous, but the commentary certainly drew positive notice among the writer's colleagues. Less than two years after submitting it, White went from first-time contributor to editor of *The New Yorker*.

Fighting an Uphill Battle

Citizen writers determined to advocate the cause of the dismissed or the downtrodden often engage in what they know upfront will be a losing battle, just as E.B. White surely knew that his opinion would not cause New York's famously unsentimental citizens to stop and take notice of the homely Bronx River. Similarly, Michael Pollan likely understands that his defense of fresh, unprocessed foods will do little to change the eating habits of most Americans. Still, the citizen critic tries mightily, hoping that readers will be galvanized by the writer's defense.

Such is the case with Henry David Thoreau, who, in his highly opinionated essay "Walking," defends the practice against those who dismiss it as idle or indulgent. The great Transcendentalist begins his defense with a short history of the activity he is prepared to defend, observing: "I have met with but one or two persons in the course of my life who understood the art of Walking, that is, of taking walks—who had a genius, so to speak, for *Sauntering*, which word is beautifully derived 'from idle people who roved about the country, in the Middle Ages, and asked charity, under pretense of going a la Sainte Terre,' to the Holy Land, till the children exclaimed, 'There goes a Sainte-Terrer,' a Saunterer, a Holy-Lander."[3] For Thoreau, walking is a noble art needing frequent practice, and so he laments the increasingly slothfulness of fellow citizens who, he claims, seem only to wax nostalgic about soulful, restorative walks they took years

15. Commentaries in Defense

ago. These same slothful people, he notes, have "confined themselves to the highway ever since."

Thoreau's opinion essay is more than a pean to the woods and wilds; its larger project is to revivify and resurrect the dying art of walking, defending its singular virtue against the rapid rise of vehicular travel. To those who would say that there's nothing worth seeing on a walk, he offers poignant rebuttal:

> My vicinity affords many good walks; and though for so many years I have walked almost every day, and sometimes for several days together, I have not yet exhausted them. An absolutely new prospect is a great happiness, and I can still get this any afternoon. Two or three hours' walking will carry me to as strange a country as I expect ever to see.... There is in fact a sort of harmony discoverable between the capabilities of the landscape within a circle of ten miles' radius, or the limits of an afternoon walk, and the threescore years and ten of human life. It will never become quite familiar to you.[4]

The argument is as much philosophical as it is practical, as Thoreau suggests that walking is actually a paradigm for life. He aims to convince readers that they would be far better spending their time in appreciation of nearby wonders than in fruitlessly chasing distant chimeras. He insists that a true saunterer might spend an entire lifetime strolling the landscape within ten miles of their home without ever running out of worthy sights to see.

Cultural Defenders

At a time when a cultural phenomenon sometimes goes viral overnight, consumers increasingly show a predilection to pile on. Consequently, a whole new lexicon of disproval, enshrined in online comments sections and chatrooms in phrases like "throwing shade," "clapping back," and "hating on," has blossomed like a dark flower on the Internet.

In fact, a valuable opportunity for opinion writing presents itself each and every time an item is put on the cultural chopping block and left for dead. If the citizen critic does indeed function as a societal counterweight, ensuring a judgmental public sees from all sides before it decides, an era of widespread canceling offers endless opportunities for reframing and rebuttal.

Disney serves as a prime example. In the 1990s and 2000s, citizen critics took the company to task for its reductive portrayals of young women, helping to prompt more, and more empowered, female protagonists in

Part III—Additional Opinion-Writing Genres

animated films ranging from *Mulan* to *Frozen*. By the early 2020s, however, a few brave opinion writers had begun to push back, suggesting the studio had pandered to the public. In his piece "In Defense of Princess Culture," cultural critic Adam Kadlac writes a lengthy rebuttal to the disproportionate venom directed at Disney princesses.

Taking us to the Magic Kingdom with his family, he shows us the many ways his 15-year-old disabled daughter Sadie derives joy, pleasure, and meaning from Disney royalty. He insists, "While the princess movies are obviously about princesses, they are really about girls and women who just happen to be princesses. And thus, like my daughter, the most compelling princesses have to live in a world full of constraints they did not create (and over which they have little direct control). Like my daughter, they are vulnerable to the opinions and expectations of others and cannot be reduced to any single trait that people might use to define them."[5] In a lengthy opinion piece penned for the online magazine *The Raven*, Kadlac suggests some girls can actually benefit from princess culture, from the drive to feel special, to transcend their circumstances, and to be taken on their own terms. The writer makes no attempt to argue that Disney's animated protagonists are the epitome of feminism, but that a silent majority of young women may find them comforting and ultimately empowering.

Voicing Your Opinion

1. Inspired by E.B. White's homage to the overlooked Bronx River, craft an opinion piece as a tribute to a person, place, or phenomenon you feel is sadly passed over or forgotten, and which you find significant value in. Perhaps you write a piece in support of mixed martial arts, defending it from its many highbrow detractors. Or maybe you pen an opinion in defense of the much-maligned roundabout American transportation planners have coopted from the British, much to the chagrin of homegrown motorists. Whatever you choose, take steps to ensure that your defense is novel, well-reasoned, and engaging, as readers will be predisposed to dispute your defense from the get-go.

2. Modeling Henry David Thoreau and Michael Pollan, write a thought-piece in defense of an aspect of everyday life, such as walking or eating, that you feel has become needlessly complicated or controversial in our post-postmodern age. For example, maybe you feel the handshake so freely given prior to the COVID pandemic deserves

15. Commentaries in Defense

to make a spirited comeback. Or perhaps the high-protein, steak-and-eggs breakfast of yore deserves a reboot in a digital age waking up to the danger of empty carbs and processed foods. The goal is to remind your readers of some basic virtue or goodness that may have slipped from their lives for reasons ranging from simple practicality, to willful neglect, to purposeful obfuscation or cover-up.

3. Modeling your work after Adam Kadlac's defense of Disney princesses, invoke a similarly maligned genre, trope, or cultural meme that deserves reconsideration if not begrudging respect. Do sitcom dads, long portrayed as inept, deserve a more positive reevaluation? Maybe the boddice-ripping romance novel long disparaged by the literati is due greater respect. Or how about those the cinematic subgenres known as slasher films? Perhaps you make the case that on-screen horror helps steel tweens and teens for the frightening challenges of adolescence.

16

Commentaries in Praise

In the early 1970s Spiro Agnew famously dismissed journalists (and other Nixon detractors) as "nattering nabobs of negativism."[1] The vice president's populist attack against pundits and press lodged itself in cultural memory not only by virtue of its alluring alliteration, but also for the popular view it dared broach: namely that writers exhibit a tendency to point out the bad rather than celebrate the good. And while it's true that sunnier, optimistic opinions are the exception rather than the rule in the nation's newspapers and magazines, their very exceptionality makes them noteworthy in a world where downbeat headlines continue to dominate newsfeeds.

An excellent contemporary example of a piece that pushes back via purposeful praise is "The Era of the Line Cook," an opinion written for *The New Yorker* by Hannah Goldfield. Goldfield begins with the premise that American food-service workers were badly disrespected during the pandemic. Disproportionately exposed to the virus via their classification as essential workers, and the victim du jour in popular TV shows in which sous-chefs and line cooks are routinely abused and berated, the workers who labor in our kitchens are due proper plaudits.

Pegging her opinion piece to the untimely death of food critic Anthony Bourdain, who famously wrote that line cooks are the unsung heroes of every eating establishment, Goldfield singles out for praise those restaurants in New York where sous-chefs generate innovative menus themselves rather than merely following recipes dictated by executive chefs. To properly appreciate the behind-the-scenes beings who toil away in the prep kitchen, the writer argues, is to grant them greater agency and creativity. Goldfield insists, "The restaurant world still harbors affection for the idea of cooks paying their dues, but the fetish for rigidly hierarchical and abusive workplaces seems to have abated in recent years."[2] And none too soon, claims the author, as the sous chefs and line cooks of the world are, in actuality, the next generation of master chefs in training.

To move beyond an unearned reputation for glibness or blitheness,

16. Commentaries in Praise

pieces written in praise usually need a high degree of novelty to succeed. Goldfield's prose ode to the invisible, often undiscovered talents hidden in prep kitchens works not just because it's tied to current events and cultural trends, but because it dares to praise someone—the lowly line cook—to whom the literati reading *The New Yorker* might not have given much thought. It's as if Goldfield leads a party of upscale diners back into the sweaty, volatile kitchen to shine a light on the unsung heroes thanklessly laboring there.

The same could be said of another recent laudatory commentary, "Sweat," by Laura van den Berg. Van den Berg begins her commentary with an emphatic value-assigning statement: "There's nothing like a sweaty Florida summer to bring you back to your body."[3] In the remainder of her piece, she works hard to develop a rhetoric of praise for a thing—humidity—that's more often derided or disparaged than enthusiastically declaimed. "Sweat" follows the aforementioned novelty prescription perfectly, waxing poetic about a popular meteorological villain—the bane of all who decry the frizziness and fuzziness of a supersaturated atmosphere. Van den Berg, who grew up in central Florida, finds in the Sunshine State's preternatural moisture a return to what is elemental and essential. She opines, "The heat brought renewed attention to my physical self—to the ways in which my body chafed and blistered; of my endurance, my thirst. Sweat didn't just root me in my body; it reminded me that this place and myself are forever entwined, that I carry it with me wherever I go." Tellingly, she subtitles her opinion "Letter of Recommendation," as her column performs just that sort of public service: a referral of something the writer begs us reconsider for the sake of an opener mind and a richer life.

Appreciative Opinions

In writing their praiseful contemporary commentaries, both Goldfield and van den Berg take a page from the playbook of social critic Bertrand Russell's early twentieth-century opinion essay, "In Praise of Idleness." Published in the October 1932 issue of *Harper's* magazine, "In Praise of Idleness" tackles head-on the so-called Protestant work ethic. Russell opens with a powerful mea culpa—admitting that he too has spent a lifetime worshipping the cult of productivity-at-any-cost. Of his recent change of heart, he duly confesses: "I think that there is far too much work done in the world, that immense harm is caused by the belief that work is virtuous."[4]

Part III—Additional Opinion-Writing Genres

A few paragraphs into this artful admission, the author puts his point still more bluntly, asserting: "I want to say, in all seriousness, that a great deal of harm is being done in the modern world by the belief in the virtuousness of work, and that the road to happiness and prosperity lies in an organized diminution of work." Hyperveneration of industriousness at the expense of idleness turns America into a kind of slave state, he argues, one that practically ensures that the intellectual curiosity of scientists, artists, and philosophers will never have the time and space to fully flower.

A philosopher by trade, Russell makes an intellectual argument in favor of idleness in his famous opinion essay, but Robert Louis Stevenson, celebrated author of *Treasure Island* among other classics, takes a more anecdotal approach to the subject in his highly opinionated "An Apology for Idlers." In it the great literary man of letters describes an early adulthood spent happily "playing truant," an experience which causes him to declare: "If a lad does not learn in the streets, it is because he has no faculty of learning. Nor is the truant always in the streets, for if he prefers, he may go out by the gardened suburbs into the country.... A bird will sing in the thicket. And there he may fall into a vein of kindly thought, and see things in a new perspective. Why, if this be not education, what is?" In the paragraphs that follow his initial shot-across-the-bow, Stevenson doubles down on the benefits of idling and the evils of too much industry, arguing:

> Extreme busyness, whether at school or college ... or market, is a symptom of deficient vitality; and a faculty for idleness implies a catholic appetite and a strong sense of personal identity. There is a sort of dead-alive, hackneyed people about, who are scarcely conscious of living except in the exercise of some conventional occupation. Bring these fellows into the country, or set them aboard ship, and you will see how they pine for their desk or their study. They have no curiosity; they cannot give themselves over to random provocations; they do not take pleasure in the exercise of their faculties for its own sake; and unless Necessity lays about them with a stick, they will even stand still.
>
> It is no good speaking to such folk: they cannot be idle, their nature is not generous enough; and they pass those hours in a sort of coma, which are not dedicated to furious moiling in the gold-mill. When they do not require to go to the office, when they are not hungry and have no mind to drink, the whole breathing world is a blank to them. If they have to wait an hour or so for a train, they fall into a stupid trance with their eyes open. To see them, you would suppose they want nothing to look at and no one to speak with; you would imagine they were paralysed or alienated; and yet very possibly they are hard workers in their own way, and have good eyesight for a flaw in a deed or a turn of the market. They have been to school and college, but all the time they had their eye on the medal; they have gone about in the world and mixed with clever people, but all the time they were thinking of their own affairs.

16. Commentaries in Praise

As if a man's soul were not too small to begin with, they have dwarfed and narrowed theirs by a life of all work and no play; until here they are at forty, with a listless attention, a mind vacant of all material of amusement, and not one thought to rub against another, while they wait for the train. Before he was breeched, he might have clambered on the boxes; when he was twenty, he would have stared at the girls; but now the pipe is smoked out, the snuff-box empty, and my gentleman sits bolt upright upon a bench, with lamentable eyes. This does not appeal to me as being Success in Life.[5]

By spilling a great deal of ink detailing just how pitiable is the workaholic, the writer argues that the idler is, by comparison, a man or woman worthy of respect if not veneration. Not only is the busy man a burden to himself, he also causes his wife and children to suffer from his malady. Comparatively, idlers are enlightened souls, for they operate under no illusion that their work will be appreciated or remembered; wisely, they have not sacrificed their youth and health on the altar of "glory and riches they expect may never come."

The citizen writer able to single out people and things for praise offers their reader a more balanced sense of self and community, one capable of adulation as well as condemnation. Indeed, locating meaning and value in that which is more often deemed unworthy could viewed as a simulacrum of love.

Voicing Your Opinion

1. Following Hannah Goldfield's column in praise of line cooks, draft an opinion piece that makes an argument for the value of the unheralded folks who work behind the scenes in an industry with which you're familiar. For example, if you've acted onstage, you might be tempted to write an opinion essay in praise of those who work backstage to make the show possible. Or, if you've ever worked big-box retail, perhaps you can speak to the invisible contributions of the late-night workers who stock the shelves long after the doors have closed to the public.

2. Inspired by Laura van den Berg's paean to the unexpected revelations of humidity, take a phenomenon you have found objectionable or annoying in the past, and argue for its reassessment or reevaluation. The more unexpected your subject, the better. For example, suppose you've always found introverts to be insular or irksome, but have recently come to a greater appreciation of their quiet wisdom.

Part III—Additional Opinion-Writing Genres

3. After the fashion of Bertrand Russell and Robert Louis Stevenson, both of whom write in praise of idlers and idleness, formulate a viewpoints piece in which you single out for adulation a group that is often subject to condemnation. Perhaps you're a Democrat who now finds unexpected value in conservative friends and colleagues. Or maybe you find virtue in an activity widely viewed as a vice: for example, gluttony. Consider writing your opinion essay to conform to the "In Praise of [fill in the blank]" template, or, following Stevenson, title it as "An Apology for," as in "An Apology for Gustatory Pleasure," or "An Apology for Cosmetic Surgery." If you opt for "the apology" phraseology, remember that you aren't apologizing in the modern sense of expressing regret or remorse for a practice or behavior, but in the spirit of the less well-known definition meaning "making a reasoned argument or writing in justification of something, typically a theory or religious doctrine."

17

Humor and Satire

In choosing to write with light, the columnist knows in advance that he or she is likely to catch the serious-minded reader off guard. The result can be positively disarming or charming—a needed jolt reminding the sober or somber reader that it's okay, on occasion, to laugh at our collective foibles. Of course, not all of our subjects lend themselves to levity. Still, surprisingly many do for the commentator with courage sufficient to risk tonal modulation.

However, it's important that the laughing not be at the audience's expense. To laugh at a reader is not nearly as desirable, or as rhetorically effective, as to laugh with them. When we are laughed at, or mercilessly ridiculed for something we sincerely believe, we grow defensive and prone to retaliation. And criticism can be especially vexing when it comes from someone outside our cultural or familial group. In many cases we'll permit an insider who shares our membership or circumstance to tackle a shibboleth in ways we would never tolerate from an indifferent critic judging us from outside our circle. "In just about every situation, we're more likely to accept information—any kind of information—when it comes from someone with similar viewpoints," Trish Hall claims, citing wisdom gleaned from her long career editing *The New York Times* opinion pages.

Religion offers a prime example. Critics have taken aim at the alleged pretense, pomp, and perversity of organized religion for centuries, but in so doing they risk being perceived as intolerant or insensitive. For the most artful citizen commentators, however, the excesses and oddities of religion can be broached affectionately and without derision. Radio raconteur and cultural critic Garrison Keillor practices this inside-out brand of cultural critique beautifully in his long-running National Public Radio program *A Prairie Home Companion*. In his weekly "Tales from Lake Woebegone" commentaries, Keillor makes Midwestern Lutherans the target of gentle and often charming barbs—slings and arrows that are absorbed rather than rejected in part because Keillor is a Minnesota Lutheran himself who knows whereof he speaks. In poking fun of his people ("God's frozen

Part III—Additional Opinion-Writing Genres

people" he once called them)¹ and their frigid Northern clime (the allegorically named "Lake Woebegone"), Keillor's veiled criticism feels comforting somehow, wrapped in a warm blanket of storytelling. Fans of Keillor's insightful and good-natured social critiques grant him the kind of immunity truthtellers truly crave.

Newspaperman and literary lightning rod Mark Twain possessed a similar gift. Famously fickle in his faith, Twain occasionally returned as an adult to worship in the Presbyterian church in which he was raised. Almost without exception, these brief yet meaningful dalliances with childhood creed elicit a charming kind of ambivalence. In straddling his two minds—one that reveres the rituals of the church, and another that finds them asinine or absurd—he produces some of his wittiest comments. In tackling his native Presbyterianism, he fully admits the thin ice he has walked out on, opining, "I hold that no man can meddle with the exclusive affairs of Providence and offer suggestions for their improvement, without making himself in a manner conspicuous. Let us take things as we find them—though, I am free to confess, it goes against the grain to do it, sometimes."²

Almost in spite of himself, Twain, the consummate issuer of opinions, is fated to go against the grain. And in "Reflections on the Sabbath," he proceeds to question several key tenets of religious doctrine, including the observance of the Sabbath itself, claiming his fellow congregants could use more rest. The same black-and-white, heaven-and-hell prescripts that attract him to Presbyterianism also, he intimates, repel him, and therein lies the rub:

> The heaven and hell of the wildcat religions are vague and ill-defined but there is nothing mixed about the Presbyterian heaven and hell. The Presbyterian hell is all misery; the heaven all happiness—nothing to do. But when a man dies on a wildcat basis, he will never rightly know hereafter which department he is in—but he will think he is in hell anyhow, no matter which place he goes to; because in the good place they progress, progress, progress—study, study, study, all the time—and if this isn't hell I don't know what is; and in the bad place he will be worried by remorse of conscience. Their bad place is preferable, though, because eternity is long, and before a man got half through it he would forget what it was he had been so sorry about. Naturally he would then become cheerful again; but the party who went to heaven would go on progressing and progressing, and studying and studying until he would finally get discouraged and wish he were in hell, where he wouldn't require such a splendid education.

The circumspect congregant is likely to find Twain's commentary on religion charming and fairly universal, since his good-natured critique of the serious and scholarly nature of the enterprise could likewise apply to Judaism, Catholicism, and countless other sects. In effect, the appeal of his comment rests in its ability to laugh with, rather than at, others similarly religiously afflicted. His viewpoints piece succeeds due to its willingness to say what so many of his readers are no doubt privately thinking. Nor is Twain's pithy commentary animated by simple or uncomplicated irony, since we can presume he means most of what he says, rather than coyly implying its opposite.

Administering a Gentle Needle

As citizen critics we do well to summon good humor when an issue needs confronting that isn't life or death. If a spoonful of sugar really does help the medicine go down, it's worth finding light in otherwise dark observations.

Humorist and cultural critic James Thurber is an acknowledged master at piquing societal foibles and faux pas in the guise of good humor, as he proves in the "Notes and Comment" piece that follows. In it he tackles rural gentrification with an understated sense of irony that refuses to succumb to the black-and-white thinking that moving to the countryside is always a virtuous phenomenon:

> All the old farms in Connecticut, at least all of them that can be seen from the highways, have been taken over by writers, painters, illustrators, poets, dancers, and actors. This marks the completion of a full circle of evolution in our country. The hardy Connecticut pioneers who fought and bled with Washington were rewarded with land grants in the Middle West. There they went after their arduous struggle, to settle the country, and there they reared their children.
> Now their descendants have come back to the old countryside. Where once Israel Putnam ploughed the hard soil, artists build smooth tennis courts, and the great-granddaughters of the soldiers of Valley Forge set up bright parasols over cunning tea tables under the elms. As we said, this completes a cycle, but we don't know whether it marks the beginning of Art and Culture in America, or just the beginning of the end.[3]

In less than 200 words, Thurber intimates to readers of *The New Yorker* that the back-to-the-land trend embraced by fops and fashionistas, should, then as now, be seen for what it is. Should the sons and daughters of the wealthy and well-heeled be ashamed of the prospect of throwing parties on land their ancestors bled for? The commentator coyly refuses to say,

Part III—Additional Opinion-Writing Genres

but it's clear from context that he finds the trend in some way objectionable, and therefore worthy of greater examination. The charm of Thurber's opinion rests in its subtlety, its slipperiness, and its sly restraint.

Bathos Brings the Mighty Back Down to Earth

Oklahoma's Will Rogers was perhaps America's pioneering social commentator of the mass media era. More often remembered for his many film, radio, and stage appearances, he was, in fact, a prolific commentator credited with thousands of opinion articles, and a *New York Times* syndicated column, to his name.

Part Native American, Rogers arrived at his ironic disposition naturally. His upbringing in Oklahoma's Cherokee Nation no doubt helped distance him from the machinations of powerbrokers in government, sport, and entertainment. This same folksy humor and everyman ethos fueled his special bond with Middle American readers who often had little recourse but to lampoon the monied class. Rogers achieved his unprecedented charm via a liminal status that allowed him to be a regular guy at the same time that he rubbed shoulders with Hollywood elites. In fact, he served as the honorary mayor of Beverly Hills, California, during the same year that his short column, "Will Rogers Says," reached forty million readers, the majority of them located in America's small towns and rural places.[4]

In the excerpt from *The New York Times* column that follows, entitled "All the Millionaires Are Optimistic" Rogers charms his way into the hearts of millions of salt-of-the-earth readers who share his doubts about the wealthy and their supposedly prophetic year-end prognostications, opining: "Now, after gathering all the returns of the New Year's, I find in hundreds of newspapers all over the United States that they devoted yards of space to what some of our Rich Men think of the business prospects of the coming year. It's the same old thing every year. It's got so a working man hates to pick up his paper New Year's morning, for staring him in the face will be: Judge Gary, the head of the steel trust, says, 'I am at heart an Optimist, and I look to the coming year with great fortitude.'"[5]

After quoting several business tycoons on their bullish views of the business climate for the New Year, America's cowboy columnist builds to the question he's been driving at all along: "Why, in the name of common sense, don't they ask someone else what they think of the coming year? What those guys think is pretty well-established. Sure they are optimistic of the future. If we had their dough we would be optimistic too."

17. Humor and Satire

Rogers's prominence at the bully pulpit of popular opinion reminds us that good humor is as much a product of technique as it is talent. His pointed questions spring from a close, common-sensical observation of the inanities of popular culture and from a simultaneous sympathy with the underdog's life predicament and populist point of view. So when he asks why the farmer or the factory worker, rather than the mogul, isn't solicited for his or her economic and social predictions each New Year, his is genuine inquiry, not an insincere set-up for a too-easy punchline. Indeed, Rogers's observations are amplifications of the questions his everyday readers are likely to raise, even though they may lack the platform to express them.

Irony and Sarcasm

While Rogers relies on a sort of aw-shucks sincerity to write winning social commentaries, literary man of letters James Thurber turns to full-on irony in humor columns penned for *The New Yorker*. His most ironic commentaries can't be taken at face value, for to follow their prescripts would very likely lead to disaster. Still, they make their point through a just-right combination of overstatement and hyperbole.

Thurber's "Polo in the Home" offers a classic example of good-natured, deeply ironic social comment. All the rage during Thurber's day, polo was the stuff of countless glossy magazine features praising the sport as the next big craze among America's jet set. Thurber enjoyed polo as much as anyone, but the genius of his take lies in the ironic premise he concocts: the idea of playing an outdoor equestrian game in a tiny New York City studio apartment. Mimicking the glib instructional tone of the many slick publications then championing the sport, he begins with a straight face:

> The adaptation of the game of polo to the home or the apartment, would seem, on first thought, to be out of the question. But no sport is worthwhile, and no progress possible if the player is not eager to be at some pains to overcome obstacles. It will be said, first of all, that the house is no place for a horse, particularly a highly-strung animal such as the polo pony invariably is. Naturally, one cannot take a horse directly into a room and begin riding him to polo balls. He should first be lead, slowly, several times, through that portion of the house which is to serve as the playing floor, and allowed to familiarize himself with the little nooks and corners, the doorways and closets.[6]

The matter-of-fact way the commentator lays down his twofold proposition—(a) that polo can be successfully adapted to a tiny apartment and

(b) that a true sportsperson must be an innovator—tricks us into accepting what is, on its face, a ridiculous prospect. When the writer begins to acknowledge the difficulty of that proposition, we think perhaps that he has finally come to his senses. By now we're aware, or should be aware, of Thurber's ironic intent, meaning that we can begin to understand his argument, namely (a) the allure of polo truly is infectious and (b) polo is singularly ill-suited to the urban life led by the majority of his magazine's cosmopolitan readers. The writer continues in a comedically understated vein: "Wear and tear on the home must be considered, of course, but how simple to remove all breakable furniture and to pad the heavier pieces that cannot readily be shifted."

Ultimately, we come to a fuller understanding that Thurber isn't to be taken literally. Instead, we would be better advised to ignore his cheeky advice entirely, thereby keeping this quintessentially outdoor sport away from the busy, crowded cities and confined to the equestrian fields where it functions best. It took only a little deft irony and strategic sarcasm to help readers realize how easy it is to be swept away by a trend that may be singularly inappropriate for their circumstance.

Voicing Your Opinion

1. Inspired by Mark Twain's and Garrison Keillor's witty takes on their own respective faith traditions, consider a group to which you belong, for better and sometimes for worse, and write a commentary about that group from the inside out. Draft your opinion with all due warmth and affection, but with a mind alive to the rich ironies you've witnessed firsthand. Take care to write in a way that also includes those who don't share your specific membership.

2. Try your hand at a purely ironic commentary of the kind James Thurber tackles in "Polo in the Home." Begin by exploring an absurd premise or predicament that still somehow rings true. For example, perhaps you imagine a family dinner in which all members gather around the same table to share an evening meal, while communicating with one another solely via text message. Your deeply ironic commentary will no doubt hold more than a grain of truth, but will be exaggerated for effect.

18

Writing in Opposition

Since strong opinions are often synonymous with unconventional or unorthodox takes, it makes perfect sense that opinion writers would be inclined to write against the grain. After all, to set oneself against something popular is sure to generate debate and dissent. A topic like "Against Super Bowl Sunday" would, for example, galvanize readers right from kick-off.

In a provocative op-ed for *The New York Times*, writer George Prochnik sets himself firmly against something many urban dwellers would be hard-pressed to live without: background noise. Speaking out against a scourge he views as a public health threat as well as a nuisance, Prochnik writes: "In American culture, we tend to regard sensitivity to noise as a sign of weakness or killjoy prudery. To those who complain about sound levels on the streets, inside their homes and across a swath of public spaces like stadiums, beaches and parks, we say: 'Suck it up. Relax and have a good time.' But the scientific evidence shows that loud sound is physically debilitating."[1] Prochnik goes on to cite a World Health Organization report that finds Western Europeans collectively losing more than one million healthy life years annually as "a consequence of noise-related disability and disease."

Prochnik's gripe is clearly contemporary, and yet his complaint echoes the sentiments of cultural critics and philosophers from the Roman philosopher Seneca to the German thinker Arthur Schopenhauer. Both men complained bitterly about the kind of cacophony that impedes deep thinking. Schopenhauer, in particular, resented distracting noise and the people who generate it, calling it "the most impertinent of all interruptions."[2] Thinking people, he insists, have always been "strongly averse to any kind of disturbance, interruption and distraction, and above everything to that violent interruption which is caused by noise."

What do Schopenhauer and Prochnik risk in condemning an enemy as seemingly innocuous as noise? They risk coming off as prudish spoilsports to readers likely to perceive their annoyance as elitist and stuffy.

Part III—Additional Opinion-Writing Genres

Readers will also be tempted to associate these noise-averse writers with any number of archetypal killjoys, from shushing librarians to ivory tower philosophers demanding absolute silence for their work. If the old maxim that writers must be liked to be listened to holds true, Schopenhauer and Prochnik, in leading with curmudgeonly critiques, risk being tuned out. And yet their willingness to go against the grain by tackling a common orthodoxy is exactly the quality that ensures their work will be robustly debated.

David vs. Goliath

When commentators, columnists, and cultural critics stand against something, they typically do so as David in a David vs. Goliath battle, since the topic we tackle is usually much bigger than we are. Often we face a juggernaut that feels as if it cannot be stopped. Take the opinion piece "Against YA" that generated such a buzz when it appeared in the online newsmagazine *Slate*. The piece generated more than three thousand comment posts on Slate.com alone, with most readers taking exception to Ruth Graham's opinion piece, in which she points out that the single largest group of buyers for young adult literature are not 12 to 17 years of age, as one might expect, but 30 to 44. She finds it disconcerting that more early middle-aged adults are reading YA than teens, and speaks strongly against the practice of older adults reading "down" in age and content: "YA books present the teenage perspective in a fundamentally uncritical way. It's not simply that YA readers are asked to immerse themselves in a character's emotional life—that's the trick of so much great fiction—but that they are asked to abandon the mature insights into that perspective that they (supposedly) have acquired as adults."[3]

In a time when YA literature is a market darling, Graham's against-the-grain stance takes real courage to write, since adult readers who do read YA are likely to feel confronted by the piece no matter how well the columnist "reads the room." And Graham reads the room with sparkling sensitivity, sprinkling conciliatory statements throughout her commentary while never losing sight of her core argument. In uniquely adept sentences like this one, she both acknowledges the naysayers and bravely disagrees with them: "Fellow grown-ups, at the risk of sounding snobbish and joyless and old, we are better than this."

When we as David tackle Goliathan subjects, we're wise to bring the heavy artillery, which in writing means not slingshots or bows and arrows,

18. Writing in Opposition

but studies, facts, and logic. Graham amplifies her credibility by first proving that she's well-versed with the genre she's critiquing. To guard against those who would accuse her of cherry-picking only those examples that support her argument, she cites multiple texts. And to diversify her appeal, she adds logos (appeal to logic) via the marketing surveys she references in support of her claim that 30- and 40-something adults drive teen fiction consumer demand.

The Commentator as Naysayer

Sometimes the most compelling "against" op-eds are composed by those who function like spies willing to partake in a practice or ritual with the intention of later calling it out. In such a case the commentator serves as the "mole," not with treacherous intent, but to see and feel what the other feels in order to better understand what they do and why they do it.

In his classic "against" treatise "Against Joie de Vivre," opinion essayist Phillip Lopate resists the happy prospect of what most would consider an unassailable virtue: joie de vivre, or "joy in living." How could a writer possibly be against the seeking of pleasure and a life well-lived? Lopate identifies the bourgeoisie dinner party as the particular locus of his displeasure, arguing that if such dinner parties truly constitute "the good life," he wants no part of it. His initial shot across the bow reads: "Over the years I have developed a distaste for the spectacle of joie de vivre, the knack of knowing how to live."[4] What rankles the writer most isn't banal happiness or everyday pleasures, but the "the stylization of this private condition into a bullying social ritual."

In his commentary, Lopate makes the case that most artifacts of "the good life" and "joie de vivre" are in fact manifestations of economic entitlement and class privilege. He opines, "Perhaps my uneasiness with dinner parties comes from the simple fact that not a single dinner party was given by my solitudinous parents the whole time I was growing up. I had to wait until my late twenties before learning the ritual. A spy in the enemy camp, I have made myself a patient observer of strange customs."[5] Along the way Lopate calls out his own hypocrisies, since to be a spy within the enemy camp is to ensure one's share of blowback and retribution. He attends dinner parties reluctantly, participates anxiously, and often leaves having experienced something perilously close to real pleasure. Only after the party does his rational, non-hedonistic mind begin to analyze the events with an ethnographer's critical eye.

Part III—Additional Opinion-Writing Genres

Bonfire of the Vanities

For cultural critics inclined to write against the grain, vanity, hubris, and entitlement serve as common targets. Opinion-makers willing to ask themselves the open-ended question "What's vain?" will find a plethora of potential subjects. Defined in a nutshell as inflated pride, vanity practically begs for puncture. Are luxury cars and gargantuan SUVs symptomatic of our hubris? If so, the citizen critic brandishes their pen. In rising up against all things gratuitous, conspicuous, and self-indulgent, the citizen cultural critic conjures the spirit of pioneering opinion writer Ida Tarbel, who once confessed, "There was born in me a hatred of privilege, privilege of any sort."[6]

In "Against Exercise," cultural critic Mark Grief tackles another shibboleth in American culture: physical fitness. While conventional thinkers would be hard-pressed to find anything objectionable about the great good of exercise, Grief takes the exerciser to task, daring to wonder aloud: "Exerciser, what do you see in the mirrored gym wall? You make the faces associated with pain, with tears, with orgasm.... But you do not hide your face. You groan as if pressing on your bowels. You repeat grim labors, as if mopping the floor. You huff and you shout and strain. You appear in tight yet shapeless Lycra costumes. These garments reveal the shape of the genitals and the mashed and bandaged breasts to others' eyes, without acknowledging the lure of sex."[7] The commentator's beef with private, self-regarding exercise turns out to be historical, cultural, and philosophical. To illustrate the solipsistic shallowness of today's exercise obsession by comparison with the past, Grief takes us all the way back to the Greek gymnasium, where exercisers practiced for public contests and received mentorship from elders rather than privately working on their pecs.

Commentators like Grief, who are characteristically willing to swim upstream, inevitably invite the ire of those who fall within their crosshairs, while also opening themselves up to charges of hypocrisy. After all, it's clear from the opinion writer's insider observations that he's spent plenty of time in gyms, so it's possible that he's complicit in the problem. Still, Grief doesn't let the Glass Houses stigma stop him from asking difficult questions of himself and others, and the resulting opinions, however controversial, surely prove enlightening.

Where one finds vanity, one finds sensitivity, and where one finds sensitivity, one inevitably touches a nerve. The opinion writer capable of touching that nerve sufficient to cause sensation or shock can be an electrifying writer indeed.

18. Writing in Opposition

When "Against" Becomes Too Much

Some critics allege our contemporary penchant for writing "against" has become too omnipresent, predictable, and reactionary, a linguistic manifestation of the philosophy Karl Marx once described as "a ruthless criticism of everything existing."[8]

If cultural critics are forever and always against, what then are they for? Writing for *The New Yorker*, critic Ivan Kreilkamp asserts that the "Against [X]" formula has become shopworn, and, furthermore, that its ubiquity contributes to an off-putting spirt of "global contrariness."[9] After the commentator "has vanquished the unlucky target of one's invective," Kreilkamp observes, "the rest of the world had better watch out." He argues that the "Against [X]" formula creates a grandiose and ambitious oppositionality, "with exile and civic death for all foes its implied goal." In the end, however, even he concedes the utility of a rhetorical form that dates back to Cicero and beyond, admitting, "We probably cannot do without 'Against [X],' however. Self-promoting and self-congratulatory as the form can be, it does offer a bracing dose of rhetorical vigor."

Voicing Your Opinion

1. Modeling Phillip Lopate and the many other writers featured in this chapter who write against off-putting social rituals, undertake an "against" opinion piece all your own. Rather than choosing a self-evident topic to oppose (i.e., "Against Crime" or "Against Racism"), consider writing in opposition to a subject widely seen as virtuous, attractive, or appealing. For example, a piece entitled "Against Coffee" on the grounds—pun intended—that it's environmentally damaging and unfair to agricultural workers would rankle the millions if not billions who find their daily cup to be one of the few routine joys in their life. Similarly, a piece entitled "Against Higher Education" would surely trouble the sizable majority who regard advanced education as a universal good.

2. Taking a page from Mark Grief's playbook, draft an opinion piece in which you stand against a practice, hobby, or habit that, despite reservations, you partake in semi-regularly, as Grief does with exercise. If it's honest, your piece will acknowledge what you value about the activity—what keeps you coming back—at the same time that it offers a chance to air your grievances with the vanity or narcissism of those

Part III—Additional Opinion-Writing Genres

who pursue it (including yourself). For example, you may love fast food or social media, but for the purposes of your "against" piece, you'll want to challenge the very thing you and others may be addicted to for all the wrong reasons, or without an entirely clear conscience.

19

Commentaries on Cultural Identity

Not so long ago the term "op-ed" conjured up images of stuffy experts writing from their ivory tower to an unwashed or ill-informed public. That misconception endured because so many of the contributors of opinion to the nation's publications of record were initially members of the so-called professional class: doctors, lawyers, engineers, politicians, scientists, public policy wonks, government officials—in short, experts in their field.

In the twenty-first century, opinion writing is as much about having a meaningful or memorable perspective as it is about credentialed expertise. Now more than ever, citizen writers avail themselves of the long-eschewed first-person pronoun to describe an issue of public interest from their own perspective and worldview. In a post-postmodern age, how we view the world—our optics—is very much a product of our identity, which in turn is impacted by such factors as race, class, gender, socioeconomics, and sexual orientation among other important considerations. These days, identity is a fundamental theme of many artifacts of citizen writing. For example, if we, like the cultural critic Richard Rodriguez, grew up in a Mexican immigrant, Spanish-speaking family, our core identity would inevitably impact how we present the world in columns and commentaries. Coming to an understanding of how our cultural heritage influences our current viewpoints is considered bedrock work for writers with strong opinions to share.

In his piece entitled "Going Home Again," Rodriguez frames his critique of American higher education within the context of his own liminal upbringing as the son of Mexican-American parents who spoke a blend of English and Spanish in the home, while being unable to read either language proficiently. One generation later, their precocious son is set to receive his PhD in English Renaissance Literature. The occasion of his advanced degree should be a purely joyful one for Rodriguez; instead, he finds himself ruminating on the "tensions, feelings, conflicts" such a mixed linguistic and cultural identity creates, writing: "I look back and remember my life from the time I was seven or eight years old as one of constant movement away from a Spanish-speaking folk culture toward the world of the English-language classroom. As the years passed, I felt myself becoming less like my parents and less comfortable with the assumption of visiting relatives that I was still the Spanish-speaking child they remembered."[1]

Here Rodriguez's upbringing isn't a sidebar to a larger public debate about assimilation, but part of a larger cultural critique wherein he examines the many ways being a "Scholarship Boy," as he calls himself, impacts perceptions of family and culture. Certainly, as a PhD the author has the academic chops to summarize the research on changes in perceived ethnic identity as a product of advanced education, but, to our point, he instead chooses to examine his subject affectively, using the first-person.

Identity as Commentator's Lens

Long before Richard Rodriguez queried his Chicano childhood as a factor in his own writerly identity, African American writer Zora Neale Hurston confronted her racial inheritance in her classic expository piece "How It Feels to Be Colored Me."

Hurston, who grew up poor in Eatonville, Florida, remembers watching the streams of Northern tourists pass through her hometown on winter vacations. For them, she was an exotic, and they eagerly paid her to sing and dance for their amusement. Far from being humiliated or shamed by their attention, Hurston writes that she was thrilled to have an audience and to make some money for her talents—two things she was denied as a child by the less amused Black community in Eatonville. Hurston begins "Colored Me" with this autobiographical vignette not just because she wants to begin in the beginning but because these early experiences shape her enduring racial awareness. From the beginning we learn that she is not bothered by White attention, though many of her Black elders are. In many ways, this racial ambivalence sticks with her well into adulthood, as she explains at length:

> But I am not tragically colored. There is no great sorrow dammed up in my soul, nor lurking behind my eyes. I do not mind at all. I do not belong to the sobbing school of Negrohood who hold that nature somehow has given them a lowdown dirty deal and whose feelings are all but about it. Even in the helter-skelter skirmish that is my life, I have seen that the world is to the

19. Commentaries on Cultural Identity

strong regardless of a little pigmentation more or less. No, I do not weep at the world—I am too busy sharpening my oyster knife.

Someone is always at my elbow reminding me that I am the granddaughter of slaves. It fails to register depression with me. Slavery is sixty years in the past. The operation was successful and the patient is doing well, thank you. The terrible struggle that made me an American out of a potential slave said "On the line!" The Reconstruction said "Get set!" and the generation before said "Go!" I am off to a flying start and I must not halt in the stretch to look behind and weep. Slavery is the price I paid for civilization, and the choice was not with me. It is a bully adventure and worth all that I have paid through my ancestors for it. No one on earth ever had a greater chance for glory. The world to be won and nothing to be lost. It is thrilling to think—to know that for any act of mine, I shall:

Get twice as much praise or twice as much blame. It is quite exciting to hold the center of the national stage, with the spectators not knowing whether to laugh or to weep.

The position of my white neighbor is much more difficult. No brown specter pulls up a chair beside me when I sit down to eat. No dark ghost thrusts its leg against mine in bed. The game of keeping what one has is never so exciting as the game of getting.

I do not always feel colored. Even now I often achieve the unconscious Zora of Eatonville before the Hegira. I feel most colored when I am thrown against a sharp white background.[2]

"How It Feels to Be Colored Me" bristles with self-possession, self-confidence, and self-knowing. Hurston claims her racial identity, not as a talisman or reward, but as a nuanced explanation of self as that self looks out to comment on the world. While some may view her take as delusional or apologist, it is, without doubt, emphatically and undeniably her own.

Embracing Culture

In his aptly named opinion essay "The Negro Artist and the Racial Mountain," writer Langston Hughes contemplates a colleague's stated wish to be known as poet in general rather than a Black poet specifically. In the commentary that follows, Hughes takes issue with his fellow literary artist, typecasting him as a "high-class" Black poet with a stunted sense of self. He is, Hughes strongly implies, a White wannabe, and a man not-so-secretly ashamed of his own racial heritage. In holding his fellow poet's worldview up for public examination, Hughes defends his own perceptions of African American art and artists, writing:

Part III—Additional Opinion-Writing Genres

For racial culture the home of a self-styled "high-class" Negro has nothing better to offer. Instead there will perhaps be more aping of things white than in a less cultured or less wealthy home. The father is perhaps a doctor, lawyer, landowner, or politician. The mother may be a social worker, or a teacher, or she may do nothing and have a maid. Father is often dark but he has usually married the lightest woman he could find. The family attend a fashionable church where few really colored faces are to be found. And they themselves draw a color line. In the North they go to White theaters and White movies. And in the South they have at least two cars and house "like White folks." Nordic manners, Nordic faces, Nordic hair, Nordic art (if any), and an Episcopal heaven. A very high mountain indeed for the would-be racial artist to climb in order to discover himself and his people.

But then there are the low-down folks, the so-called common element, and they are the majority—may the Lord be praised! The people who have their nip of gin on Saturday nights and are not too important to themselves or the community, or too well fed, or too learned to watch the lazy world go round. They live on Seventh Street in Washington or State Street in Chicago and they do not particularly care whether they are like White folks or anybody else. Their joy runs, bang! into ecstasy. Their religion soars to a shout. Work maybe a little today, rest a little tomorrow. Play awhile. Sing awhile. O, let's dance! These common people are not afraid of spirituals, as for a long time their more intellectual brethren were, and jazz is their child. They furnish a wealth of colorful, distinctive material for any artist because they still hold their own individuality in the face of American standardizations. And perhaps these common people will give to the world its truly great Negro artist, the one who is not afraid to be himself. Whereas the better-class Negro would tell the artist what to do, the people at least let him alone when he does appear. And they are not ashamed of him—if they know he exists at all. And they accept what beauty is their own without question.

Certainly there is, for the American Negro artist who can escape the restrictions the more advanced among his own group would put upon him, a great field of unused material ready for his art. Without going outside his race, and even among the better classes with their "white" culture and conscious American manners, but still Negro enough to be different, there is sufficient matter to furnish a black artist with a lifetime of creative work. And when he chooses to touch on the relations between Negroes and whites in this country, with their innumerable overtones and undertones, surely, and especially for literature and the drama, there is an inexhaustible supply of themes at hand. To these the Negro artist can give his racial individuality, his heritage of rhythm and warmth, and his incongruous humor that so often, as in the Blues, becomes ironic laughter mixed with tears. But let us look again at the mountain.[3]

Would Hughes, a contemporary of Zora Neale Hurston, criticize Hurston for what he might view as her conciliatory views toward Whites?

19. Commentaries on Cultural Identity

Would he find her writing to be overly imitative or derivative—too Anglo-centric and not sufficiently her own? It's difficult to say, but "The Negro Artist and the Racial Mountain" certainly identifies as lesser creators those writers, musicians, and artists who make inadequate use of the "unused materials ready for [their] art" precisely because they disclaim rather than claim their own cultural identity and the "inexhaustible supply of themes" it provides them.

Hughes's commentary, while impassioned and artful, is not without its own blind spots and biases. Hurston or any writer maligned or impugned by Hughes's perspectives piece might point out that he ironically stereotypes his own Black community, and that as a writer encouraging his subjects in a Saturday night habit of dancing coupled with a "nip of gin," he may be naively valorizing a class of people to which he no longer truly belongs, typecasting them after the fashion of many White writers. The takeaway? Writing about racial, cultural, or ethnic identity is an exceedingly difficult but worthwhile task, one likely to bring the citizen critic hard up against their own potential double standards, stereotypes, and savior complexes. It's precisely because such writing is self-revealing and sometimes painful that it is worth sharing.

Commentaries on Ideology

While some writers run from their ideology, sidestepping it for the sake of public palatability or propriety, opinion writers must come to examine it deeply. Why? Over the course of dozens if not hundreds of columns, commentaries, or viewpoints pieces, the commentator's creed is destined to become something of an open book to their audience. In fact, the citizen critic's distinctive worldview is what draws them to the genre in the first place.

Often commentaries concerning ideology morph into origin story pieces in which the citizen writer explains, in some de facto way, how they came to think as they do today. Anticipating reader curiosity, they commence to telling what amounts to an origin story detailing the crucial steps on their way to becoming, for instance, a democrat, or a first-responder, or a survivalist, or an advocate for a living wage or a balanced budget. Commentaries like these offer context and personal history even as they argue for the goodness, virtue, or utility of a particular philosophy or public policy. Other origin story commentaries, however, take a more surprising approach, one in which the writer explains how they changed their

Part III—Additional Opinion-Writing Genres

existing allegiances, exploded a personal or cultural myth, or took the road less traveled.

Jack London's "How I Became a Socialist" is an example of an origin story commentary with a twist, as the famous author begins with a description of a youth in which he was very much a proponent of individualism and a proper little capitalist. He recalls, "To be a MAN was to write man in large capitals on my heart. To adventure like a man, and fight like a man, and do a man's work (even for a boy's pay)—these were things that reached right in and gripped hold of me as no other thing could. And I looked ahead into long vistas of a hazy and interminable future, into which, playing what I conceived to be MAN'S game, I should continue to travel with unfailing health, without accidents, and with muscles ever vigorous."[4]

London dubs his youthful self a "Blonde Beast," an unflattering allusion to Nietzsche's nomenclature for those who seem to conquer all by "sheer superiority and strength." He confesses that he fell into individualism unthinkingly because he was strong, capable, and healthy. And because he was these things, he imagined everyone else must be, too. Work was a privilege and people who provided the work—employers—he believed were good and virtuous. London describes his youthful naivete this way:

> Work was everything. It was sanctification and salvation. The pride I took in a hard day's work well done would be inconceivable to you. It is almost inconceivable to me as I look back upon it. I was as faithful a wage slave as ever capitalist exploited. To shirk or malinger on the man who paid me my wages was a sin, first, against myself, and second, against him. I considered it a crime second only to treason and just about as bad.
>
> In short, my joyous individualism was dominated by the orthodox bourgeois ethics. I read the bourgeois papers, listened to the bourgeois preachers, and shouted at the sonorous platitudes of the bourgeois politicians. And I doubt not, if other events had not changed my career, that I should have evolved into a professional strike-breaker … and had my head and my earning power irrevocably smashed by a club in the hands of some militant trades-unionist.

It's at this point that London undertakes a life-changing trip, tramping and train-hopping his way across the country to the cities of the Eastern seaboard, where he recalls, "Men were small potatoes and hunted the job for all they were worth." London calls this class of men the "submerged tenth," and once he gets to know them he realizes that they are not so different from proletariats like himself. He continues:

19. Commentaries on Cultural Identity

> I found there all sorts of men, many of whom had once been as good as myself and just as BLOND BEAST; sailor-men, soldier-men, labor-men, all wrenched and distorted and twisted out of shape by toil and hardship and accident, and cast adrift by their masters like so many old horses. I battered on the drag and slammed back gates with them, or shivered with them in box cars and city parks, listening the while to life-histories which began under auspices as fair as mine, with digestions and bodies equal to and better than mine, and which ended there before my eyes in the shambles at the bottom of the Social Pit.
>
> And as I listened my brain began to work. The woman of the streets and the man of the gutter drew very close to me. I saw the picture of the Social Pit as vividly as though it were a concrete thing, and at the bottom of the Pit I saw them, myself above them, not far, and hanging on to the slippery wall by main strength and sweat. And I confess a terror seized me. What when my strength failed? when I should be unable to work shoulder to shoulder with the strong men who were as yet babes unborn? And there and then I swore a great oath.

London's "How I Became a Socialist" is a model of an identity-centric citizen commentary with a twist. It offers context for his present ideology, socialism, by first discussing the creed he jettisoned, capitalism, on his way toward greater enlightenment. Along the way he offers a mea culpa, admitting to his reader in so many words that his early views were ill-informed, willful, and occluded. In its way, London's published perspective follows a powerful "born-again" trope and template. As readers we're drawn to earnest first-person accounts of how, and when, a writer first saw the light, and how their life has been changed ever since. Chief among the appeals of a "How I Became…" commentary is humility. We understand from the get-go that life has taught the writer a painful if not profound lesson, and that the lesson has been learned in fits and starts, resulting, finally, in a circumspect soul eager to share their life's journey with others.

Voicing Your Opinion

1. Following the brave examples of Richard Rodriguez and Zora Neale Hurston discussed in this chapter, try a first-person opinion piece in which, using your own upbringing as an example, you elaborate on the hidden tension between cultural identity and professional identity, or, if you prefer, between familial identity and educational status. For example, you might write about how your cultural identity impacts you, and others like you, in the workplace. Or, like Rodriguez, you might examine any conflicts or coincidences between your familial identity and your educational experience. What

Part III—Additional Opinion-Writing Genres

do you see and feel about the reconciliation of these two key identities that others cannot or will not see?

2. Inspired by the opinionated Langston Hughes, craft an opinion about those in your community who seem ashamed of the cultural traditions they inherited. For example, if you grew up in an environment in which young residents were eager to leave upon graduation, how are these "leavers" or out-migrators regarded by folks who stayed close to home? In what subtle and obvious ways have they changed, perhaps appearing to put on airs? To what extent do you as a writer embrace the community that first nurtured you, and to what extent, or in what instances, do you find it necessary to distance yourself? As you generate your opinion, look for ways to treat your particular experience as representative of a group, so that you might speak for more than yourself.

3. Picking up where Jack London left off, write your own "How I became…" opinion, one that traces your evolution from a former creed, ideology, or a worldview to one that you hold now. Why did you believe what you once did? What tipping-point experience caused you to embrace a new viewpoint? How do you see the world now, compared to how you may have perceived it then? In essence, your commentary conveys a conversion narrative, one that, with any luck, will feel familiar to like-minded readers while still proving enlightening to those yet to make the leap you describe in your piece.

20

First-Person Exposé

Citizen critics have long cherished their role as muckrakers—writers dedicated to seeking out and exposing institutional and personal misconduct. Almost by definition, muckrakers dig to uncover buried truths via deep research, review of the public records, or in-person, boots-on-the-ground investigation. Coined by Theodore Roosevelt, the term "muckraker" was intended as a gentle rebuke of a press corps that, the president felt, ought to be more focused on positive news rather than on stirring up controversy. In fact, many journalists took the president's criticism as a backhanded compliment and a badge of honor for exposing misconduct others were too timid to bring to light. In the end, Roosevelt's claims galvanized the press rather than dispiriting it. And the early twentieth century soon blossomed into a heyday for muckrakers, a time when icons such as Ida Wells-Barnett, Nellie Bly, and Lincoln Steffens wielded well-honed words to keep malfeasance in check.

Investigative by nature, Lincoln Steffens focused his ire on corruption in major American cities ruled by graft and greed. Batman-like, he worked tirelessly to expose the municipal officials who failed the public trust. Steffens's sustained efforts to stop municipal misdeeds eventually landed him a recurring column in *McClure's*, one in which he featured a city-gone-wrong in each successive edition. St. Louis was one of his favorite targets, but as the excerpt below shows, he reserved some of his most pointed criticism for Pittsburgh, a steel town in the process of waking up to its own systemic corruption:

> Minneapolis was an example of police corruption; St. Louis, of financial corruption, and Pittsburgh is an example of both police and financial corruption…. The city has been described physically as "Hell with the lid off"; politically it is that same with the lid on…. There are earnest men in the town who declare it must blow up of itself soon. I doubt that; but even if it does burst, the people of Pittsburgh will learn little more than they know now. It is not ignorance that keeps American citizens subservient; neither is it indifference. The Pittsburghers know, and a strong minority of them care; they have

risen against their ring and beaten it, only to look about and find another ring around them. Angry and ashamed, Pittsburgh is a type of the city that has tried to be free and failed.[1]

Steffens follows a proven formula in his in-depth exposés, which typically begin with an overview of the target city's typography and demographics. From there he shares a history of its governance before naming its current swindlers. Thereafter he delves into the city's finances, exposing monies missing in sundry boondoggles and schemes that costs citizens millions. In cities like Chicago, Steffens's investigations galvanized angry voters and resulted in significant, albeit incomplete, reforms. Far from letting these successes go to his head, *McClure's* famed muckraker humbly concedes the limitations inherent in his method in the passage that follows:

> Ever since these articles on municipal corruption have been appearing, readers of them have been asking what they were to do about it all. As if I knew, as if "we" knew; as if there were any one way to deal with this problem in all places under any circumstances. There isn't, and if I had gone around with a ready-made reform scheme in the back of my head, it would have served only to keep me from seeing straight the facts that would not support my theory. The only editorial scheme we had was to study a few choice examples of bad city government and tell how the bad was accomplished, then seek out, here and abroad, some typical good governments and explain how the good was done—not how to do it, mind you, but how it had been done. The bad government series is not yet complete, but since so many good men apparently want to go to work right off, it was decided to pause for an instance on the reform side. I have chosen the best I have found. Political grafters have been cheerful enough to tell me they have "got a lot of pointers" from the corruption articles. I trust the reformers will pick up some "pointers" from Chicago.[2]

In articulating his modus operandi, Steffens offers something of a playbook for citizen writers seeking a sunlight cure for hidden transgressions. First, modern-day muckrakers must adapt their methods to the issue at hand, rather than using a one-size-fits-all approach. Second, the fair-minded writer of exposés must learn to look for the good as well as the bad, with the aim of brightening the contrast between them. Third, and finally, the muckraker must consider what readers are able to digest at any given moment. Since corruption is limitless, a writer risks reader exhaustion if they do not occasionally point out the bright spots in a sea of troubles.

The Art of Self-Interrogation

Investigative writers habitually direct their attention outward to the person or entity responsible for an alleged crime or injustice. Yet

20. First-Person Exposé

sometimes the enemy lies within. In such cases our own hypocrisies, double standards, and faulty memories may be the threat that needs confronting. In short, the house we clean is sometimes our own.

Such is the case with the late David Carr. In a thoroughly self-exposing article written for the publication that employed him, *The New York Times*, Carr turns his investigative talents on himself, following a long-buried paper trial of medical and legal documents leading back to the Jekyll-and-Hyde double life he lived as an avowed drug dealer who simultaneously published award-winning investigative journalism. Carr goes beyond public and private records, too, conducting uncomfortable interviews with his friends and fellow drug abusers who knew him then. Ultimately, he turns the results of his self-investigative article into the best-selling book *The Night of the Gun: A Reporter Investigates the Darkest Story of His Life. His Own.*

Commentaries in which the opinion writer uses the tools of their trade to confront themselves or to publicly declare their own wrongheadedness remain rare. Relatively few opinion writers have the courage to lay their own transgressions so thoroughly bare. But those who do tend to often discover truths that connect them more deeply to readers who have likewise summoned the courage to confront their own demons. In his self-incriminating commentary, Carr wryly observes, "When memory is called to answer, it often answers back with deception."[3] How is it, the writer wonders, that "every warm barstool contains a hero, a star of his own epic?"

His stated goal is to interrogate the hero's self-serving, self-glorying account with the same fierce energy he might summon to expose a criminal. In the end, Carr finds himself guilty of duplicity and deceit, though not without also telling his other, more redeeming story, one summarized in the subheading "I was a recovered crack addict who got custody of my twin girls, got us off welfare, and raised them."[4] Ultimately, his self-immolation is about reconciling two disparate lives, one in which he claims to have deserved "hepatitis C., federal prison time, H.I.V., a cold park bench, an early, addled death," and the other that finds him with three children and "a job that impresses."

Investigating Abuses

African American journalist Ida B. Wells-Barnett was born into slavery. As a writer based in Memphis and later in Chicago, she quickly turned the indignity of her youth into a tireless exposé of White violence

Part III—Additional Opinion-Writing Genres

in the Jim Crow South. Choosing to treat the problem concretely rather than anecdotally, Wells-Barnett put her muckraking skills to the test in her examination of lynching, ultimately publishing a work of social justice ominously titled *The Red Record* and subtitled *Tabulated Statistics and Alleged Causes of Lynching in the United States*. In *Red Record*, she publishes many pages of tables and charts documenting the instances of race-based violence White America might have hoped to forget. Taking a year-by-year approach, she documents hundreds of cases annually. And while the vast majority of incidences of race-based violence she documents occur in Southern states such as Alabama, Louisiana, and Mississippi, Wells-Barnett's evidentiary commentary records lynching in so-called Progressive states such as Illinois, California, and New York.

Wells-Barnett, who later moved to Chicago, takes particular pains to call out racial enmity in her adopted home state of Illinois, writing, "Illinois, which gave to the world the immortal heroes, Lincoln, Grant and Logan, trailed its banner of justice in the dust—dyed its hands red in the blood of a man not proven guilty of crime."[5] In a related opinion piece written for the *New York Age* entitled "Self Help," the activist writer moves away from statistical analysis to pen a piece for African Americans wondering what they can do to help themselves in a climate characterized by hate crimes and inadequate legal protections. She begins with a systematic dismissal of the methods that have proven ineffectual in pursuit of racial justice, including arguments speaking to the economic value of America's Black citizens, writing:

> The appeal to the white man's pocket has ever been more effectual than all the appeals ever made to his conscience. Nothing, absolutely nothing, is to be gained by a further sacrifice of manhood and self-respect. By the right exercise of his power as the industrial factor of the South, the Afro-American can demand and secure his rights, the punishment of lynchers, and a fair trial for accused rapists.
>
> Of the many inhuman outrages of this present year, the only case where the proposed lynching did not occur was where the men armed themselves in Jacksonville, Fla., and Paducah, Ky, and prevented it. The only times an Afro-American who was assaulted got away has been when he had a gun and used it in self-defense.
>
> The lesson this teaches and which every Afro-American should ponder well, is that a Winchester rifle should have a place of honor in every black home, and it should be used for that protection which the law refuses to give. When the white man who is always the aggressor knows he runs at great risk of biting the dust every time his Afro-American victim does, he will have greater respect for Afro-American life. The more the Afro-American yields and cringes and begs, the more he has to do so, the more he is insulted, outraged and lynched.

20. First-Person Exposé

The assertion has been substantiated throughout these pages that the press contains unreliable and doctored reports of lynchings, and one of the most necessary things for the race to do is to get these facts before the public. The people must know before they can act, and there is no educator to compare with the press.[6]

What should Black citizens do to self-advocate? Wells-Barnett calls for her fellow countrymen and women of color to support the investigative work of the Black press. She encourages boycotts of businesses hostile to the idea of racial equality. She exhorts African Americans with sufficient mobility to move to jurisdictions better able to protect their rights and to secure their safety. Only by taking action, she insists, can lynching, "that last relic of barbarism and slavery," be once and for all eliminated.

Voicing Your Opinion

1. Following the courageous muckraking of Lincoln Steffens, pen an op-ed examining a local, municipal, or regional powerbroker that you have good reason to believe is not functioning in the public interest. What anecdotal, experiential, or statistical evidence leads you to make such claims? What evidence do you have that others feel similarly? Is there a paper trail by which alleged misdeeds or malfeasance can be substantiated? Citizen writers seeking public records to substantiate their allegations might consider filing a Freedom of Information (FOIA) request.

2. Via an original work of opinion, bring an exploitative practice out of the shadows and into the light. While Ida B. Wells-Barnett tackled the horrors of lynching in America, you might, for example, call attention to human trafficking, child labor, or worker exploitation in the so-called gig economy. Taking a page from Wells's brave playbook, marshal the ugly facts of an unjust practice you hope to mitigate, reduce, or unequivocally end.

3. Investigate yourself, after the fashion of *New York Times* journalist David Carr, and write a self-exposé. Your opinion piece needn't be a self-indulgent airing of dirty laundry, but should instead reflect the genuine desire of a circumspect citizen to find fault in oneself rather than characteristically finding it in others. Perhaps we broach something in our lives we would do differently if granted a do-over. Or maybe we contemplate the darker roads we might have gone down had we not received a lucky break here or there. In the final analysis, our commentary should be an exercise in deep empathy—for ourselves and for others—and one well-illustrated with textual and perhaps photographic artifacts from the time in question.

21

Immersion Commentary

Reporters are often taught to remove themselves from the story in hope of remaining objective. And while this is good advice for deadline journalists filing conventional news stories, it's awful advice for citizen writers intending to enact the empathy principle by walking a mile in someone else's shoes.

Participatory writers seek to understand by doing, and the commentaries they pen are distinguished by their willingness to leave the writer's desk for real encounters with the issues they explore. Participatory commentators move beyond conventional interviews with others to become subjects themselves, engaging in a kind of auto-ethnography, a method better known by sociologists as participant-observation.

How do we lend a level of participant observation to our opinion writing? Some opportunities are easier than others. For example, the parent traveling with their 17-year-old to visit colleges and universities around the country might easily write a compelling participation-based opinion on the expense and privilege such visits entail. Similarly, the opinionated writer who has recently purchased an electric vehicle might write a credible piece commenting on the disproportionate challenge of traveling cross-country in an EV.

The participatory challenge grows when the problem or issue we hope to investigate becomes dangerous, threatening, or potentially illegal. Commentators willing to tackle such issues from an experiential standpoint engage in a risk-reward calculation that inevitably finds them weighing their own well-being against a reader's need to know. The bravest choose on behalf of the reader.

At the turn of the century, journalist Nellie Bly helped pioneer the participatory technique by investigating so-called swindles, often confronting fraudsters in person at corporate offices or shady backrooms. She called her regular column in the *New York World* "Putting Our Ideas to the Test," and the greatest test that crooks and charlatans faced was very often the indefatigable Bly herself. In an opinion piece titled "Another Wicked

21. Immersion Commentary

Swindle," Bly explained the logic behind her long-running column this way: "Divide the population of America into two parts and you have two classes—the swindlers and the swindled, and the census of one will equal that of the other every time."[1]

In a long career of firsthand investigations, Bly tried it all, from training elephants, to acting on the stage, to working as a spy, to reporting the horrors of world wars. Her willingness to write from the inside-out endeared her to the legions of fans who looked forward to her weekly column. In the excerpt that follows, the intrepid opinion writer participates in the illegal trade in infants then plaguing New York City:

> I bought a baby last week, to learn how baby slaves are bought and sold in the city of New York. Think of it! An immortal soul bartered for $10. Fathers, mothers, ministers, missionaries, I bought an immortal soul last week for $10!
>
> We had a war not many years ago—a long and bitter struggle, which cost many millions of lives and many millions of dollars, and it was supposed that slavery had ended when the armies disbanded.
>
> But it did not stop slavery. Slavery exists today in New York in a more repulsive form than it ever existed in the South. White slaves, baby slaves—young, innocent, helpless baby slaves—bought and sold every day in the week—bargained for before they are born—sold by their parents! The ... slaves had a John Brown to start their march to freedom. Who will start it for the baby slaves of New York?
>
> For several days before I bought a baby I advertised in a number of newspapers for a baby to adopt. I received no reply. Why? Because people who adopt babies for good purposes and in a legitimate way do not expect to buy them. Those people who have babies in the market expect to sell them, and they will not give them away.[2]

Posing as a would-be buyer, Bly visits several of the homes where babies are birthed, bought, and sold. She discovers infants sold by desperate mothers for as little as a dollar, while detailing a sinister trade where middlemen and middlewomen take the highest bid on a human soul without ascertaining the preparedness of the would-be parent. As she gleans information from the human traffickers of her day, convincing them of her interest, she must somehow keep her cool, and her cover. Still, the emotional toll her investigation exacts is palpable, as she ultimately concludes: "The inhuman, barbarous transaction made me heartsick."

Immersion-Based Commentary

In the golden age of journalism, *New York Daily News* writer Paul Gallico epitomized participant-observation on the page, putting himself

Part III—Additional Opinion-Writing Genres

in harm's way at every opportunity. For a veteran of the first world war, sport-based immersions such as boxing against world heavyweight champ Jack Dempsey or going to bat against a major league pitcher must have seemed mild by comparison.

In his opinion essay "The Feel," Gallico argues for the virtue inherent in the columnists throwing themselves into the fray, comparing the subsequent realizations to a pilot preparing for a potential emergency landing. Only then, thousands of feet in the sky and plummeting, does the airman experience "that gone feeling at the pit of the stomach and the sharp tingling of the skin from head to foot, followed by a sudden amazing sharpness of vision, clear-sightedness, and coolness that you never knew you possessed as you find the question of life or death completely in your own hands."[3] He argues that crucibles like these expose inner weaknesses suddenly and completely. The commentator who has come to know themselves completely—inside and out—Gallico believes to be the most qualified to render an opinion. The philosophy he articulates epitomizes empathy journalism, as he believes that the writer who has duked it out in the ring is, for example, the most trustworthy reporter of the power and pain of pugilism.

While Gallico excels in immersions that would surely break a less intrepid writer (he famously lasts nearly two minutes in the ring with boxer Jack Dempsey), he does not always succeed in the quest to conquer his fears. On one occasion Gallico climbs to the top of a 30-foot Olympic diving tower in Long Island, intending to experience for himself the unique feelings of vertigo and freefall known to Olympic divers. Instead, he confesses, he "flunked completely," having to crawl back from the board on hands and knees, "dizzy, scared, and a little sick" but with a newfound respect for the men and women who "hurled themselves through the air and down through the tough skin of the water from that awful height."[4] Gallico's enduring fame demonstrates the power of the writer whose opinions are rooted in practical and reciprocal understanding.

While most of Paul Gallico's participatory columns concern sports and the sporting life, the participatory method can be applied to almost any subject with convincing results.

Contemporary journalist Ted Conover smuggles himself across the Mexican border to learn the perils of illegal immigration and works as a guard at Sing-Sing to better understand the prison system. Meanwhile, in her contemporary classic "Nickel-and-Dimed," writer Barbara Ehrenreich willingly abandons her middle-class life as a magazine writer to try living on minimum wage for a year. She describes her terror at being unmasked

21. Immersion Commentary

as an investigative writer, though the results of her participant observation surprise her. She concedes, "my fears turn out to be unwarranted: during a month of poverty and toil, my name goes unnoticed and for the most part unuttered."[5] In the "parallel universe" where she became a minimum wage worker, where her father "never got out of the mines" and she failed to graduate from college, Ehrenreich is instead referred to reductively as "baby," "honey," "blondie" and "girl."

At times, the emotional drain and inherent drama of the participatory method can seem to overtake the commentator's critical analysis, though the best columnists make the difficult pivot from experience to evaluation look effortless. Ehrenreich makes the move perfectly in the concluding paragraph of her immersion-based article. Having just walked out of her job as a waitress suffering intolerable conditions, she grows circumspect, forgetting her own private indignity for the sake of broader cultural analysis: "The thinking behind welfare reform was that even the humblest jobs are morally uplifting and psychologically buoying. In reality they are likely to be fraught with insult and stress. But I did discover one redeeming feature of the most abject low-wage work—the camaraderie of people who are, in almost all cases, far too smart and funny and caring for the work they do and the wages they're paid. The hope, of course, is that someday these people will come to know what they're worth, and take appropriate action."[6]

Ehrenreich saves her takeaway for the concluding paragraph. What does she want readers to glean from her immersion? First, that welfare reform isn't as simple as some would say and, second, that the negative opinion of low-wage workers held by many conservatives is both inaccurate and uncharitable.

Writing From the Trenches

By analogy, the immersion-based commentary practiced with such distinction by Bly, Gallico, and Ehrenreich is the difference between a general commanding their soldiers at safe remove and fighting alongside them. The opinion writer willing to write from the trenches gains a new kind of credibility among readers who appreciate their willingness to take fire.

McClure's columnist Richard Harding Davis wrote from the trenches in the most literal sense, embedding himself with Allied soldiers in World War I. To plumb the common soldier's psyche, he joins his subjects on the frontlines, exposing himself to the same heavy bombardment the troops

Part III—Additional Opinion-Writing Genres

endure. In his commentary "Under Fire," Davis analyzes the bizarre ways men in the trenches cope with the threat of death, transcending mere reportage to think critically about cause and effect. "Under Fire" is an excellent example of the ways in which participant observation and astute commentary can be joined on the page:

> In times of war you constantly see men, and women, too, who, sooner than suffer discomfort or even inconvenience, risk death. The psychology of the thing is, I think, that a man knows very little about being dead, but has a very acute knowledge of what it is to be uncomfortable. His brain is not able to grasp death, but it is quite capable of informing him that his fingers are cold. Often men receive credit for showing coolness and courage in times of danger, when, in reality, they are not properly aware of the danger and through habit are acting authentically. The girl in Chicago who went back into the Iroquois Theatre fire to rescue her rubber overshoes was not a heroine. She merely lacked imagination. Her mind was capable of appreciating how serious for her would be the loss of her overshoes, but not of being burned alive. At the battle of Velestinos in the Greek-Turkish war, John F. Bass, of *The Chicago Daily News*, and myself got into a trench at the foot of a hill on which later the Greeks placed a battery. All day the Turks bombarded this battery with a crossfire of shrapnel and rifle bullets which did not touch our trench, but cut off our return to Velestinos. Sooner than pass through this crossfire, all day we crouched in the trench until about sunset, when it came on to rain. We exclaimed with dismay. We had neglected to bring our ponchos. "If we don't get back to the village at once," we assured each other, "we will get wet!" So we raced through half a mile of falling shells and bullets and, before the rain fell, got under cover. Then Bass said: "For twelve hours we stuck to that trench because we were afraid if we left it we would be killed. And the only reason we ever did leave it was because we were more afraid of catching cold!"
>
> In the same war I was in a trench with some infantrymen, one of whom never raised his head. Whenever he was ordered to fire he would shove his rifle barrel over the edge of the trench, shut his eyes and pull the trigger. He took no chances. His comrades laughed at him and swore at him, but he would only grin sheepishly and burrow deeper. After several hours a friend in another trench held up a bag of tobacco and some cigarette papers and in pantomime "dared" him to come for them. To the intense surprise of everyone he scrambled out of our trench and, exposed against the skyline, walked to the other trench and, while he rolled a handful of cigarettes, drew the fire of the enemy. It was not that he was brave; he had shown that he was not. He was merely stupid. Between death and cigarettes, his mind could not rise above cigarettes.[7]

Davis explores the irrationality of men and women under stress, but never in a holier-than-thou manner. In fact, he and fellow writer John Bass confess to behaving just as irrationally when they leave their trench despite incoming fire.

21. Immersion Commentary

Voicing Your Opinion

1. Inspired by the intrepid immersion journalism of Nellie Bly, attempt to acquire a controversial product or service by unconventional means, then write about it as a citizen. Perhaps you explore the acquisition of a pedigreed pup from a so-called puppy mill, or the cost and process of adopting a rescue dog. Or perhaps you explore the possibilities of buying prescription drugs over the internet from a country where the aforementioned pharmaceuticals are available legally without a prescription. Whatever you choose, be aware in advance of the potential predatory nature of the industry you explore, and any possible illegalities should you follow through with your purchase.

2. Attempt a popular sport or activity about which you're genuinely curious, and generate a piece of opinion writing from that participation, after the fashion of Paul Gallico. For example, suppose you want to join the millions of Americans giving the popular sport of pickleball a belated try. Or maybe you're finally ready to try the beginner's hill at a local sky resort. Oftentimes, immersion-based opinions are most richly contextualized and characterized when the writer's participations occur under the auspices of an advocacy group or club whose job it is to promote the sport and protect its integrity. For example, an immersion experience by a citizen writer turned first-time pickleballer might be scheduled at courts owned and maintained by the local pickleball club.

3. Pen a commentary after the fashion of embedded reporter Richard Harding Davis. In this case, writing "from the trenches" might mean shadowing a law enforcement official for the day. Or it might mean a visit, with permission, to a classroom to better understand the challenges educators face in the twenty-first century. Whatever figurative trench you choose to write from, resolve to be an active interpreter more than just a passive observer.

22

Polemics and Other Points of Contrast

Those who don't know better sometimes reduce opinion to so much monologuing. This misconception is understandable, as very often readers hear a single strong voice and assume the columnist has, in effect, written a drama for one.

In practice, however, few genres are as intrinsically dialogic. While most opinion pieces don't include dialogue per se, they do simulate a dynamic discussion on the page, one in which the writer is but one, albeit central, participant. Often, viewpoints pieces plead their case to an off-stage character: typically a skeptical reader. It's this delicate pas de deux that makes the op-ed, commentary, or column the epitome of public discourse. The strongly opinionated commentator may lead the dance, but, as the saying goes, it takes two to tango.

The dialogic nature of the most dynamic commentaries gets reflected in the long list of "di" words (from the Greek root meaning "two") that apply to the citizen writer's art—not just *dialogue*, but *dialectic* and, more to the point, *dichotomy*, meaning "a division or contrast between two things that are or are represented as being opposed or entirely different." Rhetoricians have deployed dichotomies for millennia to brighten the contrast between two things. Like the "Would you rather" game many of us played as kids—e.g., would you rather see the Egyptian pyramids or the Eiffel Tower?—dichotomy splits readers into two divergent camps to illustrate a point. At its worse, dichotomy can degenerate into diatribe. At its best it generates an unprecedented level of dialogic interchange between two illuminating extremes.

Much like the Greek rhetoricians of old, twentieth- and twenty-first-century opinion writers deploy dichotomy strategically. For example, writing for the *Toronto Star* during his youthful sojourn in Canada, Ernest Hemingway playfully teases Americans for the black-and-white views they hold of their neighbors to the north. Americans, he asserts, create

22. Polemics and Other Points of Contrast

stereotypes of Canadians that boil down to two distinct types, Wild and Tame. Hemingway leads with his thesis: "A typical Canadian as pictured by the man ... in the States is of two types, wild and tame. Wild Canadians mean ... blanket pants, fur caps, have rough bewhiskered but honest faces and are closely pursued by corporals of the Royal Northwest Mounted Police. Tame Canadians wear spats, small mustaches, are very intelligent looking, all have M.C.'s, and are politely bored."[1]

Hemingway's point of contrast surely holds some truth decades after he penned it, at least where North American stereotypes are concerned. In the twenty-first-century popular imagination, the "wild" Canadian still remains heavily bearded, flannel-clad and rugged—as likely to play hockey without pads on a frigid northern lake as to tap a maple tree in the dead of winter. The prototypical "tame" or civilized Canadian, on the other hand, finds a contemporary analog in the long line of elegant Canadian prime ministers such as Justin Trudeau. Of course, Hemingway realizes his dichotomy is an oversimplification made for rhetorical purposes. Canadians are far more nuanced and complicated than the Wild vs. Tame comparison-contrast could possibly capture. And yet for its admitted imperfections, Hemingway's artful classification remains essentially illuminating. It's memorable, catchy, and, ultimately revealing, in addition to serving as a surefire conversation-starter for, as he puts it, "the average American ... munching peanuts."

I've used the dichotomy strategy to positive effect in several of my own opinion pieces on national identity. In one commentary, entitled "Forget Red vs. Blue, America is Cactus vs. Philodendron," I argue that the burgeoning sales of cacti have come to symbolize the gradual desertification of American civic life, whereas the fussy Philodendron, which once served as America's houseplant of choice, requires "plant-sitting" by neighbors emmeshed in a web of interdependence. Attending to the cactus side of the dichotomy, I write: "The decided tilt toward the rugged individualism and rattlesnake politics of Cactusland is the best 'tell' yet of America's growing embrace of don't-tread-on-me ideologies. The West, where the Cactus lives freely and naturally, and where the Census tells us many young professionals and monied retirees are moving, I argue, is a harbinger of where American hearts and minds may be heading, as well as an allegory for the hazards implicit in the desertification of public life: decentralization, distance, deregulation—in short, less persnickety care and more prickliness."[2] In comparing and contrasting two of the most popular houseplants of the last forty years, my aim is to prompt a kind of intergenerational dialogue on the page that reveals, rather than necessarily judges, changing generational priorities by analogy.

Part III—Additional Opinion-Writing Genres

Polemics

If the poet Robert Frost is right that life often amounts to two roads diverging—one safer and better trod, the other less civilized and more daringly original—the commentator's art may indeed boil down to presenting the reader with two illustrative choices, often exaggerated for rhetorical effect, for debate and dialogue: stay or go, war or peace, Republican or Democrat. Such pieces are often labeled *polemics*—a term the general public often reductively associates with over-the-top arguments whipped up to stimulate public rancor when, in fact, a more accurate definition is closer to Merriam-Webster's take on the word as "the art or practice of disputation or controversy." Can a citizen writer truly make art of controversy, becoming, in effect, a controversy artist? The editors of America's most respected dictionary certainly think so.

Chicago activist Belle Squire uses the polemical strategy perfectly in her classic commentary from the *Chicago Tribune*, "Would You Rather Have a Vote or a Husband?" Embroiled in the pitched civil rights battle of their day, Squire and her fellow early twentieth-century suffragists espoused a myriad of views on the voting rights question. Some believed only White women should have the vote; others claimed only women who were citizens of the United States should cast a ballot; still others maintained that a written test should determine which women were best qualified for enfranchisement. The genius of Squire's newspaper polemic is its ability to cut through the noise to put the question directly to women: if they had to choose, would they choose between enfranchisement (the vote) or getting (or keeping) a husband? Such a question potentially serves as an invaluable litmus test revealing a woman's tolerance for sacrifice in the battle to win her civil rights. Squire leaves no doubt where she stands on the all-important question at the heart of her incendiary commentary, as she opens with:

> I want a vote; it is more dependable than a husband.
> A vote is always an asset, for it represents dignity and power.
> A husband often robs a woman of these.[3]

As a columnist, Squire refuses to pull her punches. She's unafraid to make the Faustian choice between two seemingly disparate outcomes, and would clearly like her reader to likewise declare their allegiances. While her polemic might feel coercive or bullying to some, its absolutist nature is part and parcel of its raison d'etre. She boldly calls the question, asking all those within earshot to join the cause or to be declared too mild or milquetoast to merit inclusion in the movement.

22. Polemics and Other Points of Contrast

Antithetical Treatments

In common parlance "antithetical" has come to mean the opposite or the converse, though in rhetorical studies antithesis is a figure of speech involving a seeming contradiction of ideas, words, clauses, or sentences within a balanced grammatical structure. Dating back to its Greek root, antithesis means to set against or in opposition to, though not necessarily to set apart, since antithesis puts two opposing elements side by side for further consideration. The savvy citizen writer can turn to antithesis whenever two quintessentially contrasting ideas rub shoulders. Is love the opposite of hate, or is indifference the converse of love? The opinion writer is sure to weigh in.

Social worker and writer and peace activist Jane Addams habitually views the world through a multitude of antithetical lenses: war and peace, strength and weakness, rich and poor. In the published proceedings of the annual peace conference in 1909, Addams reflects on the quintessential difference between men and women as it relates to war and peace. Her thoughts, excerpted below, demonstrate the dichotomous nature of her thinking:

> Men very early learned to do things together because they were obliged to fight together; one of the things that war bequeathed to mankind and to the male portion of mankind is this ability to go out together, to go in tribes, to go in phalanxes, to go in regiments, to go in whatever body of men was the safest to those who were fighting, and to bring the most destruction to those whom they were fighting against.[4]

Addams begins by laying out her antithetical premise for the reader to examine in full. Is it true that men are more tribal, and, if so, is their tribal nature biological, sociological, or both? Having begged the question, her antithetical pairing works nicely to advance the argument even as she continues to gently challenge its ultimate veracity:

> Whether this is true or not, I think it is certainly true that the thing which is happening now to this special generation of women is the ability and learning how to act together.
>
> At last, women are learning to pull together, to pull in bodies. We may call those bodies clubs, or we may call them benefit societies, or we may call them this, that, and the other, but they are all bodies of women as such, and they are going out to do away with such evil as they see and to bring about such good as they may be able to perform.

Addams's purpose is not to further divide men and women, which would surely be counterproductive to her stated goal of world peace, but to highlight how men and women think differently, with the intention of showing how women might draw from their counterparts' playbook to achieve solidarity. Her column perfectly illustrates the strategic use of dichotomy, since she sets the psyche of men and women side by side in yin-and-yang arrangement. The result is a dynamic dialogue between two gender identities.

Though our own era is far more gender-fluid and nonbinary than Addams's, antithesis as a rhetorical strategy endures. Consider *New York Times* best-selling author John Gray and his contemporary classic *Men Are from Mars, Women Are from Venus*. Like Addams, Gray uses dichotomy not to drive a wedge between the sexes, but to illustrate the difference between them with the ultimate goal of harmonious relationship.

Voicing Your Opinion

1. After the fashion of Ernest Hemingway, craft an opinion that explores the stereotypes two parties hold of one another, while exposing the inadequacies of both. Ideally, you will have some lived experience on both sides of the mutual stereotyping, as at the time he wrote his piece Hemingway was an American living and working in Canada. Your dichotomy-cum-commentary could tackle a subject as big as national identity or as intimate as the perceived differences between, say, an oldest and youngest sibling written by someone who sees both sides—for example, from the perspective of a middle child.

2. Inspired by activist writers Belle Squire and Jane Addams, craft a polemical or antithetical work of opinion that speaks to the illustrative differences between the sexes, or between two apparent opposites of any kind. The aim is not to enflame misunderstanding, but to distill for the thoughtful reader how one side substantively differs from the other (as well as less publicized areas of potential overlap) via the telling differences you delineate in your polemic.

23

Classification Commentaries

The opinion writer's art is fundamentally one of classification—of putting ideas, observations, and assessments into discrete bins intended to illuminate and to edify. Granted, the move toward categorization often puts the opinion-maker at odds with themselves and with their readers, since to categorize is inevitably to silo. Viewed more charitably, however, the commentator's gift for classification becomes a weapon powerful enough to expose inequity or injustice.

What good is classification as a citizen writer's superpower? The categorizer is able to group together, to organize, and to present in a logical fashion. Think of the categorizing writer as societal organizer. The opinion-maker who effectively assembles their evidence into various bins for presentation serves as a typologist, someone who categorizes according to type. By perceiving types and patterns where others see only bland monolith, the classifying writer infuses their work with a discerning kind of intelligence.

The most talented social commentators can summon their inner classifier at will. Take journalist-author Charles Dickens, who published a series of classification pieces in the magazines and newspapers of his era. To arrive at his most trenchant opinions, Dickens divides and classifies nearly every social stratum in Victorian London, simultaneously cutting them down to size. Of the so-called "cool couples" he sees at soirees, Dickens opines, "The cool couple are seldom alone together, and when they are, nothing can exceed their apathy and dullness: the gentleman being for the most part drowsy, and the lady silent. If they enter into conversation, it is usually of an ironical or recriminatory nature."[1]

While Dickens writes with an almost anthropological or zoological sense, as if objectively describing a certain species and its habitat, it's clear from context that the writer doesn't hold much esteem for the pairs he has purposefully pigeonholed. "But it must not be supposed that the cool couple are habitually a quarrelsome one," he writes. "Quite the contrary. These differences are only occasions for a little self-excuse—nothing more. In general they are as easy and careless, and dispute as seldom, as any common acquaintances may; for it is neither worth their while to put each other out of the way, nor to ruffle themselves."[2] It's not that the cool couple is irredeemably boorish or obnoxious, but that they are sufficiently complacent as to be offputtingly indifferent.

In another socially conscious sketch, Dickens crafts a takedown of the political pundit class in and around London, classifying them as "perpetually on the watch for a political allusion, or anything which can be tortured or construed into being one."[3] Then, when they find an opening for their wished-for political discourse, they pounce, "thrusting themselves into the very smallest openings for their favorite discourse, they fall upon the unhappy company tooth and nail." We can presume that the intention behind Dickens's poison pen is awareness—not only to empower members of the general public to recognize "the cool couple" or the overzealous "political gentleman," but to recognize their tendencies and qualities as manifest in ourselves, lest we unwittingly become them.

Damning Types and Typologies

Dickens's sketches of life in Victorian London are often anecdotal and wryly humorous. But the power of categorization far exceeds light comedy, as columnist Dorothy Thompson demonstrates in her resounding work of social justice, "Who Goes Nazi?" In this famous piece first published in *Harper's* magazine in August of 1941, prior to the American entry into World War II, Thompson bravely offers a typology of would-be Nazi sympathizers, referring to them by sobriquets such as "Mr. A" and "Mr. B." Drawing from recent travels throughout Germany, Austria, and France, Thompson discerns three distinct types, which she labels "the born Nazis, the Nazis whom democracy itself has created," and those who "never, under any conceivable circumstances, would become Nazis."[4]

For illustrative purposes, she bids us to imagine ourselves at a dinner party determining who among the invitees is most likely be a closet fascist. We're offered rather detailed biographical sketches of Mr. A, Mr. B, Mr. C, Mr. D, and Mrs. E in turn, with Thompson assessing the latent potential of each to succumb to the scourge of Nazism. The commentator arranges the presentation of characters in a climactic structure, beginning with Mr. A, who earns a very modest living as an editor; he's a widower loyal to his deceased wife, a Republican who crossed party lines to vote for Franklin D. Roosevelt, a veteran of the first World War, and a man of cultivated taste

23. Classification Commentaries

in the arts. He, the writer insists, would never go Nazi, presumably for his quiet virtuousness and reluctance to engage in excessive partisanship.

Next is Mr. C, whom we're told is not a born Nazi, though he bears close watching, for he's "a sensitive, gifted man who has been humiliated into nihilism. He would laugh to see heads roll." Mrs. E is saved for last in the opinion writer's climactic structure. Just because she is a woman does not mean that she would not go Nazi. Thompson reserves her most biting vitriol yet for the dinner party invitee who would no doubt draw the least suspicions by virtue of her wealth and sweetness, but who is surely, in the writer's eyes, the weakest link:

> Mrs. E would go Nazi as sure as you are born. That statement surprises you? Mrs. E seems so sweet, so clinging, so cowed. She is. She is a masochist. She is married to a man who never ceases to humiliate her, to lord it over her, to treat her with less consideration than he does his dogs. He is a prominent scientist, and Mrs. E, who married him very young, has persuaded herself that he is a genius, and that there is something of superior womanliness in her utter lack of pride, in her doglike devotion.[5]

Thompson points out early in this classification-based commentary that Nazism is not limited to German nationalists, but presents its ugly face everywhere around the world where racism, nationalism, and fascism coalesce. The typology she offers resists superficial judgment, as exactly who will "go Nazi" cannot be predicted by physical appearance or social status. The highly intellectual Mr. C, for example, is courteous and refined; in a line-up he would probably not be picked out as prime suspect. But Thompson tells us he is "a dangerous man." If he were less well-educated, she asserts, "he would be a criminal—a murderer. But he is subtle and cruel. He would rise high in a Nazi regime. It would need men just like him—intellectual and ruthless."[6]

Very few of the types Thompson sketches are what she would call "born Nazis." Instead, she presents us with a cast of representative characters not dissimilar from her readers. Her core critique is crystal clear: many if not most could potentially succumb to Nazism if their cruelty triumphed over compassion.

A Stand for Authenticity

The citizen writer's natural inclination is toward authenticity, toward honesty. In a world of pretentiousness, presumption, and propaganda, such a stance makes sense. If the commentator is guided by the twin stars

Part III—Additional Opinion-Writing Genres

of honesty and authenticity, they will be led to the truth of the matter, or, if not, at least to its heart.

Little wonder, then, that commentators and cultural critics are characteristically quick to condemn insincerity. After all, harmless artifice can quickly turn into wholesale deceit, and wholesale deceit can rapidly devolve into thoroughgoing totalitarianism. If the commentator or critic is successful at sussing out falsity, they've served—and perhaps helped save or salve—society.

In the piece that follows from the *Toronto Daily Star*, Ernest Hemingway tackles a less serious form of pretention: cultural posing by the legions of ex-patriots that settled in France during the Jazz Age. And even though hipsters are far less of a public menace than would-be fascists, he tackles the confrontation with relish.

> Paris—Paris is the Mecca of the bluffers and fakers in every line of endeavor from music to prizefighting. You find more famous American dancers who have never been heard of in America; more renowned Russian dancers who are disclaimed by the Russians; and more champion prizefighters ... per square yard in Paris than anywhere else in the world.
>
> This state of affairs exists because of the extreme provinciality of the French people, and because of the gullibility of the French press. Everyone in Canada knows the names of half a dozen French soldiers and statesmen, but no one in France could give you the name of a Canadian general or statesman or tell you who was the present head of the Canadian government. By no one I mean none of the ordinary people; shopkeepers, hotel owners and general bourgeois class....
>
> An American girl was recently billed at the Paris music halls as "America's best known and best loved dancer." None of the recent arrivals in Paris from the States had ever heard of her, but Parisians flocked to see the American "Star." Later it came out that she had a small part in a U.S. musical show some years ago.[7]

Picking up on the tagline used in the lead (spelled "lede" in journalism) sentence, the *Daily Star* titles Hemingway's column "The Mecca of Fakers in French Capital." His commentary is part cultural criticism, part diatribe, and part exposé, with its message boiling down to: "buyer beware." If Hemingway can lift the veil on the pretenders and posers of the Jazz Age, he can prevent the unsuspecting public from being taken in by a sham. He raises awareness by challenging the fakers' sincerity and by comparing himself and other genuine American products with the flimflam fraudsters flooding Paris. At root, "The Mecca of Fakers" hinges on a pair of artfully developed dichotomies: Real vs. Fake and Fidelity vs. Fraud.

23. Classification Commentaries

Voicing Your Opinion

1. After the fashion of Charles Dickens, draft a social commentary that exposes the hypocrisies of recognizable types typically encountered in habitual social settings. For example, maybe you're an environmentalist who frequently attends planning meetings with fellow eco-advocates. Write an opinion piece that dares broach some of the hypocritical character types that must be wrestled with at such meetings—for instance, the avowed environmentalist who drives a gas-guzzling SUV, or the overzealous organizer who, truth be told, prefers anarchy to activism.

2. Taking the classic Hemingway column "The Mecca of Fakers" as your model, write a typology-based opinion that unpacks various levels of posing and posers that afflict both public and private spaces. Perhaps you offer a panoramic view of the fakery that goes on inside a major cultural event like the Lollapalooza music festival in Chicago, the Burning Man gathering in Nevada, or the annual Comic-Con convention in San Diego. Note that such pieces are most effective when written by someone already inside the community they aim, at least in part, to expose. For example, Hemingway was an American man-of-letters living in Paris at the time that he cried fraud on the American wannabeism infecting the streets of the French capital. In other words, his opinion hits home because he had a front-row seat to the chicanery and charlatanism he decried.

Part IV

Publishing Citizen Writing

24

Eight Steps Post-Submission

What steps should we take once our guest opinion is safely off our desktop and in the hands of editors? How long does the publication of a freelance opinion piece usually take from start to finish, and what, if any, actions can we take to expedite the process, or at least grease its wheels? What's a reasonable pay range, or pay expectation, for a published guest opinion, and what paperwork, if any, needs to be signed before the commissioned work appears? Following are eight steps the thoughtful citizen writer might consider post-submission.

1. *Wait for it, but not for too long.* The busiest newspapers and magazines do not have time to reply to each and every submission with a "yea" or "nay." Instead, the laws of supply and demand dictate that a lack of a reply is synonymous with "not interested." This system exists in part because opinion editors know they can fairly request "exclusive submission" only if they return a verdict quickly and unambiguously to the writer. While many smaller and mid-sized newspapers are pleased to entertain simultaneous submissions (the same opinion piece sent to multiple outlets at the same time for consideration) with proper acknowledgment in a cover letter, prestige publications are more likely to demand exclusivity. For example, those submitting guest op-eds to *The New York Times* are likely to receive an automated email that reads in part: "Unfortunately, because the number of submissions is so large, we have to pass on much material of value and interest, and cannot reply to all submissions. If you do not hear from us within three business days, please assume that we will not be able to use your article. You should then feel free to offer it elsewhere."

2. *Check your email.* In the news and opinion industry, time is of the essence, which means that even though our submission may be a long shot, we should check our email frequently after uploading or emailing our guest viewpoints for consideration. In a minority of cases, a small to

24. Eight Steps Post-Submission

mid-sized newspaper may publish our piece without any follow-up contact. We may, in fact, learn of its publication only later, when a friend or colleague stops to congratulate us, or when a Google Alert suddenly appears in our inbox. Such "surprise" publications of freelance opinion are a bit of a double-edged sword. "It would have been nice to know," we might mutter to ourselves, grateful that our thoughts were read while nevertheless feeling a bit blindsided. Fortunately, such surprise publications seldom happen at major metropolitan dailies or well-established news sites, as these outlets will typically want to get back to us, pre-publication, with proposed edits, author bios, and, in some cases, a contributors agreement requiring our timely signature.

3. *Be ready to revise on a dime.* Most busy editors don't have time to coach a guest contributor or to engage in developmental editing, unless, perhaps, the opinion writer in need of coaching is a celebrity or VIP sure to generate plenty of views, clicks, and impressions. The rest of us will generally receive little more than line-edits for clarity and concision, edits that will subsequently be submitted for our approval before they go final. While editors consider it part of their job to edit freelance submissions, they are far more likely to accept work for publication if it's already polished and print-ready. In rare cases, opinion editors may contact us asking for more substantive edits; if they do, they often need our revisions back without delay. The need for quick-turnaround revisions is yet another reason why it's good practice to be in the habit of checking email multiple times per day in the days immediately after submission of freelance opinion.

4. *A submission begins a conversation.* As citizen writers submitting our opinions on a freelance basis, we want the editorial verdict to be swift and definite rather than slow and painful. Especially when we're pitching venues that forbid simultaneous submissions, we want an answer now, or yesterday. "No," is okay, we tell ourselves—it's the answer we've been trained to expect after all—so long as the rejection comes promptly and, we hope, courteously.

Our distaste for delay and equivocation is understandable, but it may not be justifiable. By analogy, if we ask our neighbor for a favor—say, to borrow their lawnmower until ours is fixed—we don't presume to also dictate the speed of their reply. They may want to hash out the details in person with us, discuss the would-be loan with a spouse or partner prior to granting their permission, or simply to come to a better understanding of our particular needs and how they might best be able to help. In other words, our request marks the beginning of a conversation, not the end.

Part IV—Publishing Citizen Writing

When we ask an editor to publish our work at their expense and risk, we're asking for a favor. When the process works at peak efficiency, we may have our answer the very day we submit, or it may take two weeks or more to hear back. Sometimes in the interim between submission and definitive judgment, an editor will seek an online conversation with us—hoping, for example, to clarify our aims for the work, our experience in the subject area, or simply to get an idea of the writer behind the words.

5. *Sign on the dotted line.* In the lucky event our opinion piece is accepted for publication by a major publication, it's possible we'll receive an agreement spelling out copyrights and licensing as it relates to the content we've produced. Sometimes this form arrives as a pdf attachment replete with legalese; other times the pertinent information arrives via email in a straightforward message for which we're asked only to acknowledge receipt. For example, following is a "terms of publication" clause I received recently from a major newspaper I'll call "X Newspaper Company":

> By filling in my name, Social Security number and contact information and sending this information to [X] by email, I confirm that I have read this entire email message, and I understand and agree to the terms listed below.
>
> This e-mail sets forth the basic understanding between you and **X Newspaper Company** (the "Company") in connection with the material you submitted for publication in the X Newspaper's Opinion pages (the "Editorial Material.")
>
> First, the Company will pay you $300 for the right to publish the Editorial Material. This is the total compensation that you will receive for this material, no matter how many times it is reprinted or reused in any form, and in any place, by the Company or anyone to whom the Company grants the right to republish or reuse Editorial Material.
>
> Second, you agree that all Editorial Material submitted by you will be original works created by you. You will use reasonable care to ensure the Editorial Material contains facts and statements that are true, do not defame individuals or infringe upon any copyright, right of privacy, proprietary right or any other right of someone else. After we have published one of your pieces, you are free to seek other outlets for it.
>
> Third, in exchange for the $300 fee set forth above, for all Editorial Material submitted by you to the Company, you grant to the Company the irrevocable, paid up, royalty-free, worldwide right to (1) publish the Editorial Material in X Newspaper and any online versions of the publication, (2) edit and create derivative works from the Editorial Material, and (3) commercially reproduce, distribute, transmit or display, and authorize republication and reproduction of, the Editorial Material (or any derivative works based on the Editorial Material) in any archival databases, microfilm, compilations, CD-ROMS and on-line or other electronic versions.

24. Eight Steps Post-Submission

Fourth, you agree that the Company has the right to use, restrict, modify and edit the Editorial Material in its sole discretion.

Fifth, you agree to indemnify and hold the Company harmless from all liabilities and claims arising out of the contents of Editorial Material. You will cooperate fully with the Company in defending against any such claim.

Sixth, this agreement will cover all articles submitted by you and published on the Commentary page of X Newspaper for a period extending from the date that you indicate your acceptance of the terms of this agreement by sending us a return e-mail with the requested information above until it is superseded by a new agreement or until termination of this agreement by you or X Newspaper. This agreement applies only to Commentary articles and not to Letters to the Editor, Counterpoint articles and other articles submitted to X Newspaper.

When I received this agreement, I made sure, prior to acknowledging it, that I would retain the right to republish my own op-ed, without formal permissions, wherever I chose—whether it be in a book like this one, in an anthology, or on a personal or professional site, without separate permissions. If the contributor's agreement you sign for your freelance column, op-ed, or commentary does not include such a clause, you should feel empowered to request it.

6. *Own your work.* Writers new to the practice of opinion writing will be glad to know that in most instances they will retain the ability to republish their commentary in their own work after first publication in the contracting newspaper, magazine, or news site. It makes sense that newspapers would maintain freelance-friendly terms that respect the needs of guest contributors who fill op-ed pages with high quality content, often without compensation. Many smaller and mid-sized newspapers will not require the guest commentator to sign any paperwork at all, while others will ask the writer simply to acknowledge a "terms of publication" blurb. Many contributor agreements make no provision for the writer to assign the copyright to the publishing company; in such instances copyright typically remains with the author.

In the more formal instances, newspapers may email the opinion writer, acting as an independent contractor, an in-house "Freelancer Agreement" that acts as a more formal publication agreement. Here is an example of the "Grants" portion of an agreement I recently received:

1. GRANT OF RIGHTS.

(a) Company's publication(s) is/are a collective work(s) as defined under the copyright laws of the United States. Each Work Freelancer prepares at Company's request is a commissioned work, and as such, constitutes a work made for hire as defined under the copyright laws of the United States. Freelancer agrees that any Work Freelancer submits to Company shall be considered a

Part IV—Publishing Citizen Writing

work made for hire for Company, and that Company shall own all rights, title and interests, including the copyright therein. If for any reason the Work is not found to be a work for hire, Freelancer acknowledges that this written Agreement shall transfer and assign ownership of the copyright in the Work to Company, or if necessary, Freelancer agrees to execute any document to effectuate such transfer of ownership of the copyright in the Work to Company.

(b) Company hereby grants to Freelancer a non-exclusive license to any and all Works (specifically excluding photographs and videos), including the right to re-sell, but only 30 (thirty) days after first-time publication of the Work by Company. Company hereby grants to Freelancer a non-exclusive license (which includes the right to resell) to photographs and videos that have not been published, posted or distributed by Company, but only 60 (sixty) days after submission by Freelancer. For the avoidance of doubt, the licensing rights granted in this paragraph shall survive termination of this Agreement.

(c) Company shall have the right to use Freelancer's name, photograph, likeness and other biographical information in any format in any media to promote Company or other publications or services that publish or will publish any Works written and/or provided by Freelancer. In addition, Freelancer waives all moral rights with respect to any Works accepted by Company for publication.

Granted, the legalese can seem a bit intimidating or off-putting at first. Lest agreements like these deter you from submitting your work, keep in mind that such agreements exist to protect the publisher, the work, and the author, not just the publisher. A close read of the "Grant of Rights" portion of this sample agreement, for example, makes it clear that the Freelancer is free to republish their work without express permission after a period of 30 days has elapsed after first publication, and that the grant of rights to The Company is non-exclusive.

7. *Make a buck, if you're lucky.* Publishing guest opinion in major publications can be lucrative, though as freelancers we would be silly to think that, at perhaps $300 to $600 per published piece, we could pay the bills on the fruits of our opinion writing alone. After all, we'll still need to plan on paying taxes on our freelance income. Meanwhile, the majority of outlets that publish our work will pay nothing for our opinions. Even some of the nation's elite news venues do not make a one-time payment to freelancers for their op-eds. Instead, they may offer the guest contributor a percentage of proceeds for the work, essentially offering compensation via royalties. Below is an example of such a payment clause in an op-ed agreement I recently received. I've replaced the specific company named in the agreement with a generic reference to "The Major Newspaper":

> Except as otherwise provided in this paragraph, The Major Newspaper hereby agrees to pay you 50% of The Major Newspaper's net proceeds from (a) any

24. Eight Steps Post-Submission

stand-alone resale of the Work for personal use; (b) any stand-alone resale of the Work for commercial or non-profit use; and (c) any stand-alone resale of the Work for editorial use. You are not entitled to any payments resulting from sales generated by the marketing, distribution, grouping or sale of the Work in association with the name or brand of The Major Newspaper, any of its associated brands, or its corporate affiliates, including but not limited to the transmission of the Work on The Major Newspaper News Service.

Payment via royalty, or not at all, helps publications address rapidly thinning profit margins. And there's yet another good reason why payment for guest opinion pieces remains modest. If the practice was highly lucrative, it would no doubt be inundated by writers for hire looking to make a quick buck regardless of whether they stood behind their words. Keeping payments modest means that personal conviction rather than corporate interests or career-building remains the primary driver of citizen opinion writing.

8. *React and Reply.* Publication marks the beginning of the writer-reader conversation. As writers, we often fear the worst in the aftermath—that readers will come with torches and pitchforks calling for our heads for a provocative piece we published. Highly engaged readers may register their feelings online in the ubiquitous comments sections that follow a published piece on a digital platform. A minority of others will reach out to us directly, since many publications require the guest writer's email address to appear as a precondition of publication. It's natural to open the inbox with an admixture of anticipation and trepidation in the days following an op-ed's appearance, assuming that our "fightin' words" have created a very public hullabaloo. However, given the multiple opportunities readers have to weigh in on content, most respondents opting for email will do so simply to say "good job," to inquire further about a fact or text mentioned in the article, or to chime in with a helpful "hey did you know?" addition, correction, or addendum.

Citizen writers differ on whether or not to interact with readers in the Comments section post-publication. Some choose to reply directly with spirited agreement or disagreement. The majority of opinion writers, however, are content to let readers have their say without further authorial mitigation or mediation. Such writers consider it their role to advance the discourse, leaving it to citizen critics to carry on the conversation post-publication.

25

A Citizen Writer's Workshop

Following are two contemporary artifacts of opinion thoroughly annotated for craft, technique, and structure. The pieces, inclusive of conventional op-ed and commentary blended with news analysis, total between 600 and 1,000 words each, making them characteristically concise. Each delineates an urgent or timely problem, details the inadequacies or inequities of the current status quo, and suggests possible solutions. While the commentaries exemplify the fundamentals discussed elsewhere in this book, they do occasionally depart from the norm, especially when adhering to the house style of the publications in which they originally appeared. For example, in the first piece that follows, "AI 'companions' promise to combat loneliness, but history shows the dangers of one-way relationships," house style dictates the writer incorporate the sort of subheadings that opinion writers often avoid.

These pieces—including one by yours truly—are fundamentally instructive without being perfect or unerring, and readers are encouraged to determine where, in retrospect, changes might be made for the betterment of the work. To aid in that process, each piece is followed by a brief summary assessment of its reach and resonance.

AI "companions" promise to combat loneliness, but history shows the dangers of one-way relationships[1]

By Anna Mae Duane

The United States is in the grips of a loneliness epidemic: Since 2018, about half the population has reported that it has experienced loneliness. Loneliness can be as dangerous to your health as smoking 15 cigarettes a day, according to a 2023 surgeon general's report.[2]

It is not just individual lives that are at risk. Democracy requires the capacity to feel connected to other citizens in order to work toward collective solutions.

In the face of this crisis, tech companies offer a technological cure: emotionally intelligent chatbots. These digital friends, they say, can help alleviate the loneliness that threatens individual and national health.

25. A Citizen Writer's Workshop

But as the pandemic showed, technology alone is not sufficient to address the complexities of public health.[3] Science can produce miraculous vaccines, but if people are enmeshed in cultural and historical narratives that prevent them from taking the life-saving medicine, the cure sits on shelves and lives are lost. The humanities, with their expertise in human culture, history and literature, can play a key role in preparing society for the ways that AI might help—or harm—the capacity for meaningful human connection.

The power of stories to both predict and influence human behavior has long been validated by scientific research. Numerous studies demonstrate that the stories people embrace heavily influence the choices they make, ranging from the vacations they plan, to how people approach climate change to the computer programming choices security experts make.

Two tales[4]

There are two storylines that address people's likely behaviors in the face of the unknown territory of depending on AI for emotional sustenance: one that promises love and connection, and a second that warns of dehumanizing subjugation.

The first story, typically told by software designers and AI companies, urges people to say "I do" to AI and embrace bespoke friendship programmed on your behalf. AI company Replika, for instance, promises that it can provide everyone with a "companion who cares. Always here to listen and talk. Always on your side."[5]

There is a global appetite for such digital companionship. Microsoft's digital chatbot Xiaoice has a global fan base of over 660 million people, many of whom consider the chatbot "a dear friend," even a trusted confidante.

In popular culture, films like "Her" depict lonely people becoming deeply attached to their digital assistants. For many, having a "dear friend" programmed to avoid difficult questions and demands seems like a huge improvement over the messy, challenging, vulnerable work of engaging with a human partner, especially if you consider the misogynistic preference for submissive, sycophantic companions.

To be sure, imagining a chummy relationship with a chatbot offers a sunnier set of possibilities than the apocalyptic narratives of slavery and subjugation that have dominated storytelling about a possible future among social robots. Blockbuster films like "The Matrix" and the "The Terminator" have depicted hellscapes where humans are enslaved by sentient AI. Other narratives featured in films like "The Creator" and "Blade Runner" imagine the roles reversed and invite viewers to sympathize with AI beings who are oppressed by humans.[6]

One reality

You could be forgiven for thinking that these two stories, one of friendship, the other of slavery, simply represent two extremes in human nature. From this perspective it seems like a good thing that marketing messages about AI are guiding people toward the sunny side of the futuristic street. But if you consider

Part IV—Publishing Citizen Writing

the work of scholars who have studied slavery in the U.S., it becomes frighteningly clear that these two stories—one of purchased friendship and one of enslavement and exploitation—are not as far apart as you might imagine.

Chattel slavery in the U.S. was a brutal system designed to extract labor through violent and dehumanizing means. To sustain the system, however, an intricate emotional landscape was designed to keep the enslavers self-satisfied. "Gone with the Wind" is perhaps the most famous depiction of how enslavers saw themselves as benevolent patriarchs and forced enslaved people to reinforce this fiction through cheerful professions of love.

In his 1845 autobiography, Frederick Douglass described a tragic occasion when an enslaved man, asked about his situation, honestly replied that he was ill-treated. The plantation owner, confronted with testimony about the harm he was inflicting, sold the truth-teller down the river. Such cruelty, Douglass insisted, was the necessary penalty for someone who committed the sin "of telling the simple truth" to a man whose emotional calibration required constant reassurance.

History lesson
To be clear, I am not evoking the emotional coercion that enslavement required in order to conflate lonely seniors with evil plantation owners, or worse still, to equate computer code with enslaved human beings.[7] There is little danger that AI companions will courageously tell us truths that we would rather not hear. That is precisely the problem. My concern is not that people will harm sentient robots. I fear how humans will be damaged by the moral vacuum created when their primary social contacts are designed solely to serve the emotional needs of the "user."

At a time when humanities scholarship can help guide society in the emerging age of AI, it is being suppressed and devalued.[8] Diminishing the humanities risks denying people access to their own history. That ignorance renders people ill-equipped to resist marketers' assurances that there is no harm in buying "friends." People are cut off from the wisdom that surfaces in stories that warn of the moral rot that accompanies unchecked power.

If you rid yourself of the vulnerability born of reaching out to another human whose response you cannot control, you lose the capacity to fully care for another and to know yourself.[9] As we navigate the uncharted waters of AI and its role in our lives, it's important not to forget the poetry, philosophy and storytelling that remind us that human connection is supposed to require something of us, and that it is worth the effort.[10]

Analysis: Anna Mae Duane's piece was shared on Facebook nearly seventy times during the first week it appeared. The author, a director of a humanities institute, effectively applies her professional body of knowledge to a topic very much in the zeitgeist. While deeply informed and historical, the commentary also manages to be contemporary. Readers are educated by this opinion piece without feeling unduly lectured by it.

25. A Citizen Writer's Workshop

What, if anything, might make the piece better? It could be argued that, as a commentary, the work is too diffuse or broad in its treatment, attempting to broach history, technology, ethics, literature, and film in a mere 1,000 words. For some readers, then, the "takeaway" may feel diluted.

Time to turn the page on children's books as graduation gifts[11]

By Zachary Michael Jack

As a writer for children and young adults, I can't help but celebrate the genius of Dr. Seuss. But as an educator of anxious college graduates who often receive multiple copies of "Oh, the Places You'll Go!" as graduation gifts, I believe it's time we diversify our books-for-grads, choosing texts whose challenges are less abstract than howling Hakken-Kraks, Giving Trees and Little Princes.[12]

It's a perennial and paradoxical phenomenon. At exactly the moment when America's youth stand poised to grapple with the perils of real adulthood—when they are old enough to go to war or to finance a car—we inexplicably give them books for children.[13]

By the time I graduated in May 1996, the infantilization of grads seemed a fait accompli, with Seuss's "Oh, the Places You'll Go!" becoming a perennial fixture in the commencement season bestsellers list, and helping to set the standard for what a graduation gift book should look and sound like.

Today, booksellers like Barnes & Noble continue to recommend Seuss, "Winnie the Pooh," "Where the Sidewalk Ends" and "The Little Prince" as the "perfect present for graduates of all ages." And once again, as of May 19, "Oh, the Places You'll Go!" resumed its annual No. 1 position in the USA Today Bestselling Books list, where it debuted in 1993 on its way to becoming a gift-giving cliche.[14]

If graduation book-buying is any measure, we Gen Xers really are becoming our parents.

I empathize with the need for nostalgia felt by the gift-givers whose grads stand on the cusp of a new and scary rite of passage. Giving a children's book to an adult receiving a degree can feel like a fun or fantastical way to allude to the challenges of the world without speaking directly to them. The artful allegories baked into children's stories and adult fables such as "The Alchemist" can help those of us afraid of being graduation buzzkills sidestep or sanitize real-world villainy.[15]

And adults deserve credit for giving books at all, in a time of dramatically declining leisure reading among teens and 20-somethings. In doing so, we remind young people of the need to value words and ideas long after assigned readings end.

For precisely these reasons, I argue that we should think twice about giving children's books as gifts for new adults. If we want to remind our grads of the need to create space and time for the difficult in busy adult lives, let's give them texts that can't be easily distilled to aphorism, or flipped through like an extended greeting card.

As a new generation crosses the commencement stage this spring, Seuss will no doubt have his day. However, as the graduates of 2022 face anew the threat of a totalitarian ruler bent on war and conquest in Europe, maybe it's time we gift them books equal to the historical moment.

In May 1945, America's graduates helped serious and somber portrayals like "Brave Men" by Ernie Pyle and "Black Boy" by Richard Wright gain a foothold atop the bestseller list. This year, the texts we select as gifts can speak volumes to our favorite graduates about what we value, what we're willing to fight for, and what may not be a laughing matter.

This year as I make my graduation list, I'm thinking of books that affirm the difficulties in our lives, like Mark Boyle's "The Way Home: Tales from a World Without Technology" or Joan Didion's "The Year of Magical Thinking." I'm thinking of the fact- and spirit-filled books that remind us of the overlooked ecologies within which we exist, like Dan Fagin's "Toms River: A Story of Science and Salvation" or "The River of Consciousness" by Oliver Sacks. I'm thinking of the rivers of race and time, too, and the titles that do the brave work of intergenerational books like "Between the World and Me" by Ta-Nehisi Coates or "Letter to My Daughter" by Maya Angelou.[16]

And if none of these will do, a blank book, sturdy and hard-bound, may be the most enduring gift of all. It's a book that can begin with thoughts on the occasion of their graduation, and one that saves the rest of the pages for them.[17]

Analysis: Timed for publication during the graduation season, "Time to turn the page on children's books as graduation gifts" originally appeared in the *Chicago Tribune*, with an average daily circulation of approximately 440,000. Additionally, it appeared in nearly a dozen newspapers around the Midwest as part of the *Chicago Tribune* News Service.

It's clear from its circulation numbers that audiences were engaged by this piece, despite (and perhaps because of) its willingness to tackle the beloved giants of children's literature, from Dr. Seuss, to Shel Silverstein, to Winnie the Pooh. Its readership was likely amplified by the reader's advisory paragraph that recommends particular books for potential graduation gifts. A potential weakness of the piece exists within its purposeful polemic. Since graduates are in a liminal stage between young adulthood and adulthood, it's possible that the ideal gift would be two books—one that speaks to the child in the young man or the young woman, and the other that speaks to the mature citizen the college graduate is in the process of becoming.

Afterword

And an Exhortation

In the end, whether we pen that long-simmering op-ed, commentary, column, guest essay, or viewpoints piece can only be a personal decision. Friends can exhort us, colleagues can encourage us, and mentors can invite and instruct, but in the final analysis it's up to us as citizens to make that fateful call.

I fervently hope you'll write that piece.

The reasons are the sum of this book. First, I believe you'll feel better about yourself and your place in this complex, ever-changing world when you put pen to paper, or fingers to keyboard, on the issues that matter most to you and to yours. Second, you'll surely regain the respect of anyone in your circle—possibly including yourself—who suspects you've become a "quiet quitter" content to complain about the condition of the universe without lifting a finger to help make it better. Third, once your piece appears, you'll have a true feather in your cap—a publication in a timeless genre that no one can ever take away from you.

Decades from now, your piece will live on not just in the drawer or folder you reserve at home for priceless personal artifacts, but in the databases and archives where content from the nation's newspapers and magazines of record is zealously safeguarded and preserved. One day, in fact, if indeed you stand up and publish your innermost yearnings and feelings as a citizen, your great-great-grandchildren are likely to rediscover you not in some nondescript record—birth, death, or marriage certificate—but alive in the passionate prose you once crafted for others, with dignity, on a difficult day on Planet Earth.

Our legacy, then, need not only be in our children, grandchildren, nieces and nephews, or brick-and-mortar communities we serve, but in the discourse communities we build with words, human connections that know no geographical bounds and that live on without the depreciation of

Part IV—Publishing Citizen Writing

material things subject to the wages of time. I hope to meet you there, on the page, in that timeless place.

But that is then, and this is now. And now, if I may be so bold, needs our heartfelt words and deeds more than ever.

Chapter Notes

Chapter 1

1. Molly McHugh, "How Many Characters Should a Tweet Be?" *Wired*, October 2, 2015, https://www.wired.com/2015/10/many-characters-tweet-ask-experts/.

2. Rosa A. Eberly, *Citizen Critics: Literary Public Spheres* (University of Illinois Press, 2000), 1.

3. Andrea Dworkin, *Letters from a War Zone* (Lawrence Hill Books, 1993), 4.

4. Paul Rogat Loeb, *The Soul of a Citizen: Living with Conviction in a Cynical Time* (St. Martin's Griffin, 1999), 38.

5. Ray Stannard Baker, "The Lone Fighter," *McClure's*, December 1903, 195.

6. Walt Whitman, "We," *New York Aurora*, April 9, 1842, 2.

7. Susan Shapiro, *The Byline Bible: Get Published in 5 Weeks* (Writer's Digest Books, 2018), 6.

8. "The New York Times Passes 2m International Digital Subscribers," *The New York Times*, June 4, 2024, https://www.nytco.com/press/the-new-york-times-passes-2m-international-digital-subscribers/.

9. Mary Pipher, *Writing to Change the World* (Riverhead, 2006), 26.

10. Walt Whitman, *Leaves of Grass* (Smith and McDougal, 1872), 95.

11. William Butler Yeats, *Per Amica Silentia Lunae* (Macmillan, 1918), 29.

12. Brian Smith, "Op-ed? Editorial? What do all these terms really mean?" *Des Moines Register*, September 13, 2018, https://www.desmoinesregister.com/story/opinion/2018/09/13/oped-editorial-opinion-section-journalism-terms-defined-des-moines-register/1224898002/.

13. "New York Times Opinion Guest Essays," accessed December 4, 2024, https://help.nytimes.com/hc/en-us/articles/115014809107-New-York-Times-Opinion-Guest-Essays.

14. "New York Times Opinion Guest Essays," accessed December 4, 2024, https://help.nytimes.com/hc/en-us/articles/115014809107-New-York-Times-Opinion-Guest-Essays.

15. "Vox First Person," Freedom with Writing, accessed November 8, 2024, https://www.freedomwithwriting.com/freedom/uncategorized/vox-first-person-personal-essays-wanted/.

16. Terry Blas, "I'm Latino. I'm Hispanic. And they're different, so I drew a comic to explain," *Vox*, August 12, 2016, https://www.vox.com/2015/8/19/9173457/hispanic-latino-comic.

17. Jonathan Blanks, "I own guns. Here's why I'm keeping them," *Vox*, October 6, 2015, https://www.vox.com/2015/10/6/9449709/gun-owner-keeping.

Chapter 2

1. Anita G. Day and Guy Golan, "Source and Content Diversity in Op-Ed Pages: Assessing Editorial strategies in *The New York Times* and the *Washington Post*," *Journalism Studies* 6, no. 1 (2005): 61–71.

Chapter 3

1. "The Difference Between News and Opinion," *The Wall Street Journal*, January 27, 2021, https://newsliteracy.wsj.com/news-opinion/.

2. "Submit an Op-ed," *Washington Post*, accessed December 4, 2024, https://helpcenter.washingtonpost.com/hc/en-us/articles/115003675788-Submit-an-op-ed.

Chapter Notes

3. "New York Times Opinion Guest Essays," accessed, 2024, https://help.nytimes.com/hc/en-us/articles/115014809107-New-York-Times-Opinion-Guest-Essays.

Chapter 4

1. "How the Opinion Pages Work," *Dallas Morning News*, January 1, 2018, https://www.dallasnews.com/opinion/2018/01/01/how-the-editorial-and-opinion-pages-work/.

2. Trish Hall, *Writing to Persuade* (Liveright, 2019), 70.

3. Sam Allock, "What Is the Best Time to Send Out a Press Release?" PR FIRE, accessed December 4, 2024, https://www.prfire.com/best-time-press-release/#:~:text=Of%20course%2C%20if%20you%20have,can%20be%20packed%20as%20well.

4. David Plazas, "Why The Tennessean does not publish anonymous op-eds," *Tennessean*, September 7, 2018, https://www.tennessean.com/story/opinion/columnists/david-plazas/2018/09/07/new-york-times-anonymous-oped-tennessean/1212127002/.

Chapter 5

1. Phillip Lopate, *The Art of the Personal Essay: An Anthology from the Classical Era to the Present* (Vintage, 1995), xxx.

2. Bill Bishop and Robert G. Cushing, *The Big Sort: Why the Clustering of Like-Minded America Is Tearing Us Apart* (Houghton Mifflin, 2008), 64.

3. Bishop and Cushing, *Big Sort*, 65.

4. Andrea Dworkin, *Letters from a War Zone* (Lawrence Hill Books, 1993), 4.

5. Dworkin, *Letters*, 6.

6. Mark Twain, "A Small Piece of Spite," *San Francisco Daily Morning Call*, September 6, 1864, accessed November 8, 2024, https://gutenberg.net.au/ebooks09/0900821h.html#TOC3_396.

7. James C. Nelson, "Just Another Day in NRA Paradise," *Counterpunch*, October 27, 2023, https://www.counterpunch.org/2023/10/27/just-another-day-in-nra-paradise/.

8. Jeff Shero, "Storm Channel 13: Hippies Turn TVs Blue," *Liberation News Service*, July 5, 1968, 13, Wisconsin Historical Society Online Collections, https://content.wisconsinhistory.org, accessed February 9, 2025.

Chapter 6

1. Mary Pipher, *Writing to Change the World* (Riverhead, 2006), 25.

2. Pete Davis, "Resist the Cult of Smart, Embrace the Call of Citizenship," *Harvard Law Record*, August 30, 2017, https://petedavis.org/op-eds-letters/.

3. Francis Pharcellus Church, "Is There a Santa Claus?" *The Sun*, September 21, 1897.

4. Max Beerbohm, *And Even Now* (E.P. Dutton, 1921), 192.

Chapter 7

1. Ambrose Bierce, "Ambrose Bierce Says: Public Opinion is Responsible for Many Fallacies," *San Francisco Examiner*, June 1, 1900.

2. Stephen Crane, "Regulars Get No Glory," *New York World*, July 20, 1898, 52.

3. Dorothy Thompson, "Our Ghostly Commonwealth," *Saturday Evening Post*, July 27, 1935, 5–7.

4. Ray Stannard Baker, "The Lone Fighter," *McClure's*, December 1903, 194.

5. Baker, "Lone Fighter," 195.

Chapter 8

1. Richard Harding Davis, "Tells Experience as War Prisoner," *New York Tribune*, September 2, 1914, 1.

2. W.E.B. Du Bois, "Returning Soldiers," *Crisis*, May 1918, 14.

Chapter 9

1. Mabel Cooper, "Mabel Writes of This and That," *Weekly Challenger*, October 6, 1973, 2.

2. C. Blythe Andrews, "Shooting of Mr. Wallace Deplorable," *Florida Sentinel Bulletin*, May 16, 1972, 4.

3. Ray Stannard Baker, "What Is a

Chapter Notes

Lynching?" *McClure's*, January 1905, 299–314.

Chapter 10

1. Zachary Michael Jack, "Men fear when women march," *San Francisco Chronicle*, January 18, 2017.
2. John Muir, "Save the Redwoods," *Sierra Club Bulletin* XI, no. 1 (January 1920): 1–4.

Chapter 11

1. Kwame Anthony Appiah, "Is It Okay to Get Food Stamps When You're Just Pursuing Your Passion?" *New York Times Magazine*, July 14, 2014, 10.
2. Elisabeth Gruner, "I no longer grade my students' work—and I wish I had stopped sooner," *The Conversation*, March 29, 2022, https://theconversation.com/i-no-longer-grade-my-students-work-and-i-wish-i-had-stopped-sooner-179617.
3. "Praise for Tiny Beautiful Things," Cheryl Strayed author page, accessed December 4, 2024, https://www.cherylstrayed.com/tiny_beautiful_things_114549.htm.
4. Cheryl Strayed, "Dear Sugar, The Rumpus Advice Column #97: You Have Arrived at the Fire," *The Rumpus*, February 23, 2012, https://therumpus.net/2012/02/23/dear-sugar-the-rumpus-advice-column-97/.
5. "Washingtonpost.com Traffic & Engagement Analysis," similarweb, accessed December 12, 2024, https://www.similarweb.com/website/washingtonpost.com/#ranking.
6. Carolyn Hax, "Friends who agreed to child-free trip are bringing kids," *Washington Post*, February 8, 2024, https://www.washingtonpost.com/advice/2024/02/08/carolyn-hax-child-free-vacations.
7. Amy Dickinson, "Ask Amy: Husband has a close Facebook relationship with younger woman," *Washington Post*, January 31, 2024, https://www.washingtonpost.com/advice/2024/01/31/ask-amy-husband-facebook-relationship/.
8. Beatrice Fairfax, "Long Courtships," *Washington Times*, October 24, 1928.

9. "Dorothy Dix: Topics in Chronicling America," Library of Congress Research Guides, accessed December 12, 2024, https://guides.loc.gov/chronicling-america-dorothy-dix#:~:text=The%20Wheeler%20Syndicate%20offers%20Gilmer,world's%20highest%20paid%20woman%20writer.
10. Dorothy Dix, "Dorothy Dix Talks," *Ogden Standard*, November 4, 1918, 5.
11. Abigail Van Buren, "Dear Abby: I wish my mom spoke to me like a parent instead of a friend," *Chicago Sun-Times*, July 14, 2024, https://chicago.suntimes.com/dear-abby/2024/07/14/dear-abby-i-wish-my-mom-spoke-to-me-like-a-parent-instead-of-a-friend.
12. Damon Runyon, "Rich Dads and Poor Dads," *Wilkes-Barre Evening News*, April 8, 1925, https://journalismhistory.com.wordpress.com/2021/06/22/rich-dads-and-poor-dads/.

Chapter 12

1. Cole Smithey, "Barbie," Smart New Media Cinema in the Round, November 25, 2023, https://www.colesmithey.com/reviews/2023/11/barbie.html.
2. Christy Lemire, "Barbie," RogerEbert.com, July 21, 2023, https://www.rogerebert.com/reviews/barbie-movie-review-2023.
3. Mark Twain, "The Great Dickens," *San Francisco Daily Alta California*, February 5, 1868, 1.
4. H.L. Mencken, "Various Bad Novels," *The Smart Set*, July 1913, 153.
5. Mencken, "Various Bad Novels," 154.
6. Mencken, "Various Bad Novels," 158.

Chapter 13

1. Paul Gigot, "The Difference Between News and Opinion," *Wall Street Journal*, accessed December 4, 2024, https://newsliteracy.wsj.com/news-opinion/.
2. Spencer Izen, "News vs. Opinion vs. Analysis," The Griffins' Nest, December 28, 2021, https://www.ehnewspaper.ca/journalism-blog/news-vs-analysis-vs-opinion-types-of-articles-in-a-newspaper.
3. Daniela J. Lamas, "I'm a Doctor and a Voter. Here's How I'm Thinking About

the Health of Trump and Biden," *New York Times* (Online), June 24, 2024, https://www.nytimes.com/2024/06/24/opinion/biden-trump-health-conditions.html.

4. Jennifer Grygiel, "Political cartoonists are out of touch—it's time to make way for memes," *The Conversation*, May 17, 2019, https://theconversation.com/political-cartoonists-are-out-of-touch-its-time-to-make-way-for-memes-116471. Reprinted by permission of *The Conversation* under Creative Commons licensing.

Chapter 14

1. H.L. Mencken, *Prejudices* (Alfred A. Knopf, 1922), 16.
2. Mencken, *Prejudices*, 12–13.
3. Mencken, *Prejudices*, 13–14.
4. David Foster Wallace, "Shipping Out," *Harper's*, January 1996, 33.
5. Ambrose Bierce, *The Cynic's Word Book* (Doubleday, Page, 1906), 9–11.
6. Ambrose Bierce, "Disintroductions," in *The Collected Works of Ambrose Bierce, Volume IX* (The Neale Publishing Company, 1911), 257.
7. Bierce, *Collected Works*, 257–58.

Chapter 15

1. "In Defense of Food: An Eater's Manifesto," Michael Pollan author page, accessed December 4, 2024, https://michaelpollan.com/books/in-defense-of-food/.
2. E.B. White, "In Defense of the Bronx River," *New Yorker*, May 9, 1925, 14.
3. Henry David Thoreau, "Walking," in *Excursions* (Ticknor and Fields, 1863), 161.
4. Thoreau, "Walking," 169.
5. Adam Kadlac, "In Defense of Princess Culture," *Raven* no. 2, accessed December 4, 2024, https://ravenmagazine.org/magazine/in-defense-of-princess-culture/.

Chapter 16

1. Will Bunch, "William Safire, 'nattering nabobs' and the power of words," *Philadelphia Inquirer*, Sept. 27, 2009, https://www.inquirer.com/philly/blogs/attytood/Nabobs_natter_about_the_passing_of_William_Safire_1929-2009.html.

2. Hannah Goldfield, "The Era of the Line Cook," *New Yorker*, June 17, 2004, https://www.newyorker.com/magazine/2024/06/24/the-era-of-the-line-cook.
3. Laura van den Berg, "Sweat," *New York Times Magazine*, June 16, 2024, 18.
4. Bertrand Russell, "In Praise of Idleness," *Harper's*, October 1932, 552–59.
5. Robert Louis Stevenson, "An Apology for Idlers," in *Essays of Robert Louis Stevenson*, ed. William Lyon Phelps (Charles Scribner's Sons, 1908), 27–28.

Chapter 17

1. Jim Harrington, "Garrison Keillor bringing new batch of stories to UC Berkeley performance," *East Bay Times*, August 15, 2016, https://www.eastbaytimes.com/2009/10/22/garrison-keillor-bringing-new-batch-of-stories-to-uc-berkeley-performance/.
2. Mark Twain, "Reflections on the Sabbath," *The Golden Era*, March 18, 1866, 3.
3. James Thurber, "Notes and Comment," *The New Yorker*, July 14, 1928, 13.
4. Tom Morrow, "Historically Speaking: Will Rogers, prolific humorist and performer," *North Coast Current*, September 11, 2023, https://www.northcoastcurrent.com/columnists/2023/09/historically-speaking-will-rogers-prolific-humorist-and-performer/.
5. Will Rogers, "All the Millionaires Are Optimistic," *New York Times*, January 13, 1924, xx2.
6. James Thurber, "Polo in the Home," *The New Yorker*, September 17, 1927, 9.

Chapter 18

1. George Prochnik, "I'm Thinking. Please. Be Quiet." *New York Times*, August 25, 2013, SR4.
2. Arthur Schopenhauer, "On Noise," in *Essays of Schopenhauer* (W. Scott, 1897), 29.
3. Ruth Graham, "Against YA," *Slate*, June 5, 2014, https://slate.com/culture/2014/06/against-ya-adults-should-be-embarrassed-to-read-childrens-books.html.
4. Phillip Lopate, "Against Joie de

Chapter Notes

Vivre," in *Getting Personal: Selected Writings* (Basic Books, 2003), 142.

5. Lopate, "Against Joie de Vivre," 146.
6. Gilbert King, "The Woman Who Took on the Tycoon," *Smithsonian*, July 5, 2012, https://www.smithsonianmag.com/history/the-woman-who-took-on-the-tycoon-651396/.
7. Mark Grief, "Against Exercise," in *Against Everything* (Pantheon, 2006), 4–5.
8. Nara Roberta Silva, "A Ruthless Criticism of Everything Existing: an Introduction to Marx," Brooklyn Institute for Social Research, accessed December 4, 2024, https://thebrooklyninstitute.com/items/courses/new-york/a-ruthless-criticism-of-everything-existing-an-introduction-to-marx-14/#:~:text=In%20the%20mid%2Dnineteenth%20century,present%E2%80%94I%20am%20speaking%20of.
9. Ivan Kreilkamp, "Against [X]," *New Yorker*, August 27, 2014, https://www.newyorker.com/books/page-turner/x.

Chapter 19

1. Richard Rodriguez, "Going Home Again: The New American Scholarship Boy," *American Scholar* 44, no. 1 (Winter 1974–75): 15–16.
2. Zora Neale Hurston, "How It Feels To Be Colored Me," *World Tomorrow*, 11 (May 1928): 215–16.
3. Langston Hughes, "The Negro Artist and the Racial Mountain," *Nation* 122, no. 3181 (June 23, 1926): 693.
4. Jack London, "How I Became a Socialist," *Comrade*, March 1903, 122.

Chapter 20

1. Lincoln Steffens, "Pittsburg: A City Ashamed," *McClure's*, May 1903, 24.
2. Lincoln Steffens, "Chicago: Half Free and Fighting On," *McClure's*, October 1903, 563.
3. David Carr, "Me and My Girls," *New York Times Magazine*, July 20, 2008, 34.
4. Carr, "Me and My Girls," 32.
5. Ida B. Wells-Barnett, *The Red Record*, 1895, 61.
6. Ida B. Wells-Barnett, "Self-Help," *New York Age*, June 25, 1892.

Chapter 21

1. Nellie Bly, "Another Wicked Swindle," *New York World*, March 31, 1889.
2. Nellie Bly, "Nellie Bly Buys a Baby," *The New York World*, October 6, 1889.
3. Paul Gallico, "The Feel," in *Participatory Sportswriting: An Anthology*, ed. Zachary Michael Jack (McFarland, 2009), 230.
4. Gallico, "The Feel," 231.
5. Barbara Ehrenreich, "Nickel-and-Dimed," *Harper's*, January 1999, 37.
6. Ehrenreich, "Nickel-and-Dimed," 52.
7. Richard Harding Davis, "Under Fire," *New York Tribune*, November 8, 1914, Part V, 1–2.

Chapter 22

1. Ernest Hemingway, "The Average Yank Divides Canadians into Two Classes—Wild and Tame," *Toronto Star Weekly*, October 9, 1920, 13.
2. Zachary Michael Jack, "Forget Red vs. Blue, America is Cactus vs. Philodendron," *Front Porch Republic*, August 4, 2022, https://www.frontporchrepublic.com/2022/08/forget-red-vs-blue-america-is-cactus-vs-philodendron/.
3. Belle Squire, "Would you rather have a vote than a husband?" *Chicago Daily Tribune*, June 22, 1913, G3.
4. Jane Addams, "Woman's Special Training for Peacemaking." *National Peace Congress, Proceedings* (1909): 252–54.

Chapter 23

1. Charles Dickens, "The Cool Couple," in: *Sketches by Boz, Volume 2* (Charles Scribner's Sons, 1898), 291.
2. Dickens, "The Cool Couple," 293.
3. Charles Dickens, "The Political Young Gentleman," in: *Sketches by Boz, Volume 2* (Charles Scribner's Sons, 1898), 225.
4. Dorothy Thompson, "Who Goes Nazi?" *Harper's*, August 1941, 237.
5. Thompson, "Who Goes Nazi," 239.
6. Thompson, "Who Goes Nazi," 238.
7. Ernest Hemingway, "The Mecca of Fakers in French Capital," *Toronto Daily Star*, March 25, 1922.

Chapter 25

1. Anna Mae Duane, "AI 'companions' promise to combat loneliness, but history shows the dangers of one-way relationships," *The Conversation*, February 12, 2024, https://theconversation.com/ai-companions-promise-to-combat-loneliness-but-history-shows-the-dangers-of-one-way-relationships-221086. Reprinted by permission of *The Conversation* under Creative Commons licensing.
2. Writer Anna Mae Duane begins with a factual journalistic hook sure to garner reader attention.
3. The thesis of this op-ed/news analysis piece is stated early.
4. Subheadings like these are the exception rather than the rule in op-eds and commentaries.
5. Quoting actual ad copy helps the commentator avoid tepid generalizations.
6. Multiple film narratives are cited as a way to concretize what for some readers remains an abstract problem
7. The writer demonstrates audience awareness, as, minus Duane's clarification, many readers would accuse the commentator of exactly the conflation she denies herein.
8. This statement might benefit from factual substantiation or, if not, the author's supporting anecdotal experience.
9. The commentator wields her pronouns strategically and well, using "you" in this sentence (in effect, excluding herself from the problem) while switching to the first-person plural "we" in the next.
10. Duane concludes by putting the finest point yet on her argument.
11. Zachary Michael Jack, "Time to turn the page on children's books as graduation gifts," *Chicago Tribune*, May 23, 2022, 14.
12. In this first paragraph I'm hoping to establish my credibility while getting right to the point of the piece.
13. In using the "go to war" and "finance a car" references, I'm seeking to make my argument concrete: that college graduates have adult obligations and responsibilities.
14. Here I aim to back up my assertion that kids' books are popular gifts for grads with a series of facts.
15. A conciliatory argument happens naturally in this paragraph, as I both write and read children's literature myself.
16. In hopes of presenting a solution to the problem identified in the commentary, I feel obliged to provide a noncomprehensive list of potential "good reads" for graduates.
17. The idea of a blank book as a grad gift is something of a "plot twist" or pivot. I use it as a reminder that the gifts we give the graduates in our lives might instead heighten their own sense of authorship and agency.

Selected Bibliography

The following sources inform and infuse this volume. In this selected bibliography, I elect to highlight principally those monographs and academic journals that provide additional historical context, praxis, or scholarly background. Readers interested in additional bibliographic information, including citations for the source material from which the many examples in this guidebook are drawn, may also consult the comprehensive endnotes at the conclusion of each chapter.

Brandt, Deborah. *The Rise of Writing: Redefining Mass Literacy*. Cambridge, 2015.

Brookes, Stephanie, and Lisa Waller. "Communities of Practice in the Production and Resourcing of Fact-Checking." *Journalism* 24, no. 9 (2023): 1938–1958.

Day, Anita G., and Guy Golan. "Source and Content Diversity in Op-Ed Pages: Assessing Editorial Strategies in *The New York Times* and the *Washington Post*." *Journalism Studies* 6, no. 1 (2005): 61–71.

Day, Christopher B. *Covering America: A Narrative History of a Nation's Journalism*. University of Massachusetts Press, 2018.

Dicks, Matthew. *Storyworthy: Engage, Teach, Persuade, and Change Your Life through the Power of Storytelling*. New World Library, 2018.

Dunlap, Louise. *Undoing the Silence: Six Tools for Social Change Writing*. New Village Press, 2007.

Eberly, Rosa A. *Citizen Critics: Literary Public Spheres*. University of Illinois Press, 2000.

Ehrenworth, Mary, Pablo Wolfe, and Marc Todd. *The Civically Engaged Classroom: Reading, Writing, and Speaking for Change*. Heinemann, 2020.

Franklin, Bob, ed. *Pulling Newspapers Apart: Analyzing Print Journalism*. Routledge, 2008.

Gartner, Michael. *Outrage, Passion, and Uncommon Sense: How Editorial Writers Have Taken On and Helped Shape the Great American Issues of the Past 150 Years*. National Geographic Books, 2005.

Golan, Guy, and Wayne Wanta. "Guest Columns Add Diversity to *NY Times*' Op-Ed Pages." *Newspaper Research Journal* 25, no. 2 (March 2004): 70–82.

Graves, Lucas. Deciding *What's True: The Rise of Political Fact-Checking in American Journalism*. Columbia University Press, 2016.

Hall, Trish. *Writing to Persuade: How to Bring People Over to Your Side*. Liveright, 2019.

Jack, Zachary Michael, ed. *Participatory Sportswriting: An Anthology, 1870–1937*. McFarland, 2009.

Kerrane, Kevin, and Ben Yagoda, eds. *The Art of Fact: A Historical Anthology of Literary Journalism*. Touchstone, 1997.

Loeb, Paul Rogat. *Soul of a Citizen: Living with Conviction in Challenging Times*. St. Martin's Griffin, new and rev. ed., 2010.

Lopate, Phillip, ed. *The Art of the Personal Essay: An Anthology from the Classical Era to the Present*. Vintage, 1995.

Pipher, Mary. *Writing to Change the World: An Inspiring Guide for Transforming the World with Words*. Riverhead Books, reprint ed., 2007.

Remler, Dahlia K., Don J. Waisanen, and

Selected Bibliography

Andrea Gabor. "Academic Journalism: A Modest Proposal." *Journalism Studies* 15, no. 4 (2014): 357–373.

Shapiro, Susan. *The Byline Bible: Get Published in 5 Weeks*. Writer's Digest Books, 2018.

Standring, Suzette Martinez. *The Art of Opinion Writing: Insider Secrets from Op-Ed Columnists*. RRP Publishing, 2014.

Index

Addams, Jane 151, 153
advice columns 3, 19, 74–84
"Against Exercise" 126
"Against Joie de Vivre" 125
The American Mercury 100
Andrews, C. Blythe 64
antithesis 46, 102, 151–52
Appiah, Kwame Anthony 74–75
Arizona Daily Sun 11
artificial intelligence (AI) 166–68
The Atlantic 38

Baker, Ray Stannard 65–66
Barbie 86–86
bathos 120
Beerbohm, Max 47–48
bias 7, 10, 28, 46, 96
Bierce, Ambrose 49–50, 54–55, 103–4
The Big Sort 37
Bishop, Bill 37
bloviation 40–41
Bly, Nellie 137, 142–43, 145, 147
The Boston Globe 14
Bronx River 107–8, 110

California 38, 71, 120, 140
Carr, David 139, 141
cartoons 96–99
censoring 8, 32, 42
charm 3, 47, 117–18, 120
Chicago, Illinois 29, 33, 55, 132, 138–40, 146, 150, 157
Chicago Daily News 146
Chicago Sun-Times 29, 82
Chicago Tribune 1, 3, 14, 28–29, 33, 150, 170
Church, Francis Pharcellus 12, 46
citizen critic 7, 66–67, 85, 88, 101, 107, 108–9, 126–33
citizen writer 1, 8, 12, 17, 36, 47, 49–50, 57, 71, 88, 102, 106, 115, 133, 147, 150–51, 160

citizen writing 1–3, 6, 8, 16–18, 20, 22, 27, 29, 33–34, 42, 63, 98, 129
civic responsibility 13, 17, 20–21, 45, 49, 54, 149
civil rights 63–64, 68, 150; *see also* voting rights
column *see* opinion column
commentary 1, 3, 6, 12–14, 17–19, 23–24, 29–34, 36, 38, 44–45, 47–52, 54–55, 59–60, 67–68, 87, 92, 94–98, 100–1, 104, 107–8, 113, 118–19, 122, 124–25, 131, 133–36, 139–41, 145–50, 152, 155–57, 163, 166, 168–69, 171
concision 6, 23, 161
contrarianism 16, 36–38, 42, 88
The Conversation 3, 28, 96
Cooper, Mabel 63, 66
copyright 3, 162–64
Counterpunch 41–42
courage 7, 9–10, 31, 54–55, 60, 66, 79, 117, 124, 139, 146
cover letter 31–34, 160
Crane, Stephen 50–52, 55
Cuba 50–52, 57
Cushman, Robert 37
cynicism 46, 57
The Cynics Word Book 103; see also *The Devil's Dictionary*

Davis, Pete 45, 48
Davis, Richard Harding 57–58, 61, 145–147
deadline journalism 12, 142
"Dear Abby" 74, 77–78, 82
"Dear Beatrice Fairfax" 80–81
"Dear Sugar" 77–78
Declaration of Independence 54
democracy 16, 49, 54, 56, 58–59, 103, 154
The Des Moines Register 13–14, 27–28
The Devil's Dictionary 103; see also *The Cynics Word Book*

Index

dialectic 148
dialogue 6, 10, 75, 148–50, 151
diatribe 144, 156
dichotomy 148–49, 152
Dickens, Charles 3, 86–88, 153–54, 157
Dickinson, Amy 78–80
Disney 109–11
Dix, Dorothy 81–82
Dr. Seuss 33, 169–70
Drudge Report 28
Duane, Anna Mae 166
Du Bois, W.E.B. 58–60
Dworkin, Andrea 7, 37–38

Eberly, Rosa A. 7
Ebert, Roger 86
editing 3, 23, 27, 161
editorial 12–14, 25, 27, 32, 46, 48, 92, 96–97, 138, 161–63, 165
Ehrenreich, Barbara 3, 144–45
email 32–33, 95, 160–63, 165
empathy 53, 64, 77, 104, 141–42, 144
essay 1–2, 13–14, 34, 89, 101, 108–9, 113–16, 131, 144, 171
evidence-based analysis 93–99
explanatory journalism 92–93
exposé 3, 137–41, 156

Facebook 79–80, 97, 99, 168
Fast Company 48
The Federalist 28
"The Feel" 144
figures of speech 102–5
first-person commentary 3, 13–14, 41, 62–65, 75, 98, 129–30, 135, 137–41
Flint, Michigan 26
Florida Sentinel Bulletin 64
free speech 1, 10, 37, 58
Freedom of Information Act (FOIA) 141
freelancing 3, 6, 12–13, 31–33, 95, 98, 160–61, 163–64
Frere-Jones, Sasha 77

Gallico, Paul 143–45, 147
Gay, Roxane 13
Germany 57–58, 154
Gerwig, Greta 85
Gigot, Paul 92
Gilmer, Elizabeth Meriwether 80–81; *see also* Dix, Dorothy
glass houses 7–8
Globe Magazine 14
"Going Out for a Walk" 47
Goldfield, Hannah 112–13

Graham, Ruth 124–25
Gray, John 152
Grief, Mark 126–27
Gruner, Elisabeth 75–76
Grygiel, Jennifer 96–99
guest essay *see* essay

Hall, Trish 28, 117
Harper's 38, 101, 113, 154
Hax, Carolyn 78–79
Hearst, William Randolph 81
Hemingway, Ernest 3, 148–49, 152, 156–57
"How I Became a Socialist" 134–36
"How It Feels to Be Colored Me" 130–31
Hughes, Langston 3, 131–32, 136
human trafficking 141–43
humor 3, 47–48, 88, 101, 119–21, 132
Hurston, Zora Neale 130–33, 135
hyperbole 121

immersion journalism 3, 145, 147
immigration 28, 34, 55, 144
In Defense of Food 106
invective 6, 9, 127
investigative journalism 139, 141, 145
irony 100–2, 106, 119, 121–22
Izen, Spencer 92

Jack, Zachary Michael 67, 169
Johnson, Cleveland, Jr. 63
Jones, Rosalie Gardiner 67–68
journalism 21, 30, 92, 139, 143, 144, 147, 156

Kadlac, Adam 110
kairos 67–68, 70–71
Keillor, Garrison 117
Kreilkamp, Ivan 127

Lamas, Daniela J. 93
Lemire, Christy 86
letter to the editor 14, 27, 46
Loeb, Paul Rogat 8
logos 70, 125
London, Jack 134–36
London, England 153–54
"The Lone Fighter" 54–55
Lopate, Phillip 36, 125, 127
lynching 59, 65–66, 140–41

Manning, Marie 80; *see also* "Dear Beatrice Fairfax"
McClure's 65, 138, 145
meme 96–99, 111

Index

Men Are from Mars, Women Are from Venus 152
Mencken, H.L. 89–90, 100–2
muckraker 137–38
Muir, John 69–71
The Muscatine Journal 11

The National Review 28
Nazism 154–55
"The Negro Artist and the Racial Mountain" 131, 133
Nelson, James C. 41
New York Age 140
New York Aurora 10
New York Daily News 143
New York Evening Journal 81
The New York Post 28–29
New York Sun 12, 46
The New York Times 12–14, 25, 28–29, 41, 74, 89, 93, 94, 96, 117, 120, 123, 139, 141, 152, 160
The New York Times Sunday Magazine 28
New York Tribune 57
New York World 50, 142
news analysis 29, 92–99, 166
news cycle 30, 101
Nietzsche, Friedrich 134
The Night of the Gun 139

objectivity ombudsman 37
O'Hanlon, Virginia 46
op-ed 1, 3, 7, 12–19, 23–30, 32–38, 42–44, 48–49, 57, 60, 67, 69, 71, 95, 98–99, 123, 125, 129, 141, 148, 160, 163–66, 171
opinion column 12, 17–19, 24, 45, 52, 57–58, 63, 66, 74, 76–83, 98, 104, 115, 120, 137, 142–43, 148, 152, 156–57, 163, 171; *see also* advice column
opinion editor 31–32, 69
oppositional writing 123–27
"Our Ghostly Commonwealth" 52–53, 55
overstatement 102, 121

Paris, France 19, 101, 156–57
participatory journalism 142, 144–45
payment 164–65
perspectives 2, 9, 13–14, 34, 45, 133
persuasive writing 3, 11, 20–21, 25, 44, 64, 102
Phillips, Jeanne 82; *see also* "Dear Abby"
Pipher, Mary 13, 45
Pittsburgh, Pennsylvania 137–38
poetry 11–13, 47, 168
polemic 9, 150, 152, 170

political cartoons *see* cartoons
political correctness 53
politics 9, 12, 28, 30, 41–42, 44, 54–55, 62, 64–65, 69–70, 93, 96–99, 134, 137–38, 149, 154
Pollan, Michael 3, 106, 108, 110
Post, Emily 74
premise 107, 112, 122, 151
Prochnik, George 123–24
product reviews 89
protest marches 67
publication 1, 11–13, 15, 23, 28, 31, 41, 95, 98, 139, 160–65, 170–71
Pulitzer Prize 1, 53, 97
Pyle, Ernie 170

racial violence *see* lynching
racism 7, 58–60, 127, 130–31, 140–41, 155
The Red Badge of Courage 50
"Regulars Get No Glory" 51
rejection 23, 95, 161
review writing 3, 85–91
rhetoric 13, 60, 98, 102, 104, 113, 117, 127, 149–52
"Rich Dads and Poor Dads" 82–83
Rodriguez, Richard 129–30, 135
Rogers, Will 120–21
Roosevelt, Franklin D. 154
Roosevelt, Theodore 137
royalties 162, 164–65
The Rumpus 77–78
Runyon, Damon 82–83
Russell, Bertrand 113–14, 116

Sacramento, California 38
The Sacramento Bee 14
St. Louis, Missouri 137
San Francisco, California 38, 40, 77
The San Francisco Chronicle 1, 69
San Francisco Examiner 49
sarcasm 102, 122
Saturday Evening Post 52
"Save the Redwoods" 70–71
Schacter, Stanley 37
Schopenhauer, Arthur 123–24
self-doubt 3, 24, 32
Shapiro, Susan 11–12
simultaneous submissions 160–61
sincerity 3, 44–46, 48, 121, 156
The Sioux City Journal 14, 27
Slate 124
slavery 114, 131, 168
Smith, Zadie 13
Smithey, Cole 85

Index

social justice 1, 12, 16, 66, 140, 154
The Soul of a Citizen 8
Spanish-American War 50
Squire, Belle 150, 152
Steffens, Lincoln 137–38, 141
Stevenson, Robert Louis 114–16
Strayed, Cheryl 3, 76–77, 79, 83

Teen Vogue 19
thesis 18, 54, 88, 107, 149
Thompson, Dorothy 52–55, 154–55
Thoreau, Henry David 108–10
Thurber, James 119, 121–22
Toronto Daily Star 156
Trudeau, Justin 149
Trump, Donald 12, 67–69, 93, 96–97
Twain, Mark 3, 38–43, 68, 86–88, 90, 118
Twitter 6

underground press 41
University of Michigan 11, 37–38
Uvalde, Texas 93–95

van den Berg, Laura 113
"Various Bad Novels" 89
viewpoints 7, 13–14, 17, 23–24, 70, 116–17, 119, 129, 133, 148, 160, 171

violence 64, 66, 68–69, 93–94, 139–40
virtue 44–45, 47, 102, 109, 111–12, 116, 125, 133, 144
voting rights 67, 140, 150
Vox 14, 28
vox populi 3, 49–56

"Walking" 108–9
The Wall Street Journal 12, 25, 28, 92
Wallace, David Foster 13, 101–2
Wallace, George 64
Washington, George 70
Washington Examiner 28
Watergate 13
The Weekly Challenger 63, 66
Wells-Barnett, Ida B. 137, 139–41
White, E.B. 108
Whitman, Walt 10, 13
"Who Goes Nazi?" 154–55
Woodward, Bob 13
Woolf, Virginia 46
Wright, Richard 170

Yeats, W.B. 13
"Yes, Virginia, there is a Santa Claus" 12, 46–48
young adult literature 124–25

www.ingramcontent.com/pod-product-compliance
Lightning Source LLC
Chambersburg PA
CBHW070357240426
43671CB00013BA/2545